THE SCOTT ORIGINALS

SIR WALTER SCOTT

From the Painting by Sir Henry Raeburn, R.A. (1808)

THE SCOTT ORIGINALS

AN ACCOUNT OF NOTABLES AND
WORTHIES THE ORIGINALS OF
CHARACTERS IN THE WAVERLEY
NOVELS

BY

W. S. CROCKETT D.D.

MINISTER OF TWEEDSMUIR

AUTHOR OF "FOOTSTEPS OF SCOTT" "THE SCOTT COUNTRY"
"ABBOTSFORD" "IN PRAISE OF TWEED" ETC. ETC.

Third and Revised Edition

GRANT & MURRAY
LIMITED
Edinburgh
1932

First Published in 1912
Second Edition, 1913
Third Edition, 1932

Printed in Scotland by GILMOUR & DEAN, LIMITED, *Glasgow*

To

Daniel Aitkenhead
Schoolmaster of Earlston

Dear Maister—From the A B C
To Greek and grand Latinity
You drave the lessons into me.

Old Homer strung his lyre langsyne,
Quintus Horatius sang divine,
In that lore-haunted school of thine

Back in those thirty years agone,
Heard I the call of " Marmion,"
And claimed the Wizard for mine own.

And oll the great heart-stirring lays
Filled up the fountain of your praise,
Ambition in my breast to raise.

You led your Scholar up the hill
Of learning, with a joyous will—
His heart is with the Maister still.

" IF anywhere in another world the blessings which men have conferred here are taken into account in distributing reward, surely the choicest in store of the Most High will be reserved for His servant Scott! It may be said of others that they have made the world wise or rich, but of him it must be said that he, more than all, has made the world happier —wiser, too, wiser through its happiness."— MARK RUTHERFORD.

CONTENTS

vii

CONTENTS

LIST OF ILLUSTRATIONS

ix

PREFACE TO THIRD EDITION

The Author of *Waverley* touched almost untapped sources when he began the writing of his great romances. Everything played into Scott's hands— the evolution of history, the study of antiquity to which he devoted much of his leisure, his flair for genealogy, his minute knowledge of his country's topography, his familiarity with rustic life, and intimate understanding of the customs, language, and spirit of the people amongst whom he lived and moved. He was fortunate in his times as an interpreter of Scottish life, for few had adventured into this rich and spacious field. Not less fortunate was he in his intellectual equipment — his prodigious memory, for instance, his observant eye, and intelligent sympathy for all things connected with his country and countrymen.

Boon assets these which stood him in good stead whenever he set his quill in motion. He was a limner who drew his pictures with swift and dexterous fingers, creating what were in truth the easeful masterpieces of literary craftsmanship. He never needed to elaborate his portraits with the exacting precision of an artist invariably touching up his canvas, altering his colours, and adding, here and there, new notes of appeal. Spontaneity governed most of his romantic work. He wrote as thoughts ran through his brain, as images rose up before his mental vision. Never was composition so magically fostered, nor, spite of its rapidity, so amazingly natural and human. The secret of the Waverleys lies largely in the fact that they were transcripts from real life, alive with figures borrowed from the realm of ordinary experience, bristling with both the best and the worst features of an everyday existence completely under the surveillance of the author's eye and ear, and illumined by the glamour of his imagination.

How did Scott manipulate those figures? For one thing he was careful not to present them as the actual counterpart of any single individual he had in view. So to speak, he distributed his traits—transferred a trait from one here and another there. He thus worked in '' composites,'' rendering identification of his several prototypes not always an easy matter. Pronounced, strongly-marked idiosyncrasies, however, seem to solve the problem in most cases. And that was just what happened when the Waverleys made their appearance. Originals were speedily discovered. This and that one, it was said, the author must have had in his mind. Robert Chambers was one of those early and fairly accurate identifiers. Nor must we forget that the author himself furnished not only hints but also made definite statements on the subject. So did Lockhart (in the Life), no doubt from recollections of conversations with his father-in-law. Scott's characters, to be sure, are his own matchless creations, but he first lived among many of them, and, as has been said, it was easy for them to reappear in his pages, and to have the immortality they otherwise could not have found.

Of the Waverley portraits the best (as all will allow) are his Scottish representations, each so faithfully drawn as to be almost an epitome of the national moods—moods by no means confined to a past age, but in many respects as true to-day as they were to Scott's view-point more than a hundred years ago.

The present volume concerns itself (with one exception) with those Scottish representations. Material which has gone to its making has been assembled from numerous sources during well-nigh a lifetime's study of Sir Walter and his work. I might have discoursed upon Originals portrayed in the few novels not included here, but I have confined myself to what are considered the best-known and the most popular. Each chapter has been revised, and fresh matter has been added. The work for a number of years has been out of print, its first publisher having left off business during the War. And now, in the centenary year of Sir Walter's death, the new owners of the copyright are of opinion that a reissue is uniquely appropriate, since no other publication deals with the subject on the same lines, or with such minuteness. Lovers of the Waverleys (and who is not their lover?) will desire to know something about the men and women of real life who strut the Waverley stage, never as puppets, and not as mere actors, but rather as people still very much alive, who continue to play their parts, amusing, instructing, and edifying generations that come and go. The wide response given to the previous editions encourages me to hope that this contribution to the increasing Scott literature of our times may fill its own acceptable niche therein.

In the making of this book I have been indebted for much kind help, particularly with regard to the Illustrations, which constitute an altogether unique Scott gallery. Under each of these, in the accompanying List, I have indicated a note as to their origin.

W. S. CROCKETT.

Tweedsmuir,
    June 6, 1932.

CHAPTER ONE

WAVERLEY
"THE BARON OF BRADWARDINE"

A

" And our old Baron rose in might,
    Like a lion from his den,
  And rode away across the hills
    To Charlie and his men."

W. E. AYTOUN.

CHAPTER ONE — WAVERLEY — "THE BARON OF BRADWARDINE"

WAVERLEY WAS SCOTT'S FIRST NOVEL. Begun at Ashestiel in 1805, and discontinued shortly afterwards, it was resumed in 1813 and published anonymously the year following. With its theme— the second Jacobite Rising—Scott was intimate and familiar. Forty years after the events occurred there were still living many who bore a valiant part therein, many who, although not actual participants, could speak with perfect knowledge of the circumstances and with all the vivacity of ancient chroniclers. To these Scott was indebted for much of his information —not, of course, that *Waverley* was in his mind at that early time. At Sandyknowe and at Kelso legends of the Highlander years lingered by hearth and hillside— linger to this day, to be sure. At Prestonpans he could hardly escape hearing local accounts of Cope, the heroic Colonel Gardiner, and others. At George Square there was no more favourite subject for the lively conversation of such men as George Constable and Alexander Stewart. Scott's youth was passed in the afterglow of the great struggle. Accordingly, when the time came for him to reduce the story of Prince Charlie's mad venture within the limits of a written romance, he found the process to be comparatively easy. All the historical data he had at his fingers' ends. Hence the astonishing rapidity with which *Waverley* was penned—quite two-thirds of it within three weeks.

Hitherto in the realm of poetry Scott had shone as

3

a star of considerable magnitude in an age when there was little brilliancy in the poetical firmament. He had his opportunity as a poet, and he made the most of it, even as at a later period—driven, it must be said, by the force of circumstance—he essayed the region of Romance in which his spurs were no less nobly won. He had none to meet him on his own ground as a poet till the greater luminary, Byron, appeared, when Scott knew that his reign in that realm was at an end. He remarked to James Ballantyne that " Byron hit the mark where I don't even pretend to fledge my arrow," although it was the author of *The Giaour* who sent a copy of his poem to the author of *Marmion* with this inscription : " To the Monarch of Parnassus from one of his subjects." But if Byron's advent meant extinction for Scott in one field of effort, it paved the way for a much higher distinction in another. And it were infinitely better to lose a bard who could never be rated among the first, or, as some critics will have it, among the second, rank of poets, and to gain instead the " King of the Romantics." We have Scott, however, as a Romantic largely because we had him first as a maker of verse. Had there been no *Lay of the Last Minstrel*, no *Marmion*, it is possible there had been no *Waverley*, no *Guy Mannering*. Scott learned his lesson as a novelist whilst he was yet raiding the Liddesdale glens or licking his cantos into shape on the Shirra's Knowe at Ashestiel. He was, indeed, " making himself " in every year before *Waverley* burst upon the scene. It was the spirit as well as the success of his poetic ventures which rendered the Waverley succession all the easier and all the more splendid. In innumerable instances one lights on passages and incidents which were the direct outcome of the time when the *Minstrelsy* was in the melting-pot. Lockhart affirmed that the *Minstrelsy* contained the elements of a hundred romances. The like may be said of Scott's great original poems. In themselves they are romances of the most first-rate character, Homeric in their epic stateliness and picturesqueness. They are the outflow of that good fortune which linked Scott to the past by an unbroken succession of traditions and personages. No man was ever more " thirled " to the haunting greatness of a history which, so to speak, wove its tendrils around his heart.

Rokeby and *The Bridal of Triermain* were the poems which immediately preceded *Waverley*. *The Lord of the Isles* and *Harold the Dauntless* followed after the first three or four of the Waverleys had appeared. Thereafter we take leave of Scott in the capacity of poet. That arena of the muse he now boldly and resolutely abandoned for those fields of fresh renown which were whitening unto the harvest.

As has been said, *Waverley* in its final stages was got quickly off the anvil. It was an unqualified triumph, the thousand copies which made up the first edition disappearing within a month, over four thousand copies being sold before the end of the year. The work appeared early in July. Contemporary criticism welcomed the novel with an exceeding good grace,

5

with the exception of the *Quarterly Review*, whose article was couched in what Lockhart calls a "captious, cavilling strain of quibble." In the *Edinburgh Review* Jeffrey sparingly employed his scalping-knife. He was generous to a degree, and was at no pains to conceal his conviction of the authorship. "It is wonderful," he says, " what genius and adherence to nature will do, in spite of all disadvantages. Here is a thing obviously very hostile and, in many places, very un-skilfully written, composed, one-half of it, in a dialect unintelligible to four-fifths of the reading population of the country, relating to a period too recent to be romantic and too far gone by to be familiar, and published, moreover, in a quarter of the island where materials and talents for novel-writing have been supposed to be equally wanting, and yet, by the mere force and truth and vivacity of its colouring, already casting the whole tribe of ordinary novels into the shade and taking its place rather with the most popular of our modern poems than with the rubbish of provincial romances."

There was no subject more germane to Scott's up-bringing and temperament than the attempt to rein-state the Stuarts upon the throne. He was, we have seen, familiar with every phase of the story. He had been over much of the ground of the struggle, had talked with individuals who had taken no insignificant part in the enterprise. Courageous enough to avow himself a Jacobite in spirit, Scott recognised, at the same time, that Jacobitism was a spent force, that no-

6

thing could have been more foolhardy than each of the Risings associated with the movement, that the state of the times and the persons mainly responsible for the project were not such as to have inspired it with any measure of hope. He was interested as a historian, as Beardie's descendant, in the Jacobite cause. He admired the splendid loyalty of the Highlanders, especially after Culloden. He was stirred by the poetic charm of the unhappy and ungrateful house of Stuart. Further than that he did not venture. Never once does he even sentimentally approve of " plunging a kingdom into all the miseries of civil war for the purpose of replacing upon the throne the descendants of a monarch by whom it had been wilfully forfeited." Waverley's reflections on receiving Rose's letter (Chap. xxviii.) are likely to be Scott's own. From a dramatic and a romantic point of view Jacobitism had its attractions. Intellectually and logically the game was not worth the candle.

Waverley * is not so vivacious, nor is it so well told as others of the series, but as a piece of historical senti-

* The title *Waverley* was derived from the Abbey of Waverley, near Farnham, in Surrey. That Scott ever visited Waverley was long doubted. Evidence, however, furnished by the Rev. O. S. C. Lang, Rector of Bentley, makes it clear that about 1803 he did see the ruin, having stayed with Mr. Lang's grandparents at Moor Park, close by. Perhaps also he consulted (in the Library of the British Museum) the *Annales Monasterii Waverleia* in the course of his investigations into the history of the Cistercian Order. It was at Waverley that the Cistercians first settled in England in 1128. The word signifies the mead, or lea, near the river Wey—Pope's " chalky Wey that rolls a milky wave."

7

ment, pathetic in its utter hopelessness, there is none in the series to match it. Its portraits, historical and imaginary, are drawn with a deft pen. As is so frequently the case with Scott, the hero, Edward Waverley, is hardly the real hero after all. He appears in every chapter, and is noble and chivalrous throughout, notwithstanding that his creator speaks of him (undeservedly) as " a sneaking piece of imbecility." He is more at home, however, on the domestic hearth than on the tented field, and with the beautiful Rose Bradwardine for his bride, to whom he owed his life, the ending of the tale is pleasant enough. Fergus Mac-Ivor is one of Scott's gallantest figures, although, as it has been said, there is just a trifle of the stage-property Highland chief about him—that touch of theatrical unreality which mars so many of Scott's heroic types. Flora Mac-Ivor, accomplished and high-souled, is one of Scott's few genuine heroines. There is a suggestion of the *Ivanhoe* Rebecca about her sense of duty, her passionate attachment to principle, her courtly renunciation of woman's tenderest prerogatives. There is no more touching scene than that in which Scott describes Flora's farewell to Edward Waverley. In his boyhood at Sandyknowe Scott had listened to the story, recounted by an eye-witness, of the execution of the Jacobite rebels at Carlisle, and to that memory we are indebted for the two most Shakespearean chapters in the novel. " Do you remember," said Flora, looking up with a ghastly smile, " you once found me making Fergus's bride-favours ; and now I

8

am sewing his bridal garment. Our friends here," she continued, with suppressed emotion, " are to give hallowed earth in their chapel to the bloody relics of the last Vich Ian Vohr. But they will not all rest together; no, his head!—I shall not have the last miserable consolation of kissing the cold lips of my dear, dear Fergus!" The unfortunate Flora, after one or two hysterical sobs, fainted in her chair. The lady, who had been attending in the anteroom, now entered hastily, and begged Edward to leave the room, but not the house. When he was recalled, after the space of nearly half an hour, he found that, by a strong effort, Miss Mac-Ivor had greatly composed herself. "Give this," she said, "to your betrothed, my dearest Rose,—it is her poor Flora's only ornament of value, and was the gift of a princess." She put into his hands a case containing the chain of diamonds with which she used to decorate her hair. "To me it is in future useless. The kindness of my friends has secured me a retreat in the convent of the Scottish Benedictine nuns in Paris. To-morrow—if indeed I can survive to-morrow—I set forward on my journey with this venerable sister. And now, Mr. Waverley, adieu! May you be as happy with Rose as your amiable dispositions deserve, and think sometimes on the friends you have lost. Do not attempt to see me again; it would be mistaken kindness." She gave him her hand, on which Edward shed a torrent of tears, and with a faltering step withdrew from the apartment, and returned to the town of Carlisle.

Macwheeble, a semi-caricature, is a type of character plentiful in the Waverleys. The redoubtable Donald Bean Lean (pronounced Bane Lane), prince of Highland caterans, and Evan Dhu Maccombich, Fergus Mac-Ivor's devoted foster-brother, with Callum Beg, his shrewd and handsome page, are all strongly limned portraits. For mine host of the Candlestick, curious, crafty, covetous, Callum exhibited a disposition rather startling to Waverley. He had no scruples about the taking of human life, and regarded the matter in a quite nonchalant fashion. Being Waverley's guide, he observed that the Englishman was annoyed by the curiosity of their host.

" If his honour thought ta auld deevil Whig carle was a bit dangerous, she could easily provide for him, and teil ane ta wiser."

" How, and in what manner ? "

" Her ain sell," replied Callum, " could wait for him a wee bit frae the toun, and kittle his quarters wi' her skene-occle."

" Skene-occle ! What's that ? "

Callum unbuttoned his coat, raised his left arm, and with an emphatic nod pointed to the hilt of a small dirk, snugly deposited under it, in the lining of his jacket. Waverley thought he had misunderstood his meaning : he gazed in his face, and discovered in Callum's very handsome, though embrowned features, just the degree of roguish malice with which a lad of the same age in England would have brought forward a plan for robbing an orchard.

"THE BARON OF BRADWARDINE"

" Good God, Callum, would you take the man's life ? "

" Indeed," answered the young desperado, " and I think he has had just a lang enough lease o't, when he's for betraying honest folk that come to spend siller at his public. . . . Ta duinhé-wassel might please himsell ; ta auld rudas loon had never done Callum nae ill."

There are no accepted Originals for any of the above, save, perhaps, for Fergus, for whom a proto-type has been found in the person of Macdonald of Tirnadrish (not Tynedrish), a cadet of the Macdonalds of Keppoch. There is, at any rate, the tradition of the window-sill at Carlisle Castle, on which the indentation of a man's fingers is said to be traceable, such fingers being those of the brave Macdonald.* The fate of the

---

* " Next night Sir Walter rested at Carlisle. . . . After that we went to the Castle, where a new showman went through the old trick of pointing out Fergus Mac-Ivor's very dungeon. Peveril said : ' Indeed ?—are you quite sure, sir ? ' and on being told there could be no doubt, was troubled with a fit of coughing, which end-ed in a laugh. The man seemed exceedingly indignant : so, when papa moved on, I whispered who it was. I wish you had seen the man's start, and how he stared and bowed. . . ." (Letter from Miss Scott, 1828. See Lockhart, ix. 226, Edin. ed.)

Fergus Mac-Ivor has a much more possible prototype in Colonel Alexander Ranaldson Macdonell of Glengarry, one of the most ty-pical Celts of his race. His pride and heat of temper were quite equal to those of the hero of fiction. He was the last Highland chief who really kept up the state and customs of ancient gaeldom to their full extent. When he travelled, he did so as a Gaelic Prince, with a full retinue of kilted attendants, not a single *arti-culus* lacking of a Highland chieftain's tail. He was a great friend of Scott's, who writes of him in glowing terms. (See Lockhart for many references.) On 14th January 1828 he was killed in the at-tempt to get ashore from the wrecked steamer *Stirling Castle*. He was buried in the cemetery of Killionan where many of the

Laird of Balmawhapple was borrowed from that of David Threipland of the Fingask family, who fell at Prestonpans in the manner described in the novel.* The incident said to have happened to Flora Mac-Ivor actually befell a Miss Nairne, one of Scott's women friends. As the Highland army rushed into Edinburgh, Miss Nairne, like other ladies who approved of their cause, stood waving her handkerchief from a balcony, when a ball from a Highlander's musket, discharged by accident, grazed her forehead. "Thank God," said she, the instant she recovered, "that the accident happened to me, whose principles are known. Had it befallen a Whig, they would have said it was done on purpose."

II

It is of one of the major and, if the phrase may be employed consistently with Scott's way of looking at life, of one of the minor characters for whom Originals have been suggested—the whimsical old Baron, and the dreamy simpleton, Davie Gellatley, who roasts eggs and makes rhymes with equal facility.

However much of a weariness the loquacious Bradwardine is in peril of becoming, there is no question as

heads of Glengarry repose. His grand ideas about the state of a Macdonald chief helped to embarrass the estates, the whole of which were sold partly in his son's and partly in his grandson's time.

* "Mr. Threipland had the misfortune, in attempting to overtake some that were running away, to be kill'd ; his horse fell, and an officer of the dragoons seeing he was alone, turn'd about and shot him."—Lord Elcho's *Affairs of Scotland* (1907).

to the excellent account which he gives of himself throughout the story. He is a man of solid accomplishments and great worth, though one of Scott's bores. More than once it is his good common sense and ready wit which save the situation. He is, for all his jargon, a noble specimen of the old Highlander, far-descended, gallant, courteous, brave even to chivalry.

Hints of an Original come from Scott himself. This was Alexander Stewart of Invernahyle, on whose valour and magnanimity at Prestonpans the plot of *Waverley* is made to turn. To Invernahyle, Scott owed much of his knowledge of Highland life and scenery. He was that "friend of my childhood who first introduced me to the Highlands, their traditions and manners," and whose visits to George Square were seasons of unbounded delight to the Scott olive-branches. To this picturesque figure, fighting his battles over again with all the garrulousness of a veteran campaigner, much of the inspiration of *Waverley* was no doubt due. Invernahyle had been "out" with Mar and with "Chairlie." There is a legend that he fought a duel with Rob Roy, wounding him slightly in the arm—enough for Rob to acknowledge defeat : "An I had known he was so cunning of fence, I had seen him damned ere I fought him." Scott says he saw Invernahyle "in arms and heard him exult in the prospect of drawing his claymore once more before he died," the occasion being Paul Jones's ridiculous descent on Edinburgh in September 1779. Invernahyle's behaviour at Preston-

13

pans, which has its counterpart in *Waverley*, is described in the Introduction to the novel, as well as in the Introduction to the *Chronicles of the Canongate*. The Appin Stewarts, determined that the victory should be a decisive one, at a particular crisis in the struggle made a furious onslaught, beating down Cope's men in all directions. Invernahyle, foremost in the mêlée, observed a Georgian officer standing alone, resolutely grasping his sword as if making up his mind to die at his post. Invernahyle called to him to surrender, and for answer received a sword-thrust which he caught in his targe. The officer was now defenceless, and would have been cut down by the miller of Invernahyle's mill, coming up at the moment, had not Invernahyle again intervened. There was nothing for it but to surrender, liberty on parole being afterwards obtained. The prisoner proved to be Colonel Charles (not Allan) Whitefoord of the Ballochmyle family, a distinguished Royalist, who may therefore stand for the Colonel Talbot of the story.*

* It is curious to find an actual Colonel (Richard) Talbot figuring in the list of those who fought at Prestonpans. As field-officer of the day, he posted the outguards the night before the battle. Colonel Whitefoord was third son of Sir Adam Whitefoord, Bart. He was visiting friends in Scotland when the Rebellion broke out. " We are alarm'd here," he writes from Edinburgh in August 1745, " with an invasion which I believe will end in smoke. Certain it is that a few people have landed in the West Highlands from a French man-of-war, but their number is so inconsiderable that they only serve to put us on our guard. Sir John Cope takes all necessary precautions, and has himself march'd with the few troops he has, to pay them his compliments on their arrival. They must be either fools or madmen, or perhaps both, to make such a rash attempt." Whitefoord volunteered to serve His

14

Brought so strangely together, both men became fast friends. Invernahyle actually visited Ballochmyle during a period of recruiting for the Highland army, spending some pleasant days with his Whig intimates, without any speaking on either side of the Civil War which was still raging. At Culloden, Invernahyle was wounded. It was now Whitefoord's opportunity to seek clemency for his honourable opponent. The most he could wring from the unwilling Cumberland was the promise of protection for Stewart's property and family. Invernahyle himself was " found with the mark of the beast in every list," a subject unfit for favour or pardon. Soldiers scoured the Appin district for weeks, in the hope of finding their man, the search party coming frequently within a stone's cast of his hiding-place. Like the Baron of Bradwardine, Invernahyle lay huddled up in a mere hole of a crag overlooking his own house. He could

Majesty in the field, without any private view, though he might have been Adjutant-General or Aide-de-camp to the Commander-in-Chief. His papers during this period include the orders given at Edinburgh, particulars as to the transports, a return of Murray's regiment, a list of the Highland clans, the order of march from Haddington, the proposed and the actual order of battle at Prestonpans, a return of the wounded and prisoners, an account of the battle of Culloden, and an elaborate defence of Cope. At Prestonpans he acted as Engineer, fired all the guns which were discharged on that occasion, remained at his post till all his powder was expended, when he was wounded and taken prisoner. After the Rebellion there is nothing of particular interest in his career. He became Colonel of the 5th Regiment of foot, on the staff in Ireland, and died at Galway, 2nd January 1753 (not 24th December 1752, as stated by the *Scots Magazine*). His portrait, in oils, is in the possession of the Whitefoords of Whitton Paddocks, Ludlow. See the *Whitefoord Papers*. Ed. W. A. S. Hewins: Oxford, 1898.

15

hear the muster-roll called every morning, the drums beating to quarters at night, and not a change of the sentinels escaped him. His bodily wants were supplied with great difficulty, a little daughter doing the needful as she had opportunity. He ventured home one night, and in the morning had a miraculous escape, being fired on and pursued to the hills whither he betook himself. When the soldiers returned, the household were called to account for having given shelter to a proscribed traitor, but an old woman stoutly maintained that the men had mistaken the shepherd for the laird. "Why then," said they, "did he not stop when we called him ? " " Because," was the ready reply, " he is stone deaf." The real shepherd was sent for, and being tutored by the way, acted the deaf man to perfection, and the storm blew over. Invernahyle was pardoned under the Act of Indemnity in 1747. He was the son of Duncan Stewart of Invernahyle, his mother being a Campbell of Barcaldine. He married Katherine Stewart of Appin, and left Dugald his successor, besides five other sons and nine daughters. His death took place in 1795 at an advanced age. He must have been a mere boy at the time of the Fifteen in which he is reputed to have had a part.*

* In 1778, he exchanged his lands of Invernahyle, Inverpholla, and Garrachoran, for the lands of Acharn, Belloch, Keill, and others. He afterwards sold Belloch and Keill. Dugald disposed of the remainder of the lands, and died at Ardsheal in 1840, leaving no issue. The present representative of the family is Charles Stewart, son of Andrew Francis Stewart, Edinburgh. See *The Stewarts of Appin.*

SIR WALTER SCOTT, BART.,
From a Painting by Graham Gilbert.

COLONEL CHARLES WHITEFOORD

The portrait of Bradwardine, like its compeers, is composite in its character. There are features in which Invernahyle has nothing in common with the " beloved Baron "—Thackeray's phrase. He was no scholar, for example, and consequently devoid of pedantic words; nor had Invernahyle fought the " foreign loons in their ain countrie "—a prime essential for the true prototype. Invernahyle's generous act at Prestonpans, his outlawry and adventures after Culloden, are constituent parts of the portrait, but as the saviour of Colonel Talbot he is rather the antitype of Waverley than of the master of Tully-Veolan.

III

It was Maria Edgeworth's father who made the statement that if no Original could be found for the Baron of Bradwardine, it " required more genius to invent and more ability to uniformly sustain this character than any one of the variety of masterly characters with which the work abounds." There were, to be sure, many brave, scholarly old Scottish gentlemen in the days following the Forty-five, who might well have sat for the picture ; but Scott, of course, could hardly have seen the best of them. Alexander Robertson of the Struan family and Colonel John Roy Stewart, the Gaelic bard, have been mentioned in this connection. But the last Lord Pitsligo is believed to answer to the part with characteristic fidelity. Pitsligo passed away nine years before Scott appeared on the scene.

His remarkable career, however, and the admirable character of the man were on everybody's lips when Scott was a boy. It is not unreasonable to suppose that Scott had Pitsligo in view in painting his picture of the rare old Jacobite. The portrait in *Waverley* offers some resemblance to him.

" He was a tall, thin, athletic figure, old indeed, and grey-haired, but with every muscle rendered tough as whipcord by constant exercise. He was dressed carelessly, and more like a Frenchman than an Englishman of the period, while, from his hard features and perpendicular rigidity of stature, he bore some resemblance to a Swiss officer of the Guards who had resided some time in Paris, and had caught the *costume*, but not the ease or manner of its inhabitants." Other similarities favour the Pitsligo identification. Take the following: "Mr. Bradwardine had travelled with high reputation for several years, and made some campaigns in foreign service. After his *démêlé* with the law of high treason in 1715, he had lived in retirement, conversing almost entirely with those of his own principles in the vicinage "—a statement which applies with absolute perfectness to Lord Pitsligo. Or take these : " To this must be added the prejudices of ancient birth and Jacobite politics, greatly strengthened by habits of solitary and secluded authority, which, though exercised only within the bounds of his half-cultivated estate, was there indisputable and undisputed." " He was of a very ancient family, and somewhat embarrassed fortune : a scholar, according to the scholarship of Scotchmen,—that is, his learning was more diffuse than accurate, and he was rather a reader than a grammarian." "Latin he could speak with as great facility as his own good Scots." It may be remarked that, like Bradwardine, Pitsligo had two bears as supporters of his shield.* The Pitsligo lands were formerly owned by the Comyns, whence probably the name of the immortal Cosmo Comyn was borrowed.

Lord Pitsligo, properly Lord Forbes of Pitsligo, son of the third peer, was born 24th May 1678. His mother was daughter of the Earl of Mar. Whilst still a minor, Alexander Forbes inherited the family title and estates. Like many a wandering Scot, scholarship and the pursuit of arms attracted him to the Continent. In Paris he fell under the spell of Madame Guyon and the Quietists, an influence which coloured his whole career. When he returned home at the age of twenty-two, he took his seat in the Scots Parliament and strenuously opposed the Union. With Union his political life came to an end. He retired to his castle at Pitsligo in the resolve to devote his days to study and deeds of charity. The call of Mar, however, found him eager and willing to take the field for the Stuarts. Pitsligo was a conspicuous figure at Sheriffmuir. When we again meet with him, it is at James's mimic Court at Rome, with other

* The Blessed Bear of Bradwardine—that *poculum potatorium* which figured so prominently in the fortunes of Tully-Veolan—had its prototype in the Glamis silver Lion whose contents Scott himself had quaffed.

Scotsmen who had fled on the failure of the Fifteen attempt. By and by, he was allowed to return to Scotland. The next twenty-five years of his life were comparatively uneventful. He spent most of his time among his books, at his favourite subjects—Mystical Literature and the Latin Classics. Bradwardine's zeal for the latter (borrowed from an actual occurrence in the career of a Highland trooper) Scott illustrates in a well-known incident : " On the road between Preston and London he made his escape from his guards ; but being afterwards found loitering near the place where they had lodged the former night, he was recognised, and again arrested. His companions, and even his escort, were surprised at his infatuation, and could not help inquiring why, being once at liberty, he had not made the best of his way to a place of safety ; to which he replied that he had intended to do so, but, in good faith, he had returned to seek his Titus Livius, which he had forgot in the hurry of his escape."

At the age of sixty-seven occurred the most extraordinary episode in Lord Pitsligo's life,—the active part he took in the Forty-five. Old though he was, and asthmatic, he joined the Prince in his rash attempt. He put himself at the head of a hundred men of Buchan. A friend's son brought a chair and put it beside Pitsligo's charger that the old man might mount without difficulty. The veteran looked at the boy and said, " This is the severest rebuke I have yet received for presuming to go upon such an expedition." The fighting blood was up, however. Pushing the stool aside, he placed his foot on the stirrup, leapt on the horse's back and rode off. Arrived in Aberdeen, he is said to have taken off his cap, to have solemnly looked up to heaven, repeating the words, "Lord, Thou knowest that our Cause is just," and then to have given the order, "March, gentlemen." When the crash came, Pitsligo lost his lands,* while managing to keep his head on his shoulders. For many a weary year he was hunted like a beast of prey amongst the Aberdeenshire wilds. A cave at Rosehearty goes by his name, and at Maud and other parts Pitsligo's hiding-places are still pointed out. Buchan has not a more thrilling romance than the tale of this fine old Cavalier's wanderings and numerous hair-breadth escapes. In beggar's garb he passed from door to door, a veritable "Edie Ochiltree." His wife sewed "pokes" for his gowpens of meal and scraps of food. His own people knew who he was, to be sure, and never were peasants more loyal—never was secret better kept. He was only "an old man in distress" if they scented danger. But in their homes they did him honour, giving him the cosiest corner at their peat-fires, and at night the best bed to sleep in. There were critical occasions. Once he was seized with an asthmatic fit just as a patrol of soldiers came

* The Master of Forbes bought back the attainted estates, but resold part of them in 1759. It is interesting to note that the remainder, in course of time, came into the possession of Sir William Forbes, the banker, Scott's friend. Upon his death, they were inherited by Scott's rival for the hand of Williamina Belsches. Lord Clinton, the great-grandson of Scott's first love, is now proprietor.

up behind him. He had no other expedient but to sit down by the roadside and beg alms of the party. One of them tossed him a coin, condoling with him on his affliction. At another time he was surprised in a cobbler's house, and obliged for the moment to assume the tools and dress of St. Crispin. Again, soldiers on the look-out for Pitsligo begged a farmer's wife to give them a guide to his suspected place of concealment. The good dame said she had no person to send with them, "unless that travelling man would take the trouble." A beggar, who was the traveller, rose up and offered to show the road. The soldiers went with him. He conducted them to the cave ; where they found no Lord Pitsligo, who, however, was not far distant, being the very mendicant himself.

By and by the persecution slackened and the search was abandoned. Pitsligo spent his last years at Auchiries, the house of his only son, the Master of Forbes, and it was there that he died, 21st December 1762. Lord Pitsligo was author of a little religious meditation—*Thoughts concerning Man's Condition and Duties in this Life and his Hopes in the World to come*—which passed through four editions, the last being published by Blackwood in 1854, with a Memoir by Lord Medwyn, and a Review contributed by Scott to *Blackwood's Magazine* in 1829. He was also the author of a volume of *Essays Moral and Philosophical*, published in 1730 and 1763, which is at once a testimony to his scholarship and piety.

Lord Pitsligo's name is honoured in Buchan to this
day. As patriot, outlaw, scholar, saint, he is, one
may almost say, Buchan's most outstanding personality. His self-sacrificing endurance after Culloden,
and the beautiful contentment of the man, are circumstances of which all Buchan natives are proud.
Scott affirmed that Pitsligo's heroism was "above all
Greek and Roman praise." Dr. King, the Jacobite
Head of St. Mary Hall, Oxford, "a severe and
splenetic judge," declared that among all his acquaintances he had known only one person to whom
he could with truth assign "the character of perfect
charitableness and perfect heroism—the present Lord
Pitsligo of Scotland." Another thinks he was "fit
to have been a martyr in the days of Nero." Still
another that he was the "most popular man in his
country, not beloved, but adored, being ever employed in doing good offices to his neighbours." And
a high contemporary authority describes him as "as-
suredly the best husband, the best father, the best
friend, and the best subject in Britain."

His burial-place is the old church of Pitsligo where
others of the family are resting, as the following inscription shows :—

Within this vault rests all that is mortal of the
Following members of the family of
FORBES OF PITSLIGO.

✠   ✠

ALEXANDER, 1ST LORD OF PITSLIGO.   Died 1636.
His wife, JOAN KEITH, daughter of William, Earl Marischal.
ALEXANDER, 2ND LORD FORBES OF PITSLIGO.   Died 1677.
His wife, MARY ERSKINE, daughter of James, Earl of Buchan.
ALEXANDER, 3RD LORD FORBES OF PITSLIGO.   Died 1690.
His children, CHARLES AND JEAN.
His wife, SOPHIA ERSKINE, daughter of the Earl of Mar.
ALEXANDER, 4TH LORD FORBES OF PITSLIGO.   Attainted 1746.
Died 1762.
His first wife, REBECCA NORTON.
His second wife, ELIZABETH ALLEN.
JOHN, MASTER OF PITSLIGO.   Died 1781.
His wife, REBECCA OGILVIE, daughter of James Ogilvie
of Auchiries.

✠   ✠

In their memory this plate is erected by their
Successor and Descendant
CHARLES FORBES TREFUSIS
OF PITSLIGO.
1893.

CHAPTER TWO

WAVERLEY
"DAVIE GELLATLEY"

" His folly served to make folks laugh,
   When wit and mirth were scarce."

SWIFT.

CHAPTER TWO
WAVERLEY—"DAVIE GELLATLEY"

IT MUST BE ADMITTED THAT *WAVERLEY* " flags " at the outset. Readers who wish to get to the story will be content to skip the first half-dozen chapters or so, for only after that does the curtain begin to rise on expectancy. As Scott observes, however, there were circumstances recorded in those introductory chapters which he could not persuade himself to retract or cancel. These " circumstances " were probably Waverley's desultory studies, his romantic readings, which are really autobiographic.

It is when the hero has ridden through the village of Tully-Veolan, when he has arrived at the mansion of that name, that interest in the story properly begins. Scott says he had no particular domicile in view in describing Tully-Veolan—the most celebrated manor-house in fiction. The peculiarities of the place, he remarks, were common to certain old Scottish seats, of which he mentions the Edinburgh Houses of Bruntsfield and Ravelston, and Grandtully Castle,* in Perthshire. But if any surviving structure may be considered an original, or closely resembling it, Traquair in Peeblesshire must carry off that honour. Bears and all, it is as like Tully-Veolan as any ancient house in Scotland can be. Scott's intimate knowledge of the place, his frequent visits to it, and the impression

* The name Tully-Veolan was devised by combining the last part of Grandtully with the last part of Ballyveolan, in Argyllshire. Similarly the place itself is a composite. Craighall, near Blairgowrie, no doubt furnished hints.

which such a history-haunted pile was likely to make on his imagination suggest the tolerable certainty of its having at least formed a study for the more finished and bolder-featured picture. The avenue in the novel was undoubtedly modelled from the avenue at Traquair, bating an archway, which Traquair never had. The twin Bears, masses of upright stone battered by the blasts of many winters, still frown on the highway, and there is about the whole scene (on which modernity has set no ruthless hand) a solitude and a repose as profound as on the day when Waverley " walked slowly down, enjoying the grateful and cooling shade, and so much pleased with the placid ideas of rest and seclusion excited by this confined and quiet scene that he forgot the misery and dirt of the hamlet he had left behind him. The opening into the paved courtyard corresponded with the rest of the scene. The house, which seemed to consist of two or three high, narrow, and steep-roofed buildings, projecting from each other at right angles, formed one side of the enclosure. It had been built at a period when castles were no longer necessary, and when the Scottish architects had not yet acquired the art of designing a domestic residence. The windows were numberless, but very small; the roof had some nondescript kind of projections, called bartizans, and displayed at each frequent angle a small turret, rather resembling a pepper-box than a Gothic watch-tower. Neither did the front indicate absolute security from danger. There were loopholes for musketry, and iron stanchions on the lower windows, probably to repel any roving band of gypsies, or resist a predatory visit from the caterans of the neighbouring Highlands. Stables and other offices occupied another side of the square."

Scott's hero almost despaired of gaining entrance into the apparently enchanted domicile. Save for the plashing of a fountain, the place was wrapt in a solemn silence :

Nor voice was heard, nor wight was seen in bower or hall.

But Waverley's quick eyes caught sight of a little oaken door set in the courtyard wall, on the other side of which he hoped to hear or see some sign of life. He found that this admitted him to the garden —"a pleasant scene" (pictured from the garden at Ravelston) ; and it was here that the curious personage whose name heads this chapter was encountered. Waverley was at once struck with the strange garb and the no less odd gestures of the figure who made his approach. "Sometimes this mister wight held his hands clasped over his head, like an Indian Jogue in the attitude of penance ; sometimes he swung them perpendicularly, like a pendulum, on each side ; and anon he slapped them swiftly and repeatedly across his breast, like the substitute used by a hackney-coachman for his usual flogging exercise when his cattle are idle upon the stand, in a clear, frosty day. His gait was as singular as his gestures, for at times he hopped with great perseverance on the right foot, then exchanged that supporter to advance in the same manner on the left, and then, putting his feet

29

close together, he hopped upon both at once. His attire also was antiquated and extravagant. It consisted in a sort of grey jerkin, with scarlet cuffs and slashed sleeves, showing a scarlet lining; the other parts of the dress corresponded in colour, not forgetting a pair of scarlet stockings and a scarlet bonnet proudly surmounted with a turkey's feather. Edward, whom he did not seem to observe, now perceived confirmation in his features of what the mien and gestures had already announced. It was apparently neither idiocy nor insanity which gave that wild, unsettled, irregular expression to a face which naturally was rather handsome, but something that resembled a compound of both, where the simplicity of the fool was mixed with the extravagance of a crazed imagination. He sung with great earnestness, and not without some taste, a fragment of an old Scottish ditty."

This was Davie Gellatley, who plays his part in the story not at all badly for a fool. The key to Davie's character is indicated by the Scots phrase put into the mouth of the major-domo in reply to Waverley's interrogation, "He is an innocent," meaning a born simpleton, yet in the possession of a degree of sanity and mother-wit which shine out on occasion, not unfrequently at the psychological moment. Persons of the Gellatley stamp were often exceedingly serviceable, as Waverley had reason to know. They could run errands, carry letters, could even be entrusted with secrets. But manual labour was anathema to the tribe. Davie " used to work a day's

30

turn weel eneugh ; but he helped Miss Rose when she was flemit with the Laird of Killancureit's new English bull, and since that time we ca' him Davie Do-little,—indeed we might ca' him Davie Do-nae-thing, for since he got that gay clothing, to please his Honour and my young mistress, he has done nae-thing but dance up and down about the *toun*, without doing a single turn, unless trimming the laird's fish-ing-wand or busking his flies, or maybe catching a dish of trouts at an orra-time."

These "innocents," or "naturals," were, as a mat-ter of fact, incapable of constant and steady exertion, though many of them were endowed with remarkable strength of limb and a robustness to be envied. Gel-latley, for instance, excelled in field sports. Scott re-presents him as a creature of warm affections, fond of animals, blessed with a prodigious memory, and a turn for music.

In days gone by there was not a town or coun-try district but had its "fool" or its "innocent." Conspicuous and pitiful figures on the village street many of them were—the butt of schoolboys, and of older tormentors. Thanks to the more humane con-ditions of modern life, such scenes are now almost, if not altogether, impossible. Davie Gellatley oc-cupies a position which did not fall to the "daft Jamies" and the "simple Sandies" of the street. In Scotland, the fool was a common appendage of early Court life, and down to a late period he con-tinued to hold his place in the establishments of

31

various wealthy noblemen. There was the Earl of Wemyss's fool, Willie Howieson, a Haddington "innocent," whose services at Gosford were not unlike those of Gellatley at Tully-Veolan. It was compassion, rather than custom, which fostered the good fortune both of Howieson and the fictitious Davie. They were, however, relics of an era when the laird and his followers must needs be entertained by the rude humour and buffoonery of the jester in the absence of more refined relaxations. Only Gellatley is more than jester. He amuses, yet he wins confidence also, and in a variety of circumstances renders the most genuine help to Bradwardine and Miss Rose. One must laugh at his whimsicalities ; spite of his crazedness, his heart is in the right place. Like Caleb Balderstone, Andrew Fairservice, and others of the kidney, he lives not less by his loyalty than by his jokes and oddities, his happy tricks and song-snatches. His mother, old Janet Gellatley's verdict about him "whom she loved, her idiot boy," was as good as any : " Davie's no juist like other folk, puir fallow, but he's no sae silly as folk tak' him for." But *Alexander ab Alexandro* and Macwheeble had their own suspicions of Davie, in whom they saw more of knave than of fool.

Surely Morritt of Rokeby was mistaken in assuming as the Original of Davie Gellatley, William Stewart Rose's valet, David Hinves. Except for the Christian name, there was little other likeness. Hinves, a bookbinder by trade, and Methodist local preacher to boot, came into Rose's service as the result of a

LORD FORBES OF PITSLIGO
"Baron Bradwardine"

[see page 18

DAFT JOCK GRAY
"Davie Gellatley"

sermon which Rose heard him preach under a tree in the New Forest. Master and man they lived together for forty years without so much as a quarrel arising between them. Scott (who presented Hinves with all his works) declared that he was as much a piece of Rose as Trim was of Uncle Toby. Hinves may have furnished hints for the portrait of Gellatley, but the one was certainly not a transcript of the other.

II

Throughout the Border country, Daft Jock Gray is considered the true Original of Davie Gellatley. There is no gainsaying the fact that Jock answers to his literary double in an astonishing number of ways. It is Jock's lineaments which look out from the pages of the novel—Jock's quaint, queer self who has apparently been limned in the simpleton of Tully-Veolan. Scott knew him as a visitor at Ashestiel, and in the first days at Abbotsford. Everywhere on his native heath Jock was known as " the ladle," or " Jock the ladle." This cognomen he derived from a song which he rehearsed at the Border fairs and wherever his peregrinations carried him—

> " There cam' a man doon frae the mune,
>   Doon frae the mune, doon frae the mune ;
> There cam' a man doon frae the mune,
>   An' they ca'd him Wullie Wud.
>   An' he played upon a ladle,
>   A la-dle, a la-dle ;
>   He play'd upon a la-dle,
>   An' his name was Wullie Wud."

There were two Jock Grays—*père et fils*. No more
" kenspeckle " couple tramped the Border highways
and byways from Berwick to the Beild, from Ettrick
Kirk to Roxburgh Castle. The best account of the pair
is from the pen of Thomas Aird, who refers to them
in his *Old Bachelor*. Bowden was one of their howfs,
and Aird's parents were kind to the wanderers.

" The father was one of the very smallest of men,
but one of the Truest Bluest of Covenanting Scotland's ' True Blue '; and being thus, almost of course,
an Old Light Anti-burgher, he was compelled to toddle
to the sacraments of this denomination many a weary
mile, their congregations being very thin-sown throughout the south of Scotland. As he made it a point of
conscience not to miss one of these solemn occasions
in the three counties already referred to, he was seen
far and wide on his periodical tramps along the Scottish Border; while, moreover, twice a year, he ascended to the metropolis to sit down under Paxton or
M'Crie, with feelings akin to those of the old Hebrew
who went yearly up to the Passover at Jerusalem.
In all such pious pilgrimages his son, Jock, was his
constant attendant, or rather follower. Here marched the old little Presbyterian in front, often with the
Bible in his hand ; never failing in his track, but always fifty yards or so behind, daft Jock, bare-headed,
brought up the rear : Wherever old Johnie was seen,
daft Jock was not far behind : Wherever daft Jock
was seen, old Johnie was not far before. If any passing stranger bestowed a penny on the poor idiot, he

immediately trotted up to his sire with his unvarying
'Father, there's a penny,' and having deposited it
with the old man, who never begged himself, but yet
never declined any offerings thus vouchsafed to Jock,
he immediately fell back again to his proper place in
the rear with the utmost deference. At night, on
their way, they drew to stated places of sojourn, where
some shepherd Gaius of the hills, or village elder,
or most commonly some pious sympathetic matron
'had them' (as John Bunyan phrases it) to a decent
bed in the 'bauks' after supper : But never before
the ordinance of family worship was observed, at
which little Johnie never failed to act as priest, his
spiritual gifts being great, and his desire to exercise
them not small. Many a knotty argument in the
Bostonian divinity, and many a fierce pressing of the
Covenant on the lukewarm disciples of these degenerate times, varied throughout the evening the tongue-
doughty champion-ship of the tough old Seceder."

Though bred a weaver, Jock senior abandoned the
loom for the easier and more romantic calling of an
itinerant vendor of small wares, *videlicet*, packman.
A native of Ettrick, he lived for a time at Cross-
lee, where his son was born. Then he moved down
the valley to Lochstocks, near Selkirk, and finally to
a house in Selkirk Loan. There paralysis laid hold
of him about the beginning of 1837, and he died in
little more than a month, at the advanced age of
eighty-six years. All that could be learned at the
time about his forebears was that he was grandson on

his mother's side to John Currie (native of Berwickshire) who was minister's man to Boston of Ettrick, and one of his pious elders (see Boston's *Memoirs*). Old Jock was twice married. His first wife, Euphan Robertson, was the mother of Davie Gellatley's prototype. His second wife left him in a pet, whereupon the two Jocks took to the road for the remainder of their days.

Jock junior, who was born about the end of 1776, was nothing more than an idiot—but a most favourable specimen of the class. He was, of course, incapable of receiving instruction. He resisted every attempt to set him to some simple employment. He was intolerably lazy. People on the whole were kind to him, and he was much attached to those who showed him kindness. As befitted one who was a Baron's "fool," Jock has a somewhat glorified description in *Waverley*, but his appearance at all times was unique and conspicuous. He wore knee-breeches; his stockings were fastened by the flashiest red garters tied neatly in a rose-knot. He had a penchant for the most glaring colours, for the cart-wheel type of buttons, for the tallest of tall hats. Thus garbed, he was his father's constant way-fellow. During one of their trips to Edinburgh, Smellie Watson, R.S.A., got hold of daft Jock, and painted a capital portrait of the "innocent." The picture was exhibited at the Scott Centenary Exhibition (1871), but had been lost sight of for many years. It has now been recovered, and is in the hands of the representatives of the late Mr.

Ralph Dundas. A mere glance must deepen the conviction that it was Jock's veritable physiognomy which entered into the immortal portraiture of the fool of *Waverley*. Jock's is a rather handsome face, but symptoms of the weak and stagnant brain are obvious.

Jock passed away in the house of a Mrs. Hall at Selkirk, 10th June 1837, about four months after his father—not within a week, according to Dr. Russell's account. The two Jocks rest somewhere in Selkirk's old graveyard, the spot long since forgotten.

The Jock Gray anecdotes are legion. There is the story of Jock at Ettrick Kirk—a real incident. Jock mounted the pulpit early one Sunday morning. When the minister appeared and found his place forestalled, he quietly said, " Come down, sir ; come down." " Na, na," was Jock's reply, " come ye up, Mr. Paton. Come ye up. They are a stiff-necked and rebellious people and it'll tak' us baith."

Jock was a noted kirk-ganger, but the most restless being who ever darkened the doors of a Border sanctuary. Dr. James Russell tells how in Yarrow Kirk, which Jock frequently attended, Jock would come in with a big " dunt " of bread-and-butter and cheese in his hand, munching and moving about from pew to pew. Frequently old Dr. Russell (father of Dr. James) was forced to pause during the service and reprimand Jock for his antics, or peremptorily order him to sit still. On one occasion Jock was sadly discomfited. Pushing his way into the Eldinhope servants' seat, he made as if he were about to speak to some of them. Fearful of his conduct, the plough-man planted a big hob-nailed boot on the bare feet of the natural. Imagine the consternation when poor Jock wailed out, " Oh my taes, my taes ! "

One day Jock took his place in the pew beside Henny Scott, a Yarrow body who was rather afraid of the half-wit. When Henny moved a little farther up the seat, Jock moved also, and the game went on until he had her firmly pinned against the wall and in a state of collapse. The poor old soul made for the manse after the service, totally unnerved, and ex-plained her sad state to Mrs. Russell as being due to fear that Jock would kiss her !

Dr. Robert Russell accosted Jock on one occasion : "John, you are one of the most idle boys in the par-ish. You might at least herd a few cows." " Me herd cows ! Me herd cows ! I dinna ken corn frae gersh."

At Midlem Kirk (an Auld Licht citadel) the snoring of an elderly worshipper stirred Jock into one of his humorous moods. Making for the sleeper, he seized his spectacles, transferred them to his own nose, and glared into the unconscious man's face, until some intuition awoke him, when he was nearly distracted at the great eyes adorned with " specs " peering down his throat !

Lodging at Kershope one night, father and son were installed at the fireside. At supper the elder Jock said one of his long graces. But either he was unduly prosy or young Jock was uncommonly hungry, and while the old man was roaming through the Psalms in a penitential mood, Jock advised him to be done, every now and again lifting the pot-lid and sniffing the savoury morsel within.

Jock possessed extraordinary powers of mimicry. His imitations of the styles of preaching which he heard in his rounds were perfectly marvellous. " I recollect an amusing incident," says the late Alexander A. Hogg of Hawick; " it occurred when the students were attending Professor Lawson's Hall in Selkirk. One day some half-dozen or more of them forgathered with Jock. Proffering a few pence, they readily got him to give nearly his whole budget of clerical imitations—Nicol of Traquair; Pate of Innerleithen ; Campbell of Lilliesleaf ; Jolly of Bowden ; Russell of Yarrow, and others. ' Now,' said one of them, ' before you go away we must hear Leckie of Peebles.' A son of Leckie's was present, who was evidently uneasy and not at all pleased with the proposal. But before he could interfere Jock sang out in solemn tones, ' Oh ye wicked people of Peebles ! if it were not for Sir John Hay of Hayston, you would all go to the devil together.' Young Leckie's face flushed crimson, and he made good his escape amid the merry laughter of the light-hearted youths."

Like Davie Gellatley, Jock was dotingly fond of music. He had a repertoire of verses and tunes of his own composition, and one of his ballads actually survives in print. It is nothing more than a jingle of names of persons and places familiar to him in his rounds. Jock seldom sang the song in the same way, being, it is said, partial to omissions and additions—

" There's daft Jock Gray * o' Gilmanscleugh,
    And Davie o' the Inch ;
  And when ye come to Singley,
    They'll help ye in a pinch.
      And the laddie he's but young,
        And the laddie he's but young :
      And Robbie Scott ca's up the rear,
        And Caleb beats the drum.†

There are the Taits o' Caberston,
    The Taits o' Holylee ;
  The ladies o' the Juniper Bank,‡
    They carry a' the gree.
      And the laddie he's but young, etc.

There's Lockie o' the Skirty Knowes,
    There's Nicol o' Dykeneuk,
  And Bryson o' the Priestrig,
    And Hall into the Heap.
      And the laddie he's but young, etc.

The three Scotts o' Commonside,
    The Tamsons o' the Mill,
  There's Ogilvy o' Branxholm,
    And Scoon o' Todgiehill.
      And the laddie he's but young, etc.

The braw lads o' Fawdonside,
    The lasses o' the Peel ;
  And when ye gang to Fairnielee
    Ye'll ca' at Ashestiel.
      And the laddie he's but young, etc.

There is Lord Napier o' the Lodge,
    And Gawin in the Hall,
  And Mr. Charters o' Wilton Manse,
    Preaches lectures to us all.
      And the laddie he's but young, etc.

* The name should be *Scott*. His brother was farmer of Gilmanscleugh. Jock Gray never lived there.

† Caleb Rutherford, town-drummer of Hawick. See Robert Murray's *Hawick Characters*.

‡ Misses Thorburn. Their brother is referred to under " Dandie Dinmont," Chapter III.

"DAVIE GELLATLEY"

There are three wives in Hassendean,
  And ane in Braidie-Yairds,
And they're away to Gittenscleuch,
  And left their wheel and cairds.*
    And the laddie he's but young, etc.

There's Bailie Nixon, merchant,
  The Miss Moncrieffs and a' ;
And if ye gang some further east
  Ye'll come to Willie Ha'.
    And the laddie he's but young,
      And the laddie he's but young ;
    And Robbie Scott ca's up the rear,
      And Caleb beats the drum."

With all his oddities and his harmless "knavery,"
Jock was a kindly-affectioned creature ; and it is his
humaner traits—his simplicity and loyalty—which
reappear in those of the fool Davie Gellatley.

Gellatley's commission from Rose Bradwardine to
Glennaquoich, his behaviour among the ruins of
Tully-Veolan, and rapturous glee over his grand new
bedizenment at the end, are among the most finely-
imagined and touching passages in the novel. " He
danced up with his usual ungainly frolics, first to the
Baron, and then to Rose, passing his hands over his
clothes, crying, ' Bra' bra' Davie,' and scarce able to
sing a bar to the end of his thousand-and-one songs for
the breathless extravagance of his joy." Daft Jock
Gray never rose to such heights. He was only a poor
wandering simpleton all his life, and having crossed
the orbit of Scott in the days when the novelist was
in the making, literature is richer because of him, poor
simpleton though he was.

* Hand-cards for carding wool.

CHAPTER THREE

GUY MANNERING
"DANDIE DINMONT"

" True worth and reverence in his mien,
His manners simple as the day."

PROFESSOR VEITCH.

CHAPTER THREE   GUY MANNERING "DANDIE DINMONT"

IN THE WAVERLEY ORDER OF MERIT *GUY Mannering* is easily in the first class. As a mere story it is possibly the best of the series. No novel of Scott's shows greater constructive skill, although its author's greatest feat in rapid writing. The romance differs from its predecessors in being purely a tale of private life, unconnected with any historical data, religious or political. Its chief interest centres in a number of fictitious characters and incidents, some of which have a slight foundation in fact. According to Lockhart, Scott took as a basis for the story, Train's account of an astrologer storm-stayed among the Galloway wilds and obliged to accept the hospitality of a friendly farmhouse for the night. The gudewife, about to become a mother, was in her travail. All that the astrologer foretold of the infant, his adventures abroad, and return home to recover a lost inheritance, were said to have actually come to pass. Scott had listened to a similar story from the lips of John MacKinlay, his father's Highland servant. It is this which he prints in the Preface to the *magnum opus*; but the Durham *Garland*, which Scott heard in his boyhood, contains more of the main fable of *Guy Mannering* than either Train's or MacKinlay's narratives.

Additional to these, the celebrated Annesley trial, in which claim was made to the title and estates of the earldom of Anglesey, constituted, perhaps, the nearest approach to an original foundation for the novel. Even the names of the witnesses examined have been appropriated with very slight modifications. Henry Brown, for instance, becomes Henry Bertram, *alias* Vanbeest Brown. An Irish priest, Abel, recalls the inimitable Abel Sampson. Macmullan and Macmorlan are nearly related ; and the names Jans and Kennedy and Barnes appear unaltered. A remarkable expression applied to Annesley, that " he is the right heir if right might take place," has probably served as a hint for the motto of the Bertram family, " Our right makes our might." Lockhart does not doubt that Scott had read the Annesley record, as well as Smollett's edition of the story in *Peregrine Pickle*. He cannot, however, explain the silence of the Introduction.

There is another plausible source for the *Guy Mannering* plot. This is found in the great Dormont suit which was actually in the Court of Session immediately prior to the commencement of the novel. Scott was unusually interested in the affair, and it was the subject of a long letter to Lady Abercorn on 21st May 1813. Briefly, the facts are these: Carruthers of Dormont married a lady whose fidelity he had afterwards reason to suspect. He sought divorce, but ere the proceedings could be finished, she bore a daughter of whom Carruthers was legally the father. He declined to see the child, and sent her to be brought up in a remote part of the Cheviots, and in complete ignorance as to her origin. Somehow she learnt the secret of her story. Reaching womanhood,

46

she married Henry Rutledge, the son of a neighbouring impecunious laird, and getting into difficulties, had recourse to old Dormont, to whom she compounded her rights for the sum of £450 (not £1200 as Scott says). By and by, a son and daughter were born. Within a few years both parents died in poverty. The boy was sent by a friend to the East Indies. A bundle of papers handed to him at parting he left unopened at a lawyer's. In India the youth prospered exceedingly. In course of time he revisited his native country. He came to Cumberland where he had been born, crossed the Border into Dumfriesshire, and took a shooting-lodge within a short distance of Dormont, his ancestral home. At the village inn of Dalton where he lodged, the landlady, struck by his name, gossiped with him about his family history. He knew nothing of the facts disclosed by the worthy dame, but impressed with her tale, sent for and examined his neglected packet of papers. He thereupon sought legal opinion and was advised by Lord President Blair, who was then Solicitor-General, that he had a claim worth presenting to the Court. The decision was favourable, and the true heir, returning from India a second time, celebrated his victory by giving a dinner party to his friends and counsel, and "I am sorry to add," says Scott, "was found dead in bed the next morning, having broken a blood vessel during the night." *

* See also in Miss Goldie's *Family Recollections* the story of the missing heir of Orcharton, a reputed groundwork of the novel.

On the face of it, the Dormont case is as likely as not to be the germ out of which grew Sir Walter's romance of the missing heir—that favourite theme of balladist and fiction-monger since ever Homer sang his *Odyssey*, and probably long before that. The appeal on behalf of the Rutledges was thrashed out in the Court of Session in 1811–1812, and was still pending in 1813. Scott was cognizant of the whole case before it went to the House of Lords, hence, no doubt, the rapidity with which the story sped from his pen. Of great novels written at white heat, *Guy Mannering* is the most conspicuous example. With the exception of *Count Robert* and *Castle Dangerous*, the Waverleys were all composed without effort, the chapters flowing from Scott's quill as easily as the Tweed ran past the windows of Abbotsford. Here is a novel of fifty-eight chapters and comprising (say) 170,000 words, begun and completed " within six weeks at a Christmas." Scott had only heard the tale of the astrologer in November, and by the beginning of February *Guy Mannering* had gone through the mill, and the public were buying it by the thousand—two thousand copies at a guinea each being sold on the day of publication.

The strength of the story is in its wealth of remarkable characters beyond the author's own group of heroes and heroines. The latter are four in number, none of them very interesting or attractive. Neither Harry Bertram, on whose disappearance the mystery turns, nor Charles Hazlewood, Lucy's lover, has a tithe of the interest that belongs to Dominie

48

Sampson or to Dandie Dinmont. Julia Mannering (painted from Charlotte Carpenter at the time of the Gilsland courtship), a veritable Medea in appearance with piercing dark eyes and jet-black hair, is a very fascinating damsel. So also is Lucy Bertram, what little we see of her for her habitual demureness, but neither of them cuts a striking figure. It is the redoubted Meg Merrilies with her haunting songs and incantations, her dishevelled locks, her sibylline communications, who is the real heroine of the story, and whose unbroken courage and invincible fidelity win our unswerving regard. It was characteristic of Scott to borrow so many of his best figures from life's humbler walks, from classes despised and overridden. He declares, indeed, that he was more at home among mercenaries, and moss-troopers, and outlaws, and poachers, and gypsies, and beggars, than in the company of all the fine ladies and gentlemen under a cloud whom he adopts as heroes and heroines. It was Scott's catholic gift of sympathy which enabled him to break down the barrier of class distinctions, and enrich his novels with those characters of humble life which are on the whole the finest he has drawn. Scott is for ever master of the tragedy and pathos of humble life—a life which, at Lasswade, and Ashestiel, and Abbotsford, it may be said he had under his daily inspection.

Nowadays the Scots peasant is a familiar figure in literature, but none of his modern delineators can be mentioned in the same breath as Scott, who paints him absolutely as he is, with no false sentiment or extravagance. The strength of Scott lies, there can be little doubt, in his pictures of Scottish life and character. He knew his countrymen thoroughly, and the nature of the life they lived, and he put his knowledge into language of remarkable felicity. In the characterisation both of nature and of human nature Jeffrey said that Scott was successful of all writers subsequent to Milton.

Of Originals apart from those to be noted, Tod Gabbie (Gabriel Faa) the gypsy fox-hunter was studied from Tod Willie, the huntsman of the hills above Loch Skene. The demoniacal Dirk Hatteraick was the Dutch smuggler, Yawkins. Tib Mumps was Margaret Carrick or Teasdale, of Gilsland, whose grave is still seen in Denton Churchyard ; * and Colonel Mannering, as Hogg affirmed, was just Walter Scott painted by himself. Glossin, the villain of the piece, is no doubt a copy of Gifford, the designing lawyer in the Annesley Case ; and Godfrey Bertram, who, like Gratiano, speaks an infinite deal of nothing, is thought to be drawn from the last Godfrey M'Culloch of Cardoness.†

* " Here lieth the Body of Margaret
Teasdale of Mumps Hall who died
May the 5, 1777, aged 98 years.
What I was once some may relate,
What I am now is each one's fate,
What I shall be none can explain
Till He that called call again."

† On the Gatehouse and Creetown road which winds along the shores of Fleet and Wigtown Bays—" the finest shore road in

II

Scott had high qualifications for being the author of *Guy Mannering*. As has just been said, the hearts and ways of the peasantry were well known to him. He was at home in the whole gamut of the agricultural world, so that when the inspiration drew him thither, there was a spontaneity, a fresh and radiant natural-ness about his work which a town-bred man could not have realised. It is this feature which makes *Guy Mannering* so successful—its glow and spirit, the sense of out-of-doors-ness which blows like a pure and fragrant breeze through every chapter.

The manners described in the novel had either al-together disappeared or were greatly modified in Scott's day. He was illuminating a period at least fifty years earlier. Speaking of the farming class, he says that they are " a much more refined race than their fathers. Without losing the rural simplicity of

Britain"—are the reputed scenes in *Guy Mannering*, though Scott, not committing himself, merely smiled when he heard the sugges-tion. Gatehouse-of-Fleet, at one end, is supposed to be the " Kippletringan " of the novel, and Creetown, at the other, " Portanferry." Either Cardoness or Barholm is " Ellangowan Auld Place " (though the building itself is evidently modelled from Caerlaverock). Cassencary is " Woodbourne," and the " Kaim of Derncleugh " is located in the neighbourhood of Skyreburn. Half-way between the two extremities mentioned and by the rocky shore at Ravenshall, is " Dirk Hatteraick's Cave," accessible only when the tide is out. The " Gordon Arms at Kippletringan," where Mannering puts up after his return from the East, is the Murray Arms of to-day. The Masons' Lodge, where the sale of Ellangowan is detailed in chap. xiv. of the novel, adjoins the hotel. This is all a piece of guesswork, but the resemblances are striking.

manners they now cultivate arts unknown to the former generation, not only in the progressive improvement of their possessions, but in all the comforts of life. Their houses are more commodious, their habits of life regulated so as better to keep pace with those of the civilised world; and the best of luxuries, the luxury of knowledge, has gained much ground among their hills during the last thirty years. Deep drinking, formerly their greatest failing, is fast losing ground; and while the frankness of their extensive hospitality continues the same, it is, generally speaking, refined in its character, and restrained in its excesses."

At the distance of a century after Scott's time, the most sweeping change is in the matter of the farms themselves. The extraordinary diminution in the number of independent holdings is a momentous and vexing feature in modern Scottish life. The number is stated to be only one-half of what it was in the *Guy Mannering* period, or even in Scott's day. Two, and three, and more smiling Charlieshopes have been merged into a single tenancy with an accompanying depopulation—that to-day's curse of Scotland. In a letter dated 1771, one clergyman (Muschet of Tweedsmuir) tells how seven farms in his parish were annexed by a single individual, and no fewer than fourteen families turned adrift as no longer necessary under the new conditions. Sixty years ago, the number of people engaged in the cultivation of the soil amounted to two millions; now, there are little more than half a million. A system so deplorable cannot be too much deprecated. On all hands the hope is expressed for a speedy reversal of such an unhappy state of affairs. The salvation of many a rural parish will only be found in a solution of its land problem. With the return of the land to its original and proper place in the fortunes of the people one of the most vital triumphs in Scottish history will be vindicated. Spite of that haunting "yerd-hunger" which in the end ruined Scott, he was not untouched by the pathos of the empty glens of Tweed and Yarrow. It required no prophet's vision to convince him of what was coming. He knew that Goldsmith's lines rang sadly true :

> " But a bold peasantry, their country's pride,
>   When once destroyed, can never be supplied."

Guy Mannering contained Scott's own favourite among his men characters, the honest sheep-farmer, Dandie Dinmont, the best rustic portrait, as the *Edinburgh Review* said, " that has ever yet been exhibited to the public,—the most honourable to rustics, and the most creditable to the heart as well as the genius of the author, the truest to nature, the most complete in all its lineaments."

We get our first glimpse of Dandie in the little Cumberland alehouse which afforded the last chance of refreshment to the traveller northbound by the wild and thief-haunted Waste of Bewcastle. At the inn we also meet Meg Merrilies, and Vanbeest Brown, the metamorphosed Harry Bertram. As the farmer rose to go, Meg warned him of danger ahead from Border bandits. Dandie scouted the suggestion, to discover, to his cost, the singular candour of the old hag. He was waylaid, and would have fared badly, but for the timely appearance of Bertram (with Wasp), who was making the journey on foot into Dumfriesshire. Having mastered their assailants, the pair mounted on Dumple ("Dumple could carry six folk if his back were long enough "), made off like whitrets [weasels], and without further mischance gained the boundary line, and were soon at Dandie's home among the hills. " Descending by a path towards a well-known ford, Dumple crossed the small river, and then, quickening his pace, trotted about a mile briskly up its banks, and approached two or three low thatched houses, placed with their angles to each other, with a great contempt of regularity. This was the farm-steading of Charlieshope, or, in the language of the country, 'the toun.' A most furious barking was set up at their approach by the whole three generations of Mustard and Pepper, and a number of allies, names unknown. The farmer made his well-known voice lustily heard to restore order ; the door opened, and a half-dressed ewe-milker, who had done that good office, shut it in their faces, in order that she might run ' ben the house ' to cry ' Mistress, mistress, it's the master, and another man wi' him.' Dumple, turned loose, walked to his own stable-door, and there pawed and whinnied for admission, in strains which were answered by his acquaintances from the interior. Amid this bustle Brown was fain to secure Wasp from the other dogs, who, with ardour corresponding more to their own names than to the hospitable temper of their owner, were much disposed to use the intruder roughly.   In about a minute a stout labourer was patting Dumple, and introducing him into the stable, while Mrs. Dinmont, a well-favoured buxom dame, welcomed her husband with unfeigned rapture.   ' Eh, sirs ! gudeman, ye hae been a weary while away ! ' "

The chapters which follow are founded on Scott's Liddesdale experiences between the years 1792 and 1799.   At the Michaelmas Circuit at Jedburgh in the first-mentioned year, Scott, a newly-fledged advocate, made the acquaintance of Robert Shortreed (afterwards Sheriff-Substitute of the county), son of Thomas Shortreed, an extensive farmer in Jed Forest. He was Scott's senior by nine years, and had spent the whole of his life by Jed Water.   Shortreed was an authority on ballads.   It was this circumstance that drew the twain together.   For ever since Scott as a boy came under the spell of the *Reliques*, the study of ballads engrossed much of his attention, and was become a sort of passion with him.   He longed to do for the Border what Bishop Percy had done for his own land. The material, therefore, must be gathered before it was too late, ere the memory of the minstrels and their stock-in-trade had vanished.   Scott was aware that in Liddesdale some of the old "riding ballads" were still extant.   He had also the wish to see the Castle of Hermitage and to explore a district which, though it is part of Roxburghshire, he was comparatively

55

ignorant of. Robert Shortreed, however, knew every foot of it. He had many friends there, and was the best guide Scott could have had. The pair set out from Abbotrule, the residence of Charles Ker, one of Scott's intimates. They would probably go up the Rule to Bonchester Bridge, strike off towards the Slitrig, climb Limekiln Edge, and make the descent by the path parallel with Whitterhope Burn, on the east of which lies the Nine-Stane Rig of Leyden's *Lord Soulis*, and a little further over,

> " The brown ruins scarred with age
> That frown o'er haunted Hermitage."

Or they might proceed by Southdean and Dykeraw to Jed Head and the Raven Burn, and on to the ridge where they would join the almost obliterated Wheel-Causeway redolent of Edward the First's victorious marchings. Thence, following the course of the Peel Burn, the valley of the Liddel would be reached. There is another road they may have taken—by Hyndlee and over the steep, tortuous Note o' the Gate (spelled Knot o' the Gate in the novel) and Singden, then down the Dawston Burn (reminiscent of Jock o' Dawston Cleugh) to Saughtree and Liddelside.

That Liddesdale did not produce the fruits anticipated by the travellers seems tolerably certain from some of Scott's letters and from the *Minstrelsy* itself. They unearthed a few treasures, but what they lacked in the shape of ballad discovery had other agreeable compensations. They formed heaps of friendships. They encountered an endless round of hospitalities, and, not least, they laid in magnificent stores of health and strength. It is doubtful if Scott ever again experienced days more peacefully delightful. Regarding these rambles ("raids" was the word Scott favoured) the memoranda furnished to Lockhart by Scott's lively companion is the best of commentaries. That need not be repeated here, save to recall Shortreed's oft-quoted statement that Scott was "makin' himsel' a' the time; but he didna ken, maybe, what he was about till years had passed." Ostensibly, Walter Scott's object in raiding Liddesdale was to collect matter for the *Minstrelsy*, which even then was simmering in his brain. Or did the Liddesdale peregrinations suggest a bolder and a higher flight? The gains of Liddesdale, at all events, were turned to excellent account in after years. Not only *Guy Mannering*, but quite two-thirds of Scott's romances were the fruit of that raiding epoch which did so much to develop and make possible the Scott who, as Taine has well said, gave Scotland a citizenship in literature.

According to Shortreed, Willie Elliot of Millburnholm (now Millburn) was the great Original of Dandie Dinmont. Millburnholm, the Charlieshope of the novel, was situated a short distance north of the bridge which spans the Hermitage Burn on the west side of the road leading to Hawick. The farmhouse is no longer in existence, its site being occupied by a couple of workmen's cottages, and the farm itself has been merged in the one adjoining. The place was one of the first visited by Scott, and intimacy with Willie

57

Elliot was maintained in every summer that followed. Shortreed's account of the first interview is exceedingly happy. Scott, as was said, had just turned advocate, and "advocates were not so plentiful, at least about Liddesdale." Of course there was the usual bustle, not to say alarm, when the honest farmer was informed of the quality of one of his guests. When Scott dismounted, Elliot received him with great ceremony and insisted upon leading his horse to the stable. Shortreed accompanied Willie, however, and the latter, after taking a deliberate peep at Scott out by the edge of the door-cheek, whispered : "Weel, Robin, I say, deil hae me if I'se be a bit feared for him now ; he's just a chield like ourselves, I think." Half a dozen dogs of all degrees had already gathered round the advocate, and his way of returning their compliments set Elliot at once at his ease.

If Elliot of Millburnholm is to be regarded as Dandie's prototype, he was at that time a man still on the sunny side of forty, having been born in 1755. He was the son of the former tenant, Robert Elliot, and his mother was a Scott of Greenwood. He married Elizabeth Laidlaw, of Falnash, and lived to 1827.* A son and daughter, Robert and Jean, survived him. "When a lad I frequently saw Willie Elliot and his wife," wrote a nonogenarian in 1902. " Willie was the good and generous soul that Dandie

---

* Willie Elliot's grave may be seen in the lonely kirkyard of Unthank in the Ewes valley. A great " throuch " covers his remains, and the inscription is becoming illegible.

was, and Mrs. Elliot had not a few of Ailie's characteristics. She was a pleasant woman."

Lockhart does not confirm Shortreed's claim. All
he says is, "There can be little doubt that he sat for
some parts of the portrait." The race of Dandies
and Ailies was then powerful in the land, and almost
any of them might have stood for the picture of the
bluff, but honest-hearted, and faithful farmer and his
good-natured spouse. In a note to the novel, Scott
indeed declares that the character of Dinmont was
drawn from no particular person, and he asserts that
a dozen at least of stout Liddesdale yeomen with
whom he was acquainted, and whose hospitality he
shared in his rambles, might well lay claim to the
honour.

In his lifetime, it does not appear to have been suggested that Elliot was Dandie's Original. It was otherwise with James Davidson of Hyndlee, who carried
the name of Dandie with him to the grave. Yet
Scott and Davidson never met until more than a year
after the novel had established the man's celebrity
all over the Border. "I have been at the Spring
Circuit" [at Jedburgh], wrote Scott to Terry, "and
there I was introduced to a man whom I never saw
in my life before—the genuine Dandie Dinmont. Dandie is himself modest, and says, 'he believes it's only
the dougs that is in the buik, and no himsel'.' In
truth, I knew nothing of the man except his odd
humour of having only two names for twenty dogs."
Shortreed—one of Davidson's intimates—would no

59

doubt tell Scott about the Hyndlee terriers. That
Scott ever saw them in their own native haunts
there is no evidence whatever ; nor for the stupid
story which represents Davidson as exclaiming ire-
fully : " I wish to goodness that hirpling auld body
would only come this way again. I wad thraw his
neck for him." Contrariwise, Davidson was flattered
with the Dandie compliment, but he never read the
" buik." " Ailie used to read it to him, and it set
him to sleep." As for Dandie's fox-hunting proclivities, does not Scott give himself away with
regard to Davidson when he adds in the note aforesaid that " his passion for the chase in all its forms,
but especially for fox-hunting, as followed in the
fashion described in chapter xxv., in conducting
which he was skilful beyond most in the south
highlands, was the distinguishing point in his character " ? Apparently there was more of Dandie in
the Hyndlee farmer than Scott meant to admit. An
English lady of rank and fashion, being desirous to
possess a brace of the celebrated Mustard and Pepper
terriers, expressed her wishes in a letter which was
literally addressed to Dandie Dinmont, under which
very general direction it reached Davidson, who was
justly proud of the application, and failed not to
comply with a request which did him and his favourite attendants so much honour.

James Davidson's death took place at Bongate,
Jedburgh, 2nd January 1820. He was in his fifty-
fifth year. He lies buried under the shadow of Oxnam

Kirk. The ruling passion for sport was said to be strong even on the eve of dissolution. Baillie of Mellerstain's fox-hounds had started a fox opposite his window a few weeks before, and as soon as he heard the sound of the dogs his eyes glistened; he insisted on getting out of bed, and with much difficulty got to the window and there enjoyed the fun, as he called it. " When I came down to ask for him," says the minister who attended him, "' he had seen Reynard, but had not seen his death. If it had been the will of Providence,' he added, ' I would have liked to have been after him ; but I am glad that I got to the window, and am thankful for what I saw, for it has done me a great deal of good.' Notwithstanding these eccentricities, I sincerely hope and believe he has gone to a better world, and better company and enjoyments."

III

Lockhart brings a third representative of the incomparable Dandie into the arena. " I have the best reason to believe," he says, " that the kind and manly character of Dandie, the gentle and delicious one of his wife, and some, at least, of the most picturesque peculiarities of the menage at Charlieshope were filled up from Scott's observation years before this period of a family with one of whose members he had, through the best part of his life, a close and affectionate connection. To those who were sufficiently intimate with him I have perhaps already sufficiently indicated the early home of his dear friend William Laidlaw among the braes of Yarrow."

Scott visited Blackhouse in the autumn of 1802, when he made the acquaintance of Laidlaw, the "dear Willie" of the happy Abbotsford days. Laidlaw's father, James Laidlaw, and his mother, Catherine Ballantyne, were an altogether superior couple, intellectually above the average of their class, and possessed of characteristics not quite compatible with their alleged portraits in *Guy Mannering*. James Laidlaw was a singularly shy man, totally different from the Dandie of romance. Mrs. Laidlaw answered more to Ailie, and the most that can be said is that Blackhouse and its circle merely served to heighten the delightful traits of rustic character in the delineation of Dandie Dinmont's home at Charlieshope. William Laidlaw himself, be it noted, is not the prototype Lockhart has suggested, although several of Scott's biographers have hastened to that conclusion.

Other claims advanced by Robert Chambers and others, are for Mungo Park's brother, Archie of Lewinshope, on the Yarrow, and John Thorburn, of Juniper Bank, near Walkerburn. Park, whose wife was an Ailie, was a man of unique strength and stature. He had all the careless humour and boisterous hospitality of the Liddesdale farmer. On the appearance of the novel, his neighbours put him down as the Dandie Dinmont of real life, and he was so addressed by his familiar associates. Relinquishing his farm, he became a collector of Customs at Tobermory, and died there in 1831, aged about fifty.

Thorburn was a humorous, good-natured farmer, very fond of hunting and fishing, "and a most agreeable companion over a bottle. He was truly an unsophisticated, worthy man." Many amusing anecdotes are told of him, and numerous scenes have been witnessed in his hospitable abode akin to that described in the novel as taking place upon the return of Dandie from Stagshawbank Fair.

All this, however, is but further proof of the compositeness of the portrait. Neither Willie Elliot, nor James Davidson, nor the Blackhouse Laidlaws, nor any of the others, are to be accepted as individual characterisations. There were so many of the class that identification is out of the question unless Scott himself had expressly afforded the clue, which he does not do. Dandie Dinmont is nothing more than a type of the large-hearted Border farmer of a day now long by. Drawn by the deftest artist in fiction, the portrait has passed into the realm of historical representations, and other years will only add to its value.

CHAPTER FOUR

GUY MANNERING
"DOMINIE SAMPSON"

E

" I do present you with a man of mine,
    Cunning in classics and the mathematics."
                                SHAKESPEARE.

CHAPTER FOUR GUY
MANNERING "DOMINIE SAMPSON"

IN AND AROUND MELROSE THERE IS THE
constant tradition that Scott found his Dominie
Sampson in the son of the parish minister of his time.
Lockhart has been quoted as authority, but Lockhart
nowhere expressly makes the statement. The most
that he does is to reflect the opinion of the Melrosians
themselves : " Nor did Dominie Thomson," he says,
" quarrel in after times with the universal credence
of the neighbourhood that he had furnished many
features for the inimitable personage whose designation so nearly resembled his own." There is, however, little doubt as to the correctness of the identification. A good case, to be sure, may be argued for
a second claimant, James Sanson ; whilst a third
has been put into the field in the person of John
Leyden, Scott's coadjutor in the making of the *Minstrelsy*. The most that may be said for Leyden is
that he perhaps furnished hints for the character
of Dominie Sampson. The claim made for him can
hardly be taken seriously. On the other hand, if
contemporary opinion is to have any weight—and it
must be remembered that Scott offered no contradiction to it—the balance of evidence is in favour of
the Melrose representative. It is worthy of note that
in the correspondence of Mrs. Hughes, of Uffington,
a shrewd visitor to Abbotsford in its palmy days,
there is no hesitation to regard Thomson and Sampson
as one and the same.

The father of the prototype—also the Rev. George Thomson—was ordained minister of Melrose in the year 1788, and served the cure for close on half a century. During two-thirds of that period he was in the position of an assistant and successor, the senior minister dying in 1811, Thomson himself in 1835. Mrs. Thomson, the prototype's mother, was Margaret Gillon, a daughter of the Manse of St. Boswells. An incident in the career of the elder Thomson demonstrates the sturdily independent character of the man —a not inconspicuous trait in his son's character. His absentee colleague having asked for an augmentation of stipend, the junior minister claimed part, on the ground that he performed the whole of the pastoral duties. The Court listened to his petition and awarded him the entire augmentation. But the stipend was still scantily meagre, and being a family man, the hardship of his case came to be a matter of common talk in the almost famine times that prevailed. Such a condition of affairs having reached the ears of the philanthropic Dr. Johnston of North Leith, that most estimable divine at once organised a subscription, and having obtained a considerable sum, forwarded it with a letter to the Manse of Melrose. Immediately upon receipt, Thomson wrote to his Leith friend gratefully acknowledging his kindness, but desiring that every penny should be repaid to the donors, as "he and his family were content to live on their humble fare without eleemosynary assistance, no matter from what source it might be proffered." Thomson (still dealing with the father) was an exceedingly guileless person. Forgathering one day with an unknown pedestrian making his way to Lauder, he handed him his watch with a request that it might be left at the watchmaker's there for repair. Needless to say, neither watch nor stranger were seen again.

George Thomson, the Dominie, was educated at Melrose, and at the Nest, Jedburgh, and afterwards at the University of Edinburgh. On 2nd April 1816 he was licensed as a preacher by the Presbytery of Selkirk, and to the end of his days he was never anything more than a probationer. For a time he was his father's helper, and preached regularly to appreciative congregations, said one who could still remember his appearances in the pulpit. He had in him a vein of geniality and kindliness and was popular with the parishioners, despite his extraordinary and well-nigh unpardonable eccentricities. But for these he might have "wagged his head in a pulpit o' his ain," for he was clever enough otherwise, was "one of the most intelligent young men of his time." He lived, however, in a condition of chronic absent-mindedness. Not even Lawson of Selkirk could rival him upon that score. The Dominie confessed that his mind wandered greatly when in the pulpit. Once he fancied himself a General on horse-back meeting a woman with a basketful of eggs who caused his horse to shy and throw him from the saddle. At this point he suddenly ceased preaching, and to the dumbfounderment of his hearers exclaimed, " There is a grand army officer thrown by an old woman selling eggs." Thomson was a tall, handsomely-built man, vigorous and athletic to a degree. Lockhart describes him as a " dauntless horseman and expert at the singlestick." Unfortunately, he was minus a leg, the result of a boyish wrestling bout, and the spirit with which he refused at the time to betray the name of the companion who had occasioned his mishap, and the courage by which he ever afterwards struggled against its disadvantages, raised him to a special share in Scott's favour, who often said, " In the Dominie, like myself, accident has spoiled a capital lifeguardsman." This defect notwithstanding, he was a wonderful walker, and could cover great distances with surprising rapidity. He is alleged to have walked from Edinburgh to Melrose in nine hours, finishing the day by climbing to the top of the Eildons, a performance which a man possessed of both limbs might find it difficult to beat. Though so good a pedestrian, he dearly loved a ride on horseback, and many stories are told of his escapades in that connection. Even on Sundays when a pony was brought to the church door for the use of a rheumatic worshipper, George would mount the animal, take a ride round the town, and return to the kirk door where the owner was impatiently awaiting his appearance. One fine Sunday morning he hired a pony from Andrew Marr, innkeeper in Melrose, to ride to Lilliesleaf, where he was to take duty for the day. When the service was over,

George set out for home, but at Bowden Moor he dismounted and did the remainder of the journey on foot, leaving the pony to its own sweet will. As the day wore on and there was no sign of the return of his beast, Marr went down to the Manse to make inquiries. There he saw George, who excused himself with the remark that as he thought the animal would be the better of a bite of grass he had left it on Bowden Moor. Fearing the loss of his mare, Marr went off in search of her, and found her, as George had said, quietly browsing at the foot of the Eildons.

Thomson was very fond of children. His sermon-ettes to the young people of Melrose were said to be models of their kind. Like his counterpart in the novel, he was at his best with young persons, and with them he was ever a beloved and popular figure :

" God bless him for it ! " said Bertram, shaking the Dominie's hand ; " he deserves the love with which I have always regarded even that dim and imperfect shadow of his memory which my childhood retained."

" And God bless you both, my dear children ! " said Sampson ; " if it had not been for your sake I would have been contented—had Heaven's pleasure so been —to lay my head upon the turf beside my patron."

About the year 1812, George Thomson was install-ed as " Dominie " at Abbotsford. " I am relieved," Scott wrote to Terry, " of the labour of hearing Walter's lesson by a gallant son of the church, who with one leg of wood, and another of oak, walks from and to Melrose every day for that purpose." Of

Scott's four children, Sophia, the eldest, was passing into her teens; Walter was eleven, Ann about nine, and Charles five. The Dominie's business was mostly with the boys, with Walter in particular, who was being prepared, it was hoped, for the law. For how many years Walter was under the sway of Dominie Thomson is not very clear from Lockhart's pages. At sixteen, however, he was a Cornet of the Selkirkshire Yeomanry. At eighteen he joined the 18th Regiment of Hussars. Towards the close of 1820 Walter is informed (in a letter from his father) that "Dominie Thomson has gone to a Mrs. Dennistoun, of Colgrain, to drill her youngsters. I am afraid he will find a change; but I hope to have a nook open to him by and by— as a sort of retreat or harbour on his lee." It would appear, therefore, that Thomson was tutor at Abbotsford for seven summers in all. The "nook" which Scott desired to find for him was never visualized, despite many valiant attempts. Patronage was at its height in the Church of Scotland, and though Scott numbered among his friends many patrons of livings, he was never able to influence them successfully on Thomson's behalf. We have him writing (1819) to the Duke of Buccleuch for the Kirk of Middlebie: "It is doomed this letter is not to close without a request. I conclude your Grace has already heard from fifty applicants and I come forward as the fifty-first in behalf of George Thomson, being the grinder of my boys, and therefore deeply entitled to my gratitude and my good offices as far as they can go. He is nearer Parson

72

Abraham Adams than any living creature I ever saw
—very learned, very religious, very simple, and extremely absent. His father, till lately, had but a sort of
half stipend, during the incumbency of a certain notorious Mr. [Maclagan], to whom he acted only as
assistant. The poor devil was brought to the grind-
stone (having had the want of precaution to beget a
large family), and became the very figure of a fellow
who used to come upon the stage to sing 'Let us all be
unhappy together.' This poor lad George was his saving angel, not only educating himself, but taking on
him the education of two of his brothers, and maintaining them out of his own scanty pittance. He is a sensible lad, and by no means a bad preacher, a staunch
Anti-Gallican, and orthodox in his principles. Should
your Grace find yourself at liberty to give countenance
to this very innocent and deserving creature, I need
not say it will add to the many favours you have conferred on me; but I hope the parishioners will have
also occasion to say, 'Weel bobbit, George of Middlebie.' Your Grace's aide-de-camp, who knows young
Thomson well, will give you a better idea of him than
I can do. He lost a leg by an accident in his boyhood,
which spoiled as bold and fine-looking a grenadier as
ever charged bayonet against a Frenchman's throat.
I think your Grace will not like him the worse for having a spice of military and loyal spirit about him. If
you knew the poor fellow, your Grace would take uncommon interest in him, were it but for the odd mix-
ture of sense and simplicity, and spirit and good
73

morals." But a day or two afterwards Scott confessed to Adam Ferguson that he had "little expectation of success in his suit." "If the Duke mentions him to you pray lend him a lift. With a kirk and a manse, the poor fellow might get a good farmer's daughter, and beget grenadiers for His Majesty's service. But as I said before, I dare say all St. Hubert's black pack are in full cry upon the living, and that he has little or no chance. It is something, however, to have tabled him, as better may come of it another day." That "another day" never dawned for the Melrose probationer. There could have been only one obstacle —the pitiful eccentricity of the man. A passage in Scott's Diary, 28th December 1825, reveals the tender solicitude of the author of *Guy Mannering* for his Abbotsford protégé: "Last night George Thomson came to see how I was, poor fellow. He has talent, is well-informed, and has an excellent heart ; but there is an eccentricity about him that defies description. I wish to God I saw him provided in a country kirk. That, with a rational wife—that is, if there is such a thing to be gotten for him,—would, I think, bring him to a steady temper. At present he is between the tyning and the winning. If I could get him to set to any hard study, he would do something clever." Without kirk, without wife also. After his father's demise, the Dominie became a teacher in Edinburgh, where, on the morning of the 7th January 1838, he was discovered dead in bed. There is a story that the socket of his wooden leg contained a hundred sovereigns of his savings. In chronicling his death the *Edinburgh Advertiser* said that Thomson was " an excellent classical scholar, a very superior mathematician, and a man of uncommon general information. He had remarkable simplicity of character, indeed from a moral point of view he was the most amiable, downright, and honest of human beings. In fine, there was displayed in him an utter negation of anything like duplicity and malevolence. One peculiarity he had in common with many men of strong original mind, he was very absent, remarkably so ; and we are not sure but some of the eccentricities which he exhibited and the cause of which may be traced to his absence of mind were the occasion of his advancement in life not having been at all commensurate with his merits and attainments. It was impossible to know the man without feeling a regard, ay, a love, for him. The milk of human kindness in his own breast flowed in no scanty stream ; and the warmth of his feelings, which it was not his nature to disguise or repress, was calculated to endear him to all who enjoyed his friendship." His remains repose close to the great east oriel of Melrose Abbey. It has been stated that the prototype must often have preached in the Abbey when a portion of it was used as the parish church. That, however, is a mistake, the church on the Weir Hill having been opened in 1810, while the son of the minister was still a boy.

Several reminiscences and anecdotes taken down from the lips of very old people in Melrose may be given a more permanent record. Of the Dominie's pulpit appearances, for example, it is told how one day he was to occupy his father's place. The bell had ceased ringing, but the preacher had not appeared in the vestry. One of the elders stepped outside to look for him, when he was seen to emerge from the manse, fully gowned, and to make his way in a bee-line to the kirk door, leaping tombstone after tombstone by the help of his wooden leg and a walking-stick. (The same objection applies to this anecdote as to the Abbey preaching—he was not a preacher until 1816.) The most extraordinary exhibition was in the pulpit itself. He knew that some of the congregation did not relish read sermons, and he fell on a plan by which he imagined he could read and not be detected in the act. He wrote out his sermon on one side only, on separate sheets of manuscript. These he carefully arranged in the Bible, to be quietly drawn down into the pulpit as occasion required. This did well enough for a time, but waxing eloquent, an accident happened, and the mass of paper fell at his feet. The old-fashioned box-pulpit was narrow; the wooden leg did not lend itself to easy stooping, and in the endeavour to recover his fallen notes the unfortunate man got completely stuck, and had to be released from a somewhat humiliating position. One day he journeyed to Stow to preach. Arrived, he found to his horror he had forgotten his sermon. He would not be able to go on with the service, he said to the elders. He was assured that all that was necessary, in addition to the devotional exercises, was a short explanation of the passage read. Thus comforted, George ascended the pulpit, but the explanation grew and expanded into a discourse so eloquent and impressive that at the end of the service the elders came to him exclaiming that " whenever he came to Stow again to be sure to forget his paper." The Dominie was an ardent Freemason. He took an active part in the affairs of the Melrose Lodge, one of the oldest in the kingdom, coeval with the Abbey. One night when presiding at one of these meetings, he suddenly seized hold of a sword and pushing the point of it through a loaf of bread which was lying near, brandished it in front of his astonished brethren exclaiming, " Gentlemen, I present to you the staff of life upon the point of death." He often dined and spent the evening with some of the leading families in the neighbourhood. Having accepted an invitation to The Pavilion, he made his way to a roadman's cottage instead, where he astonished the inmates by bowing and shaking hands with them all. They had never seen him looking so " grand " (he was in evening dress), and it was not until the gudewife spoke that matters began to right themselves : " Dear me, Maister George " (he was always " Maister George " in Melrose), " what has come owre you the nicht ? " Looking round for a moment, he gradually realised the situation, and explained that he had come to dine with Lord Somerville, and thought he was in the presence of his Lordship and his family. The Dominie's happiest hours, however, were those spent at Abbots-

77

ford. There he was treated as one of the household. He sat at table with Scott and his guests, and performed chaplain's functions after his own unconventional fashion. Lockhart describes how at the Abbotsford Hunt dinner Thomson "said grace, as Burns says, ' As long's my arm,' beginning with thanks to the Almighty, who had given man dominion over the fowls of the air, and the beasts of the field, and expatiating on this text with so luculent a commentary, that Scott, who had been fumbling with his spoon long before he reached his Amen, could not help exclaiming as he sat down, ' Well done, Mr. George ! I think we've had everything but the view holla ! ' "

In 1819, when Prince Leopold (afterwards Leopold I. of the Belgians) visited Abbotsford, George Thomson was invited to meet him, and was much chagrined at Scott's refusal to allow the repetition of a long Latin grace which he had prepared for the occasion. At the Abbotsford " handselling," he sang Laidlaw's pathetic lyric "Lucy's Flittin'," and in the course of the evening, when the whole company were assembled in the new dining-room, John of Skye took his station, and old and young danced reels to his melodious accompaniment until they were weary, while Scott and the Dominie looked on with gladsome faces, and beat time now and then, the one with his stick, the other with his wooden leg.

It would of course be absurd to try to identify George Thomson in all the many strange characteristics of his reputed counterpart, Abel Sampson. The Introduction to the novel, in which Sampson is referred to as "a poor, modest, humble scholar, who had won his way through the classics, but fallen to leeward in the voyage of life," corresponds but remotely with the facts of the case. For Thomson, notwithstanding he was a "stickit minister," was by no means a failure. He could always keep his head above water, and he passed away in comparative comfort. It is not generally known that he penned the description of Melrose in the New Statistical Account of Scotland (1834), one of the best of the series, and some of his still extant sermons show him to have been a man of more than average ability, with a true insight into human nature, and possessed of a high ideal of duty. Julia Mannering's description of the habits of the fictitious Dominie is hardly in keeping with one who was considered fit company for the Abbotsford table—for one who was for years its familiar guest : " He pronounces a grace that sounds like the scream of the man in the square that used to cry mackerel—flings his meat down his throat by shovelfuls, like a dustman loading his cart, and apparently without the most distant perception of what he is swallowing—then bleats forth another unnatural set of tones by way of returning thanks, stalks out of the room, and immerses himself among a parcel of huge worm-eaten folios that are as uncouth as himself!" Nor in the description of his personal appearance as a "tall, gaunt, awkward, bony figure, attired in a threadbare suit of black, with a coloured handkerchief, not overclean, about his sinewy, scraggy neck, and his nether person arrayed in grey breeches, dark-blue stockings, clouted shoes, and small copper buckles," can we imagine that we have the counterfeit presentment of the Abbotsford tutor. Not so much in appearance, as in disposition, has Scott limned George Thomson in the fanciful, affectionate scholar of *Guy Mannering*. It is the simple, unadulterated character of the man that shines throughout the novel. He is a most amusing oddity forsooth, is constantly attempting and doing the most foolish, outré things, yet is he in many respects not only a notable but a noble figure. He has with some truth been compared to the great hero of Cervantes. What Dr. Johnson said of Don Quixote may be applied not inappropriately to Dominie Sampson: "However Cervantes embarrasses Don Quixote with absurd distresses, he gives him so much sense and virtue as may preserve our esteem, wherever he is, or whatever he does; he is made by matchless dexterity commonly ridiculous, but never contemptible."

Had Johnson lived to read and enjoy *Guy Mannering* he would probably have thought that, in describing the Dominie, Scott had shown a " dexterity " equally " matchless " to the Spanish author, for may we not say of the Dominie that if his character and conduct are often eminently " ridiculous " both as to subject and act, they are " never contemptible " in

THE REV. JAMES SANSON

[see page 81

ADAM ROLLAND
"Pleydell"

[see page 89

either motive or spirit. Here is a man utterly deficient in those qualities of sagacity, prudence, and common sense usually essential to worldly prosperity, and generally so requisite to obtain the esteem and respect of others ; and yet, as a kindly critic puts it, though Sampson is destitute of these qualities, the wisest man of honour and principle who ever read the book cannot study his character without some admiration for it, and of which he would own that many infinitely superior to the poor Dominie in sense and shrewdness were totally unworthy.

But however much of a caricature Dominie Sampson may be, is there not some honour and glory in being even caricatured by such a master as Walter Scott? Thomson himself was rather proud of the fact. It is said some of his friends resented it. Nevertheless *Guy Mannering*, as one of the masterpieces of the novelist's art, has won its immortality very largely because of this boldly executed and essentially honest, good-natured figure, in whose hands is bound up so much of the destiny of the story.

II

JAMES SANSON

According to Robert Chambers, a second Original has been found for Dominie Sampson in the Rev. James Sanson, minister of the preaching station at Leadhills, in Lanarkshire, towards the close of the eighteenth century. Here the points of resemblance are quite as remarkable. There is the similarity of the name, as well as Sanson's constant use of the word "pro-di-gi-ous, pronounced syllabically, without moving a muscle of his countenance." It was Scott's early friend, John Irving, W.S., who as a boy took notice of this peculiarity and related it to Scott.

Of Sanson's somewhat chequered career little information is available. He was a native of Lauderdale, son of the tenant of Bridgehaugh Mill, in the parish of Legerwood. He was first of all a pupil at the country school of Legerwood, then at Earlston School, whose teacher, John Mill, was a notable classical scholar. Thereafter he passed to the Universities of Edinburgh and Glasgow, and at the latter of these he completed his theological curriculum. Sanson was, all accounts say, a diligent student, excelling in linguistic attainments and philosophy. He was licensed as a preacher by the Presbytery of Earlston, 24th November 1778, and became an acceptable, an admired pulpiteer. In this, both Sanson and Thomson were a long way ahead of the Dominie, whose only appearance in public, it will be recollected, ended so disastrously. Additional to his ministerial duties, Sanson, like Thomson, acted as tutor in a number of private families. Living no doubt very economically after the manner of his rearing, he managed to save a sum of twenty-five pounds, a small fortune in those days to a youth of Sanson's habits. This he devoted to an excursion into England on foot. He made his way to Harwich, crossed to Holland, travelled through a considerable portion of Germany, and returned to Scotland after a lengthened absence, having only spent about a third of his twenty-five pounds! How he maintained himself during his sojourn was never revealed. He seldom spoke on the subject, and it was thought that much of his time was spent in the monasteries, where the monks were ever ready to show acts of kindness to men of such profundity of learning as Sanson undoubtedly showed.

In 1784 he became tutor in the Manse of Earlston. There he remained for several years. The Rev. Laurence Johnston was minister of the parish, and Sanson acted as his helper. There are no traditions in Earlston respecting Dominie Sanson; indeed few of the inhabitants have heard his name. From Earlston, he removed to Elliston, St. Boswells, the residence of Thomas Scott, uncle of Sir Walter, who was factor on the Crailing estate. While superintending the education of that gentleman's family, Scott's cousins, he was appointed to the charge of Carlanrig Chapel (now the parish of Teviothead) which he held in conjunction with his tutorial work. Next, on 22nd January 1788, we find him ordained at Earlston for service at Leadhills, where he was employed as Lord Hopetoun's chaplain among the miners. Here, "with an admirable but unfortunate tenaciousness of duty, he patiently continued to exercise his honourable calling to the irreparable destruction of his own health." His death took place in 1795. Sanson's burial-place cannot be discovered. Diligent search has been made both in

Leadhills and Crawford churchyards without success. Probably (supposing him to be interred in either of these places) no memorial was erected over his remains, or any such monument has long since been defaced or altogether crumbled away. Robert Chambers says that he was a man " of the greatest stature, nearly seven feet high, and otherwise proportionately enormous. His person was coarse, his limbs large, and his manners awkward; so that, while people admired the innocence and simplicity of his character, they could not help smiling at the clumsiness of his motion and the rudeness of his address. His soul was pure and untainted, —the seat of many manly and amiable virtues." John Irving described him to Scott as a "tall, awkward and bashful gentleman, fond of curling and bowling, and devoted to books of all sorts and sizes." *

III

It is unlikely that Scott adopted John Leyden as his Original in depicting the eccentric though worthy Dominie. Leyden began his career as a country schoolmaster at the Luggie, Clovenfords, and blossomed into a minister of the Kirk, but was like Abel Sampson, a "stickit minister." He was a tutor too, the most profound linguist of his time, and a voracious bookworm. Leyden's voice was "raucous, naturally loud and harsh, and (in a dispute) exaggerated into what he

* See a lengthy correspondence in *The Scotsman*, February to March 1903, on the subject of Dominie Sampson. Some interesting particulars are given of James Sanson.

84

himself used to call his saw-tones, which were not very pleasant to the ear of strangers. His manner was animated, his movements abrupt, and the gestures with which he enforced his arguments rather forcible than elegant; so that, altogether, his first appearance was somewhat appalling." Physically, however, Leyden and Sampson were poles asunder. Leyden was of middle size, thin, muscular; his features well-proportioned; his cheek a clear hectic red.

Between Scott and Leyden there existed the most genuine friendship till the close of the latter's brief life in 1811. It fell to Scott to pen the Memoir of his quondam literary associate for the *Edinburgh Annual Register*. Leyden is mentioned more than once in *The Lay*:

> " His bright and brief career is o'er,
>   And mute his tuneful strains;
>   Quenched is his lamp of varied lore
>   That loved the light of song to pour;
>   A distant and a deadly shore
>   Has Leyden's cold remains."

In *St. Ronan's Well* Josiah Cargill is made to utter a similar sentiment. So that, if for nothing but the memory of a dear friendship, can we conceive of Scott caricaturing his dead ally, spite of any honour in being so caricatured? No doubt there are resemblances between Leyden and Sampson. Both were poor, both were learned, both were bookmen, both ridiculed astrology, and both were Cameronians. On the principle that Scott's portraits were "composites" less or more, it is probable that Leyden was made to furnish *hints* for the character of the Dominie. But that is all that can be said.

Lancelot Whale, Scott's dominie at Kelso, son of Andrew Whale, schoolmaster of Earlston, has been spoken of in this connection ; and there are others with whom the name is associated. But if the honour is to be divided, it can only be divided between Thomson and Sanson.

CHAPTER FIVE

GUY MANNERING
"PLEYDELL"

" So wise, so grave a tongue,
    And loud withal, that would not wag, nor scarce
Lie still without a fee."

BEN JONSON.

THE FIRST WE HEAR OF PLEYDELL IS IN his capacity as Sheriff of the county conducting the inquiry into Kennedy's murder. He is not mentioned by name, for his appearance then is purely official and ephemeral. He does not make his début as the redoubted Counsellor till well on in the story, when Mannering and Dinmont are introduced to the saturnalia in which Pleydell was principal actor. It is from Scott himself we derive the information which connects one of his own old friends with this character. In June 1830 Scott visited at Luscar * and set down in his Diary that he " saw with pleasure the painting by Raeburn, of my old friend Adam Rolland, who was in the external circumstances, but not in frolic or fancy, my prototype for Paul Pleydell." Pleydell is pictured as a lively, sharp-looking gentleman, with a professional shrewdness in his eye, and, generally speaking, a professional formality in his manners. Earlier in the tale he is said to be " well born and well educated; and, though somewhat pedantic and professional in his habits, he enjoyed general respect." As a veteran of the law, he was " thirled to the old road, and was one of those praisers of the past time, who, with ostentatious obstinacy, affected the manners of a former generation. He was a good scholar, an excellent lawyer, and a worthy man." Thus far

* Scott indicates Anstruther as the place where he saw the portrait. That, of course, is a mistake.

the Rollandic part of the prototype, though the description might stand for that of a number of Edinburgh lawyers of the time. We have Scott's statement, however, that the particular person he had in view was Adam Rolland. The rest of the characterisation belongs to another and a totally different personage, of whose identity Scott gives not the slightest clue. He goes on to say of Pleydell that "his professionalism, like his three-tailed wig and black coat, he could slip off on a Saturday evening, when surrounded by a party of jolly companions, and disposed for what he called his altitudes."

To combine in a single character, as Scott was so fond of doing, the habits and foibles of two or more individuals who may be at opposite poles of temperament, is disconcerting enough. There was no possible resemblance between Rolland and Pleydell "of the High-Jinks," for whom another Original must be found. A well-established tradition of the Parliament House points to Andrew Crosbie as the undisputed prototype—a limb of the law, who, in the heyday of his power, enjoyed as great a reputation as Rolland had in his.

To take Rolland first. Adam Rolland—who must not be confounded with his nephew of the same name, Principal Clerk of Session and Scott's colleague —had passed his eightieth year when *Guy Mannering* appeared. Rolland's father was Laird of Luscar and Gask in Fifeshire. Born in 1734, Adam received his earlier education at Dunfermline. He studied law at Edinburgh University, and was called to the Bar in 1757. The legal profession, he said, was never to his liking, and he only adopted it in deference to the opinion of friends. A great luminary he became nevertheless. He did not shine as a pleader in public, for he seldom opened his mouth in Court, but confined himself to written pleadings and the giving of opinions, a branch of professional employment in which he is averred to have had no rival. Had he desired it, he might have become a Judge of the Supreme Court; but though urged many times, he could not bring himself to relinquish his quiet sphere for one so prominent and in which public speaking was a necessity. Retiring from business about 1799, he was appointed Deputy-Governor of the Bank of Scotland, and died at his Edinburgh residence in Queen Street, on 18th August 1819. He never married. It is said that but for his extreme shyness he would have asked (not unsuccessfully) for the hand of Miss Gray of Teasis. That lady died first, bequeathing to him all her possessions and her burial-plot in St. Cuthbert's Churchyard, where by and by he was laid beside her.

Two pen-portraits of Adam Rolland have come down to us, exhibiting a study in contrasts almost as startling as those which exist between the prototypes, Rolland and Crosbie, themselves. The *Edinburgh Magazine* (September 1819), in chronicling the death of Rolland, refers to him as " an accomplished gentleman, an elegant scholar, an eminent lawyer, a Christian from conviction, a man of unsullied probity and honour, of liberal and munificent habits and an ardent lover of his country. He was an acute observer of men and manners, had an inexhaustible fund of anecdote, which he never introduced but with point and effect. He had an exact and critical knowledge of the Latin language, and the English language he made it his peculiar study to speak, as well as to write, with purity and elegance. He was a zealous Presbyterian and regularly attended public worship until his deafness rendered him incapable of hearing. The Sunday he carefully kept sacred both from business and company. Amid the unceasing round of engagements, great, he said, was the benefit he had derived from that rule which gave him the command of a portion of time to himself. As to his personal appearance, he was little above the middle size, erect, without any tendency to stoop, even in his declining years ; his features, as well as person, elegantly formed, with a graceful demeanour and fine expression of countenance ; exact in his dress, without any approach to frivolity—a finished gentleman of the former age— but without any of that peevish nonconformity with the present time, which is often the weakness of age, and which lessens that usefulness which men so respectable as Mr. Rolland have always in their power, and which he never failed to exercise to his friends, his neighbours, and the public. He took a warm interest in the public and private occurrences of the day, and was always ready to countenance by his

name, and aid by munificent donations, every charitable plan that appeared to him to be recommended
by its utility.   His charities, both of a public and private kind, were liberal and extensive, and many who
were relieved by his bounty will lament his death."

Now take this from Lord Cockburn's *Memorials* :
" Another Edinburgh character ceased in 1819 to
be gazed at by men.   This was Adam Rolland, advocate, sometimes said to have sat to Scott for his
picture of Pleydell ; a worthy but fantastic personage. His professional practice had been very extensive, but only as a consulting and a writing counsel ;
for he never spoke, nor honoured the public by doing
anything in its presence. Divested of buckram, he
was a learned and sound lawyer, and a good man,
much respected by his few friends.   But there are
many men to whom the buckram is everything, and
he was one of them.   It was by his outside that he was
known to the world. He was old at last ; but his youth
was marked by the same external absurdity that adhered to him through life, and I presume followed him
into his coffin.

" His dresses, which were changed at least twice
every day, were always of the same old beau cut ;
the vicissitudes of fashion being contemptible in the
sight of a person who had made up his own mind as
to the perfection of a gentleman's outward covering.
The favourite hues were black and mulberry : the stuffs
velvet, fine kerseymere, and satin. When all got up, no
artificial rose could be brighter or stiffer.   He was like

93

one of the creatures come to life again in a collection of dried butterflies. I think I see him. There he moves, a few yards backwards and forwards in front of his house in Queen Street ; crisp in his mulberry-coloured kerseymere coat, single-breasted ; a waistcoat of the same with large old-fashioned pockets ; black satin breeches with blue steel buttons ; bright morocco shoes, with silver or blue steel buckles ; white or quaker-grey silk stockings ; a copious frill and ruffles ; a dark brown, gold-headed, slim cane, or a slender green silk umbrella : everything pure and uncreased. The countenance befitted the garb : for the blue eyes were nearly motionless, and the cheeks, especially when slightly touched by vermilion, as clear and as ruddy as a wax doll's ; and they were neatly flanked by two delicately pomatumed and powdered side curls, from behind which there flowed, or rather stuck out, a thin pigtail in a shining black ribbon. And there he moves, slowly and nicely, picking his steps as if a stain would kill him, and looking timidly, but somewhat slyly, from side to side, as if conscious that he was an object, and smiling in self-satisfaction. The whole figure and manner suggested the idea of a costly brittle toy, new out of its box. It trembled in company, and shuddered at the vicinity of a petticoat. But when well set, as I often saw him, with not above two or three old friends, he could be correctly merry, and had no objection whatever to a quiet bottle of good claret. But a stranger, or a word out of joint, made him dumb and wretched."

" It is difficult to account for his practice ; for

though industrious, honourable, kind, and timidly judicious, he had slender talents, and no force, and the age in which he acted was one in which I should have thought that neither Bar nor Bench would have had any patience with gilded filigree. I wonder Braxfield did not murder him by a single grunt. However, I suppose that there must have been something more in him than I am aware of, else he could not have been the oracle that some people held him. When I was about to begin my legal studies, I was reckoned a singularly fortunate youth, because he had condescended to intimate that he would advise me how to conduct them. I was therefore ordered to wait upon him. I did so, and after being eased of some of my awe by a kind reception, and a few very simple jokes, the lesson commenced. It consisted entirely of a short discourse by the sage, for I sat nearly dumb ; and its result was more than once summed and repeated, as if to make me recollect the very words. These I do not now remember ; but surprise has prevented my ever forgetting their tone and import, which were exactly to this effect—' In short, my young friend, philosophy is the vice of the age. Take my advice, and read nothing whatever but Scotch and civil law, except the first volume of Blackstone, the introduction to Robertson's *Charles the Fifth*, Hume's *History of the Stewarts*, and De Lolme ; never have a pen out of your hand, and keep a commonplace book on Locke's plan '—a volume of which, kept by himself, he showed me as a specimen. In so far as

95

kindness and pedantry went, he may be supposed to have had some resemblance to Pleydell ; but nobody who knew, or indeed ever saw, Rolland can imagine his descending to High Jinks, especially in a tavern."

Lord Cockburn's sketch was penned at least a dozen years after Rolland's departure. There are corroborations of the *Advertiser's* remarks, but one would scarcely associate both notices as appertaining to the same person. The truth is that Cockburn wrote unadvisedly. He did not care for Rolland. His account was biased, perverted, strained. Moreover, he was ignorant of Rolland's real character. Rolland belonged neither to the Beau Nash nor the Georgian School of dandies. He had his foibles, his idiosyncrasies, amongst them a pronounced love of externals, but not to the extent indicated by Lord Cockburn's impressionism. The latter has entirely failed to grasp the inner and better traits of Rolland, and as for his legal acumen, he relegates him to a quite ordinary place, whereas Rolland stood in the front rank as a pleader, withal a silent one. Making every allowance for Rolland's eccentricities, Lord Cockburn's picture must be confessed to be little more than a caricature.*

II

ANDREW CROSBIE

As already said, Andrew Crosbie has been generally held to represent the " High-Jinks " Pleydell. Scott,

* It may be interesting to note that the wife of Principal Rainy, Susan Rolland of Luscar, was granddaughter of Scott's friend,

ANDREW CROSBIE
"Pleydell"

GEORGE CONSTABLE
" Jonathan Oldbuck "   [see page 119

however, could not have known much about him personally, for Crosbie had been dead thirty years before
the publication of *Guy Mannering*, when the future
author was a lad of fourteen. Memories of Crosbie
lingered about the Parliament House. His portrait still
adorns its walls, and in Scott's young advocate days
Crosbie's meteor-like career was one of the chief traditions of Bench and Bar.

Crosbie was a native of Dumfries, son of Andrew
Crosbie, and grandson of John Crosbie, both Pro-
vosts of the burgh. His mother was a Grierson of
Barjarg (related to the Lag family) and his uncle-
in-law was Lord Justice-Clerk Tinwald. The Cros-
bies had long been connected with the county. They
were lairds of Holm (now Goldielea), a sweet spot, a
short distance from Dumfries. Andrew Crosbie—
Pleydell's transcript—was born in 1736. Little is
known of his early life. He was admitted to the
Faculty of Advocates the same year as Rolland. Unlike Rolland, he devoted himself heart and soul to his

Adam Rolland, W.S., and great-grandniece of Pleydell's prototype :

Adam Rolland of Gask and Luscar, =
    d. 1763.

Adam Rolland, "Pleydell," *d.* 1819.   Rev. Robert Rolland, Culross ▬

Adam Rolland of Gask and Luscar, W.S., =
    Principal Clerk of Session.

Adam Rolland of Gask and Luscar, =
    W.S.

Susan Rolland = Rev. Principal Rainy, D.D.

Dr. Adam Rolland Rainy, M.P.

studies, and quickly won his way to recognition as the most daring and eloquent pleader of his time. In 1784 he became Vice-Dean of Faculty, and might have been President of the Court of Session but for his untimely death, brought about largely by his inveterate love of tavern-haunting. When Crosbie flourished it was the fashion for members of the Bar to transact whatever business was not actually required to be done at Court, in the taverns and coffee-houses with which the Lawnmarket and High Street of Edinburgh a-bounded. No lawyer could be found at his own abode. " The chief thing was to find out his tavern and he would be sure to be there." Crosbie's favourite haunt was Clerihugh's (the name in the novel), a well-known howf in Writer's Court at the close of the eighteenth century. It was here, on that notable Saturday night described in the thirty-sixth chapter, that Mannering and Dinmont, having turned from the High Street " into a dark alley, then up a dark stair, then into an open door " (this is hardly a picture of the real Clerihugh's), found themselves bewildered in presence of orgies which had lasted from well on in the afternoon. " With some difficulty a waiter was prevailed upon to show Colonel Mannering and Dinmont the room in which their friend, learned in the law, held his hebdomadal carousals. The scene which it exhibited, and particularly the attitude of the counsellor himself, the principal figure therein, struck his two clients with amazement." Pleydell was " enthroned as a monarch in an elbow-chair placed on the dining-table, his scratch wig on one side, his head crowned with a bottle-slider, his eye leering with an expression betwixt fun and the effects of wine, while his court around him resounded with such crambo scraps of verse as these :

' Where is Gerunto now ? and what's become of him ?
Gerunto's drowned because he could not swim, etc. etc.'

" Dinmont was first in the room. He stood aghast a moment, and then exclaimed : ' It's him, sure enough. Deil o' the like o' that ever I saw ! ' "

At the period treated of in the novel scenes such as that now described were common to the life of the capital. Some English reviewers of *Guy Mannering* fell foul of the author for his " exaggerated " sketches of Edinburgh society. Scott, however, declared that he was not overstepping the bounds of accuracy in depicting the manner in which the lawyers of long ago united the worship of Bacchus with that of Themis. In illustration, he quotes an episode in the career of Lord President Dundas the Elder. Dundas, when Lord Advocate, was called to draw up an appeal. The time was Saturday at noon. The Court had risen. Dundas had just changed his dress. His servant and horse were at the foot of the close to carry him to Arniston. It was scarcely possible to get him to listen to a word. The agent, however, pretending to ask a question or two which would not detain his Lordship more than half an hour, proposed an adjournment to a neighbouring tavern. Thither they went. The learned counsel was soon involved in a spirited discussion of the case. At length it occurred to him that he might as well ride home in the cool of the evening. The horses were stabled. Dinner was ordered, and the bottle circulated freely. At nine o'clock at night, after he had been honouring Bacchus for so many hours, the Lord Advocate called for paper, pen, and ink, began to dictate the appeal, and continued at his task till four o'clock the next morning. By next day's post the solicitor sent the case to London—a *chef-d'œuvre* of its kind ; and in which it was not necessary to correct five words. This, it will be recalled, is what actually happened with Driver, Pleydell's drunken clerk.

" Oh, drink never disturbs him, Colonel ; he can write for hours after he cannot speak. I remember being called suddenly to draw an appeal case. I had been dining, and it was Saturday night, and I had ill will to begin to it ; however, they got me down to Clerihugh's, and there we sat birling till I had a fair tappit hen under my belt, and then they persuaded me to draw the paper. Then we had to seek Driver, and it was all that two men could do to bear him in ; for, when found, he was, as it happened, both motionless and speechless. But no sooner was his pen put between his fingers, his paper stretched before him, and he heard my voice, than he began to write like a scrivener ; and, excepting that we were obliged to have somebody to dip his pen in the ink, for he could not see the standish, I never saw a thing scrolled more handsomely."

" But how did your joint production look the next morning ? " said the Colonel.

" Wheugh ! capital ! not three words required to be altered ; it was sent off by that day's post."

But Clubdom as practised in Crosbie's day was to prove his undoing. The potency of the bottle not even this most brilliant of men could master ; and it was that which killed him in the end. He had too many " High Jinks " shrines. A songster, and raconteur of the first water, a born talker, whose *bon mots* bristled with wit and wisdom, he was the life and soul of each of them. The Crochallan Fencibles, which met in Danny Douglas's, at the head of the Anchor Close, was the most famous of those old drinking institutions. Founded by Smellie, the printer-philosopher, it was the great resort of the literary life of the capital, numbering Burns and Boswell amongst its members. It was there that Crosbie met Dr. Johnson during the latter's visit to Scotland in 1773. It is no mean praise to Crosbie that he was almost the only one who had the courage to stand up to the Dictator. Boswell describes Crosbie as " My truly learned and philosophical friend," and other references to him occur in the Life. Crosbie's death took place 25th February, 1785. It is said that he died of a broken heart, following the failure of the Douglas and Heron Bank, of which he was a director, and in which most of his fortune, made at the Bar, was involved. Robert Chambers declares that he passed away in a state of comparative destitution and friendlessness, in the garret of a great house* he had built for himself in St. Andrew Square, and adds that he was borne to the grave in Greyfriars churchyard by a handful of unconcerned strangers. He left a widow, Elizabeth Barker, who, on 2nd July 1785, was granted aliment of £40 annually from the Faculty of Advocates, " in consideration of her poverty-stricken circumstances."

---

* " This very expensive and whimsical edifice was little more than roofed in when the Bank stopped payment."—Ramsay's *Scotland and Scotsmen*, vol. i.

Principal Robertson said one day at a dinner : " Crosbie, were your town and country houses to meet, how they would stare at each other ! " Holm was only thatched and of a single story. Crosbie's mansion, at what is now No. 35 St. Andrew Square, is the first house to the north of the Royal Bank,—the offices of the Scottish Union and National Insurance Company. After Crosbie's day, it became the Douglas Hotel, and here Sir Walter spent his last night in Edinburgh. For a full account of Crosbie, where many new facts are noted, see *Andrew Crosbie*, by Frank Miller (Annan, 1925).

CHAPTER SIX

GUY MANNERING
"MEG MERRILIES"

" Old Meg she was a gypsy,
  And liv'd upon the moors ;
Her bed it was the brown heath turf,
  And her house was out of doors.

An old red blanket cloak she wore ;
  A chip hat had she on.
God rest her aged bones somewhere—
  She died full long agone ! "

KEATS.

THE GYPSY PART OF *GUY MANNERING*
Scott gathered from his grandfather's memory of
Jean Gordon of Yetholm, and from his own knowledge of gypsy life. The Gordons derived their
surname from the village of Gordon in Berwickshire,
of which the Duke of Richmond and Gordon is still
the "superior." Whether the Gordons of gypsy blood
are sib to the "gay Gordons" or not, or simply took
the name, it can at least be said that they have
shown much of their spirit. Jean Gordon, immortalised by Scott, was the most conspicuous representative of her class in her day. She is perhaps the best
known of all the gypsy race—queen of a wild world
all her own.

Kirk-Yetholm, on the immediate boundary between
the counties of Roxburgh and Northumberland, has
been the headquarters of Scottish gypsydom since the
middle of the sixteenth century. It was about then
that the gypsies appeared on the Border for the first
time. They came into the country boasting the high-
sounding designation of "Lords and Erles of Litell
Egypt," and the natural inference was that they were
really natives of the Orient who for some unexplained
reason had either been driven or were self-exiled from
the banks of "Nile's redundant stream" to find new
homes in the valleys of the Tweed and Clyde. By
others again they have been identified, not as Egyptians, but as descendants of the Lost Ten Tribes of
105

Israel. With the Jew they certainly have many things in common, and their complexional resemblance is striking. By that keen student of prophecy, Dr. Keith, they were considered a proof of the fulfilment of Ezekiel's words, " I will scatter the Egyptians among the nations and will disperse them through the countries." Grellman's theory that the gypsies reached Europe from India some time after the Tamerlane rebellion in 1417, has been disproved by firmly established facts. More acceptable perhaps is the Behram Gur theory, upheld by such authorities as Sir Henry Rawlinson and Sir Richard Burton. Behram Gur about 420 A.D. imported twelve thousand Jat minstrels from India into Persia, and their descendants emigrating gradually westward, entered Europe as late as the beginning of the fourteenth century. Be that as it may, a veil of mystery hangs to this day over the genesis of the gypsy race, nor is it likely to be dispelled.

The Scottish gypsies had their own septs and dignities, and preserved them for many a day. Their royal house was that of the Faas. The Faas figure not unfrequently in historical records, and they were allied by marriage with some of the best families. Sir John Faa of Dunbar, who made himself notorious by carrying off the Countess of Cassillis, was the hero of the ballad, " The Gypsy Laddie." Gypsy blood ran in the veins of Mrs. Carlyle, who was not slow to proclaim the fact. (Does not a cross between John Knox and a gypsy explain many things ?) Principal

Lee and Principal Story were both the offspring of gypsy ancestry, the one of pure Herefordshire stock, the other of a family connected with Jean Gordon's village of Yetholm. Dr. Robert Gordon, a distinguished divine of the Free Church of Scotland, belonged to that same sept. It has been alleged that there was a gypsy strain in Sir Walter himself, through the Rutherfords, a gypsy name at all events. May that not account for his familiarity with the breed ? Scott, like George Borrow, was the gypsies' friend. He allowed them considerable latitude about Abbotsford. The description of the gypsy camp in Crabbe's *Tales*, which is absolutely perfect both in its moral and physical expression, might have been fully realised many a summer's day and night on Tweedside within sight of the smoke of Sir Walter's home. Not seldom had he to do his duty when members of the fraternity appeared before him in a judicial capacity; that never interfered with his numerous kindly acts to the nomads. One of the few things Tom Purdie could never "thole" was Scott's partiality for gypsy camp-fires and caravans, and his fondness for gypsy children. "If folk but kenned them as I ken them," he said, "there would be less trock wi' sic a crew." But Scott was much too romantic a person not to have his imagination quickened in presence of this curious and speculative people. Their exclusion from the Waverley Gallery would have been a lamentable omission. Scott lived at a time when the gypsy fortunes were beginning to wane. A Meg Merrilies would be an impossible creation nowadays. For the gypsy *qua* gypsy is an almost vanished quantity. Police Acts, with the County Councils and Education Committees, have been quietly metamorphosing him, and within a few years he will be undistinguishable from the rest of the community.

Jean Gordon, undoubted prototype of Meg Merrilies,* greatest of gypsy blood in the realm of fiction, was born at Kirk-Yetholm about the year 1670. In her teens she wedded a Faa and had a numerous progeny. All her sons, with one exception, are said to have perished at the hands of the hangman. Her husband, Patrick (not George) Faa, was banished to the American Plantations for the crime of fire-raising, and in the same year the son who was not hanged was murdered at Huntlywood, near Earlston, by a neighbour gypsy, Rob Johnstone. Whilst a candidate for the gallows, Johnstone contrived to escape from Jeddart Gaol, and not for twelve months was he captured and brought back to undergo the death sentence, 28th August 1728. The story that Jean hunted him to Holland is apocryphal. It does not appear that she had any hand in the affair. Jean's own career alternated between acts honest and dishonest. Like the

* It is unnecessary to discuss the claim made for Flora Marshall, the Galloway gypsy, to be Meg's Original. Here are Scott's own words on the matter : " I cannot grant that the idea of Meg Merrilies was, in the first concoction of the character, derived from Flora Marshall, seeing I have already said she was identified with Jean Gordon. But I am quite content that Meg should be considered as a representative of her sect and class in general, Flora as well as others." Mrs. Carlyle thought that Margaret Euston, wife of Matthew Baillie, might stand for the Original of Meg Merrilies.

foxes, she studied to keep her own hole clean, and she carefully refrained herself, and sought to prevent others from committing depredations on those who showed hospitality. But her children were not of the same virtuous kidney, and Jean was frequently mortified at their ungrateful behaviour. Three of the sons with their wives were convicted of sheep-stealing at Jedburgh, in May 1730, and all of them went to the scaffold. This is the trial mentioned in the Introduction to *Guy Mannering*. The jury were said to be divided, but one of their number who had slept during the discussion, suddenly awoke and gave his vote for condemnation in the emphatic words, " Hang them a'." Jean herself got into trouble more than once after that. At the Jedburgh Circuit of 1732 she presented a petition setting forth that she had been indicted as an Egyptian and common vagabond, that she was old and infirm, and was willing to quit Scotland entirely. " Her Grace," says Baron Hume, who reports the case, "was banished accordingly, with certification of imprisonment and scourging should she return." The English Border now became her favourite haunt. It was there that the adventure happened which is also narrated in the Introduction to the novel, and has its counterpart in Brown's indebtedness to Meg Merrilies for shelter and protection in the den at Derncleugh (chap. xxvii.). The story is to this effect.—The tenant of Lochside (Robin Oliver), who had often shown kindness to Jean during her Yetholm days, but who had not seen her for years, was returning from

Newcastle with the money for his rent in his pocket. He was in danger of being benighted amongst the Cheviots on the road leading over Shiell Moor to the head of Bowmont Water. A light glimmering through the window of a barn that had survived the steading to which it once belonged, guided him to a place of shelter, and when he knocked at the door it was opened by Jean Gordon. Jean set up a shout of joyful recognition, "Eh, sirs! the winsome gudeman of Lochside! Light down, light down; for ye maunna gang farther the night, and a friend's house sae near." Oliver was obliged to dismount, and accept the gypsy's offer of supper and a bed. No sooner had he entered the lonely dwelling than Jean stalled his horse in a dark corner, and set about providing him with a plentiful repast. She then inquired what cash he had about him, and made earnest entreaty to take charge of it overnight. He complied, keeping back a few shillings in his pocket to avert suspicion. By and by he lay down for the night. Some little time after, the gang with whom Jean had taken up returned. They soon discovered the stranger's presence, and demanded who and what he was. " E'en the winsome gudeman of Lochside, puir body," replied Jean. "He has been at Newcastle seeking siller to pay his rent, honest man, but deil-be-licket he's been able to gather in, and sae he's gaun hame wi' a toom purse and a sair heart." " That may be, Jean," replied one of the banditti, "but we maun ripe his pouches a bit, and see if the tale be true or not." Jean set up her throat against this breach of hospitality. Oliver heard their stifled whispers and light steps by his bedside, and knew they were rummaging his clothes. When they found the money which Jean's foresight had made him retain, they held a consultation if they should take it or not, but the smallness of the booty, and the vehemence of Jean's remonstrances, determined them in the negative. They caroused and went to rest. As soon as day dawned, Jean waked her guest, produced his horse, and guided him for some miles till he was on the high-road to Lochside. She then restored his whole property; nor could his earnest entreaties prevail on her to accept so much as a single guinea. Meg's words to Brown on the morning of his departure after Kennedy's death were almost certainly suggested by this incident : " Many's the awmous your house has gi'en Meg and hers : and she has lived to pay it back in a small degree," and she placed the purse in his hand.

Scott would get his first impression of the gypsy character when at Sandyknowe. In the Smailholm district the gypsies had several favourite camping-places, Sandyknowe itself being one. Not far off were the famous Mellerstain Entries (in Earlston parish), one of the most delightful old country lanes in the Border—little frequented, splendidly sheltered by overhanging woods, with fountains of pure water at hand, on its wide and grassy sides abundance of the richest and choicest herbage, a ready store of fuel for the gathering, game galore, and everywhere nooks cosy and inviting. Scott, as boy and man, was often

111

at Mellerstain, and may have seen as many as sixty carts "lowsed" there at one time; but indeed almost anywhere between Yetholm and Earlston companies of gypsies might be encountered any day or night from Whitsunday to Michaelmas.

It was Scott's grandfather who had the Charterhouse Moor experience mentioned in the Introduction to *Guy Mannering*. Riding home one night, Robert Scott fell among a band of gypsies who were carousing in a hollow of the moor surrounded by bushes. They instantly seized his horse's bridle with many shouts of welcome, exclaiming that as they had often dined at his expense he must now stay and share their good cheer. "My ancestor," says Scott, "was a little alarmed, for, like the gudeman of Lochside, he had more money about his person than he cared to risk in such society. However, being naturally a bold, lively-spirited man, he entered into the humour of the thing, and sat down to the feast, which consisted of all the varieties of game, poultry, pigs, and so forth, that could be collected by a wide and indiscriminate system of plunder. The dinner was a very merry one; but my relative got a hint from some of the older gypsies to retire just when the mirth and fun grew fast and furious; and, mounting his horse accordingly, he took French leave of his entertainers, but without experiencing the least breach of hospitality. I believe," adds Sir Walter, "Jean Gordon was at this festival." That, however, is unlikely. Jean would be dead long before. It was probably her granddaughter, Madge Gordon (no doubt incorporated in Scott's picture of Meg), who formed the conspicuous figure of the party. Scott encountered Madge at least once during his boyhood, and never forgot the impression. " My memory is haunted by a solemn remembrance of a woman of more than female height, dressed in a long red cloak, who commenced acquaintance by giving me an apple, but whom, nevertheless, I looked on with much awe. I conceive this woman to have been Madge Gordon." Madge (or Meg) Gordon, who married a Young, was the facsimile of her grandmother. She was a remarkable personage of a very commanding presence and stature, being nearly six feet high. She had a large aquiline nose, penetrating eyes, even in her old age, bushy hair that hung around her shoulders from beneath a gypsy bonnet of straw, a short cloak of a peculiar fashion, and a long staff nearly as tall as herself. When she spoke vehemently (for she made loud complaints), she used to strike her staff upon the floor and throw herself into an attitude which it was impossible to regard with indifference. She used to say that she could bring from the remotest parts of the island friends to avenge her quarrel, while she stayed motionless in her cottage ; and she frequently boasted that there was a time when she was of still more considerable importance, for there were at her wedding fifty saddled asses, and unsaddled asses without number.

Jean Gordon's last years were spent in begging

from door to door. But the old spirit was upper-most, despite age and frailty. She chanced to be at Carlisle soon after the Forty-five. On going up Rickergate, Jean spied the heads of some of the rebels upon the top of the Scotchgate. Being a staunch Jacobite, she gave loud vent to her political partiality in such unmeasured terms of contempt for the House of Hanover and loyalty to that of Stuart that the rabble of the city, as zealous in their attachment to the king *de facto*, when there was no longer any danger from the wild Highlanders, as they had been pusillanimous the year before, when they tamely surrendered to Prince Charlie, inflicted upon the aged woman no slighter penalty than that of ducking her to death in the Eden. It happened to be a Fair Day, and the town was crowded. Jean, with characteristic bravado, moved boldly through the throng singing with broken voice :

> " To wanton me, to wanton me,
>   Ken ye what maist wad wanton me !
>   To see King George hung up at Rome,
>   To see King Jamie croon'd at Scone,
>   To see England taxed and Scotland free :
>   This is what maist wad wanton me.
>
>   But to daunton me, to daunton me,
>   This is what sair does daunton me,
>   To see an ill-faur'd German loon
>   Keep wrangfu' haud o' Scotland's croon,
>   And a' laid low that high should be :
>   This is what sair doth daunton me."

Rascaldom gathered thick about her, and the poor old gypsy, without a friend either to support or rescue her, was mercilessly pelted with mud and stones.

Those who came within her grasp, indeed, paid for their forwardness, for Jean was a stout woman still, and not easily "dauntered." But her assailants succeeded in dragging her down the street and plunged her headlong into the river. As often as she got her head above water, she shouted, " Up wi' Chairlie yet ! " and as long as she had voice left, she continued to exclaim, " Chairlie yet ! Chairlie yet ! " till she was left to her fate. Strange to say, she managed to crawl to the side and take shelter under a hedge, where next morning she was found dead, exhaustion and exposure having brought about her end.* What purports to be her grave at Denton among the Cumberland Hills is not the grave of Meg Merrilies, but of Meg Carrick, Tib Mumps, the Mump's Ha' landlady. Meg Merrilies's last resting-place is unknown.

* Such is the Carlisle tradition. Scott, it will be remembered, makes Madge Wildfire meet her doom in this fashion, though Madge lived a few hours after her ducking, and died in a hospital.

CHAPTER SEVEN

THE ANTIQUARY
"JONATHAN OLDBUCK"

" No shop is so easily set up as an antiquary's."

SCOTT

CHAPTER SEVEN   THE ANTI-
QUARY   "JONATHAN OLDBUCK"

ON THE 22ND DECEMBER 1815 WE HAVE SCOTT
writing to his friend Morritt of Rokeby, "My literary
occupation is getting through the press the Letters of
Paul, of whose lucubrations I trust soon to send you
a copy." Exactly a week later James Ballantyne is
informed in playful doggerel that the book is finished :

> " Dear James—I'm done, thank God, with the long yarns
>   Of the most prosy of Apostles—Paul ;
> And now advance, sweet Heathen of Monkbarns !
>   Step out, old quiz, as fast as I can scrawl."

The Antiquary had been bargained for some while
previously. At that time there was only " a very general sketch " before the writer, but " when once I get
my pen to paper it will walk fast enough." Obviously
more pains were taken with this novel than with its
predecessors, that is, if by " a general sketch " we are
to understand that Scott first outlined the narrative,
which is quite likely. Elsewhere he says that usually
he had written into the middle of one of the novels
without having the least idea how it was to end—
the *hab nab at a venture* style of composition. One
can scarcely imagine *The Antiquary* being so constructed. Scott must have known his plot from the
beginning, and how certain characters introduced
early on the scene were to turn out as they did in the
course of the story.

The novel made its appearance in May 1826, and
sold at the rate of a thousand a day for the first week.
In the Preface the unknown author announced that it

completed a series of fictitious narratives intended
to illustrate the manners of Scotland at three different
periods : *Waverley* embraced the age of our fathers ;
Guy Mannering that of our youth ; *The Antiquary*
refers to the last ten years of the eighteenth century.
The tale keeps to familiar ground throughout. We
never get far away from Fairport (Arbroath).* Like
its predecessors, its delineation of Scottish life leaves
nothing to be desired. Without the romantic associations of *Waverley* or the adventurous element which
is so conspicuous in *Guy Mannering*, there are
scenes and characters in *The Antiquary* in which
it surpasses both these productions. And if less exciting than the others it cannot be said to be less
pleasing or less fascinating. Lovel and his lady, Miss
Wardour, the nominal hero and heroine, are a colourless pair. As Pope would say, they have " no character at all." Scott has apparently little interest in
them, and they play only a secondary part in the
story. It is the sturdy-looking Antiquary and the rag-
ged, boisterous bedesman, Edie Ochiltree, who are the
principal personages here. Probably in none of his
other characters has Scott drawn so literally from individuals of real life as in these two instances. Some
of the incidents are dramatic enough : the Wardours'
escape from the rising tide ; the confession of the
mad crone Elspeth of the Burnfoot ; the funeral

---

* There is no warrant for identifying Fairport with Portobello
or Mussel-Crag with Musselburgh. The locale is clearly north of
the Forth, the Arbroath coast offering perhaps as good a likeness
as any to the scenery depicted.

scene in Mucklebackit's cottage, and the recognition
of Lovel by his father.   Sir Arthur Wardour (said to
be modelled from Sir John Whitefoord, Bart.) is an
eminently silly type of aristocrat—a foolish old Tory
with whom we lose all patience. Dousterswivel,* the
German quack, is clever in a way, but his humour is
too much forced. The most genuinely diverting episode in the novel, apart from the exposure of Monkbarns's foibles, is the village post-office scene.

Of all the Waverleys there are few in which Scott's
benevolent and kindly sympathy for the toiling poor
is more marked than in the case of *The Antiquary*.
Take, for example, Maggie Mucklebackit's unanswer-
able retort to Monkbarns when the latter, in reproof
of her attachment to an occasional dram, hopes that

* Scott admits that part of the narrative relating to Dousterswivel was founded on actual fact, an Earl of Traquair being similarly imposed upon by a foreigner who wanted to open up lead
mines, as he alleged, at Bold, on the Tweed, below Walkerburn.
Robert Chambers points out an Original in the person of Peter
Stranger, or Japhet Crook, who lived in the reigns of Queen Anne
and George I.   This consummate knave has been condemned to an
infamous immortality by Pope, who, in his Third Moral Essay,
speaking on the value of riches, asks :

   " What can they give ? to dying Hopkins, heirs ?
      To Chartres, vigour ? Japhet, nose and ears ? "

This in allusion to the latter having suffered personal mutilation
for practising an infamous fraud on an unsuspicious old gentleman,
by which the latter was induced to execute a will in his favour to
the exclusion of his natural heirs. Japhet is said to have migrat-
ed into Eskdale and by trickery similar to that of Dousterswivel,
induced the Duke of Buccleuch to enter into some large and ruin-
ous mining operations. The " Glenwithershins," where these
operations were conducted, was a place near Gilnockie—Johnie
Armstrong's Tower.

121

the distilleries will never be permitted to work again :
" Ay, ay, it's easy for your honour and the like o'
you gentlefolks to say sae, that ha'e stouth and routh,
and fire and fending, and meat and claes, and sit dry
and canny by the fireside ; but an ye wanted fire and
meat and claes, and were deeing o' cauld, and had a
sair heart, whilk is warst o' a', wi' just tippence in
your pouch, wadna ye be glad to buy a dram wi't, to
be eilding and claes, and a supper and heart's ease
into the bargain, till the morn's morning ? " Or this
when the Antiquary, returning from laying Steenie's
head in the grave, finds the gruff old father vainly endeavouring to repair the " auld black bitch o' a boat "
which had swamped with its crew, and congratu-
lates him upon being able to make such exertion after
so great a deprivation : " And what would you have
me to do," answered the almost desperate old man,
" unless I wanted four children to starve because ane
is drowned ? It's weel wi' you gentles, that sit in the
house wi' handkerchers at your een when ye lose a
friend ; but the like o' us maun to our wark again, if
our hearts were beating as hard as my hammer."

The whole tone of the novel is redolent of what
may be termed popular feeling. Curious to find
Scott a whole-hearted and willing democrat here.
He puts into the mouth of Oldbuck expressions
which are the antithesis of his own political creed.
He is in sympathy with reform of every kind. The
French Revolution he likens to a " storm or hurri-
cane, which, passing over a region, does great damage

in its passage, yet sweeps away stagnant and un-
wholesome vapours, and repays, in future health
and fertility, its immediate desolation and ravage."
Above all, it is by his profound interest in the fortunes
(or the misfortunes) of the labouring poor that the
novelist reaches high-water mark and binds himself
to the great heart of the people.

II

As to the Original of the Antiquary of Monkbarns
there is no dispute. Scott informs us he was "George
Constable, an old friend of my father's, educated
to the law, but retired upon his independent property and generally residing near Dundee. He had
many of those peculiarities of temper which long afterwards I tried to develop in the character of Jonathan
Oldbuck."

It was at Prestonpans, in the year 1777, in his
delicate boyhood, that Scott made the acquaintance
of the future prototype. Constable was greatly intimate with the family of the Scotts in Edinburgh,
but young Walter was mostly at Sandyknowe in
those days. They never met in the George Square
house until after his return from the Border. As
appears from the Ashestiel fragment, Constable was
not so decided an enemy to womankind as his representative Monkbarns. On the contrary, Scott was
sure that his Prestonpans friend exhibited rather
a soft side—a *tendresse*—towards "his kind and
123

affectionate Aunt Jenny," who even then was a most beautiful woman, though somewhat advanced in life. Constable was bordering on sixty at the time, and Janet Scott must have been over fifty. But nothing came of the "constant philandering" which even a child of six had wit enough to recognise. Constable continued his bachelorhood, and Scott's aunt was Miss Janet to the end of her days. She survived Constable little more than a year. Of the Prestonpans visit Scott had some pleasant recollections. It was to Constable that he owed his introduction to Shakespeare—to such characters as Falstaff and Hotspur. At a later period Constable and he were often in each other's company, a fondness for antiquarian pursuits being the bond between them. Indeed, Lockhart states that it was Constable's leanings in this direction which inspired Scott with a similar liking (was not the inspiration from another source?). Constable spent many of his Edinburgh Sundays with the Scotts—ever a welcome break in the austerity of the day to the younger generation, who coaxed Constable to turn the conversation from its severely Calvinistic tone to subjects of history and auld lang syne. He remembered the Forty-five and told many excellent stories, all with a strong dash of peculiar caustic humour. Constable presented Scott with Adelung's Dictionary at the commencement of his German studies, "and in other ways," adds Scott, "he was very kind to me." The tale of *The Two Drovers* was derived from the old lawyer, who was present at the trial. Constable, however, had gone the way of all the earth before the Waverleys burst on the astonished world.

The name Constable, imported from Yorkshire, is still common to the counties of Fife and Forfar, and some parts of Perthshire. In the Burgess Roll of Dundee (preserved in the City Charters) it is found as early as 1563, and appears frequently up to 1800. Burgesses of the name were engaged principally as brewers, as fleshers, and masons.

George Constable, the Antiquary, was the son of John Constable, "trader in Dundee," and his mother was Barbara Kirkcaldy. The father died 23rd April 1773, leaving two sons and five daughters. Of George the elder (in the novel Monkbarns is a younger son), born in 1719, there is little or no information as to his earlier life. He became a solicitor, and practised in Edinburgh for a number of years with considerable success. In 1789 the lands of Wallace-Craigie, a small property on the outskirts of Dundee, came into the market, and fell to the Edinburgh lawyer's bid for the price of £2170. The mansion, which was little better than a farmhouse, has long since disappeared in the marvellous growth of the jute city within the last century. The estate itself has been completely built over, and the annual feu-rental is very much in excess of the original purchase-money. Wallace-Craigie stood about the position of the present Middle Street. It is curious to think of this as the place where Scott forgathered with the inimitable Monkbarns, and

125

became acquainted with the scenes depicted in *The Antiquary*. Wallace-Craigie could only have represented the house of Monkbarns in a general way—as true to Monkbarns as its owner himself approximated to Jonathan Oldbuck, for here again it was the character of the Antiquary and not his actual surroundings which claimed the author's attention in presenting to the world a figure so wholly admirable and so welcome. That the laird of Wallace-Craigie should be recognised (as he was by George Chalmers, a friend of Scott's father and Constable) in the livery of Oldbuck was a matter of astonishment to Scott. "I thought," he says, "I had so completely disguised the likeness that it could not be recognised by any one now alive," and then he goes on to explain that "there is not a single incident in the novel which is borrowed from his real circumstances except the fact that he resided in an old house near a flourishing seaport, and that the Author chanced to witness a scene betwixt him and the female proprietor of a stage coach, very similar to that which commences the history of *The Antiquary*. An excellent temper, with a slight degree of subacid humour; learning, wit, and drollery, the more piquant that they were a little marked by the peculiarities of an old bachelor; a soundness of thought rendered more forcible by an occasional quaintness of expression, were, the Author avers, the only qualities in which the creature of his imagination resembled his benevolent and excellent old friend."

But to those who knew of the pilgrimages to Wallace-Craigie, as well as the foibles of its master, the identification was not so difficult. Constable died at Wallace-Craigie on 13th April 1803, in his 84th year. The Original of the Antiquary's "most discreet sister Griselda, who disdains the simplicity, as well as patience, annexed to the poor old name of Grizel," is held to be Constable's sister, Matilda. George, son of David Constable, brother of the Antiquary, a Colonel in the Bengal Artillery, was the prototype of the hot-headed Captain Hector M'Intyre.

Additional to his friend Constable, Scott, in composing the portrait of Monkbarns, was perhaps thinking of John Ramsay of Ochtertyre. On a Highland excursion in 1793 Scott visited Ochtertyre and made acquaintance with Ramsay, which continued till the death of the latter in the year when *Waverley* was published. A copy of the Bürger Ballads was sent to Ochtertyre in 1796, and Lockhart prints Ramsay's letter acknowledging the gift and commending the translations. Ramsay was an enthusiastic antiquary, and was the means of recovering many prehistoric and Roman remains, and other antiquities, in his neighbourhood. For Scottish traditions and memories of the Forty-five there were few better authorities, and to him Scott was, no doubt, indebted for more than one incident in the *sturm und drang* of the romances.

Dr. George Gleig (a Scott biographer), who knew Ramsay intimately, says that Ramsay certainly stood with Constable as the model from which the character of Oldbuck was painted. "When I knew him he was an old man, and having lived as he died, a bachelor, he had fallen with living alone into slovenly habits. When receiving company his appointments were those of a gentleman of the old school—coat, usually blue, with bright metal buttons, a high collar, and lace frills at the wrist. I think he wore the hair powdered but I am not quite sure, though of his carefully-tied queue I have a clear remembrance ; breeches and blue stockings with silver buckles on his shoes were also worn on these occasions. At other times his legs would be encased in worsted stockings to which it appeared as though he sometimes forgot to append garters. . . . I think of him as a man of middle stature, well made, and with an intelligent expression of countenance." *

In one particular, however, Ramsay differed from the Laird of Monkbarns: he was not the woman-hater that Oldbuck was. He had, indeed, both in youth and manhood been a great admirer of the sex, and so much " of the old Adam remained with him that he used to exact a kiss from each of his young lady visitors, for which he rewarded her with a peach—his well-walled and sheltered garden being renowned for the excellency of the peaches it brought to maturity."

Alexander Gordon, author of the *Itinerarium Septentrionale*, undoubtedly furnished Scott with some of the colouring for his immortal picture of Jonathan

* Introduction to *Scotland and Scotsmen in the Eighteenth Century*, ed. by Alexander Allardyce.

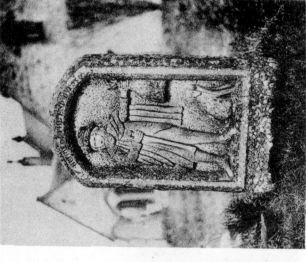
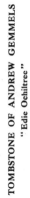

TOMBSTONE OF ANDREW GEMMELS
"Edie Ochiltree"

[see page 140

THE BLACK DWARF'S COTTAGE, MANOR

[see page 143

Oldbuck. It was Gordon's tome which Monkbarns had with him on the journey to Hawes Inn, and he always professes a deep respect for the authority of "Sandy Gordon." Scott has transferred some passages in the *Itinerarium* to the pages of the novel.

But Sir Walter himself, in some important respects and in spite of significant differences, was his own half-conscious delineator in this superlative figure. Scott, like Ramsay, was not averse to the influence of the gentler sex. And to say that he was niggardly in money matters was the last fault that could be charged against him. At the same time it cannot but be remembered that Scott's early love disappointment did beget in him a soreness on the question of the relation of the sexes comparable to that impatience of the "eternal woman" which, in the fictitious old bachelor, originated in a similar misfortune. And careless and lavish as Scott was in the disbursement of large amounts, his account books had always a column for his turnpike money. Then there is the ruling passion of both for ballads. Take Elspeth's death-bed scene: Oldbuck and his friends come to take the old hag's confession. As the Antiquary lifted the latch of the hut Elspeth is heard chanting forth an old ballad in a wild and doleful recitative. "His foot refused to cross the threshold when his ear was thus arrested, and his hand instinctively took pencil and memorandum-book."

"'It's a historical ballad,' said Oldbuck eagerly, 'a genuine and undoubted fragment of minstrelsy !

Percy would admire its simplicity—Ritson could not impugn its authenticity. . . .'

"'I wish,' he said, when they were inside, 'she would resume that canticle or legendary fragment: I always suspected there was a skirmish of cavalry before the main battle of the Harlaw! Hush, hush! she has gotten the thread of the story again,'—and as he spoke she sung: . . .'

"'Chafron!' exclaimed the Antiquary, 'the word's worth a dollar,'—and down it went in his red book."

It was quite in keeping with Scott's character that he should poke fun at Monkbarns's foibles, and the ludicrous mistakes into which he fell (as at the Kaim of Kinprunes*)—those occasional " mares'-nests into which a passion for antiquities may betray even the acutest of amateurs": " Monkbarns is no that owre wise himself, in some things : he wad believe a bodle to be an auld Roman coin, as he ca's it, or a ditch to be a camp, upon ony leasing that idle folk made about it. I hae garr'd him trow mony a queer tale my-sell, Gude forgie me," says Edie Ochiltree, admitting that in life's ordinary affairs Oldbuck's wisdom could not be called in question.

* The hero of the story " Prætorian here, Prætorian there, I made it wi' a flaughter-spade," was the grandfather of Scott's friend John Clerk of Eldin.

CHAPTER EIGHT

THE ANTIQUARY
"EDIE OCHILTREE"

" O heard ye o' the bauld blue-gown,
    Auld Edie Ochiltree ?
Weel kent in ilka country town,
    Auld Edie Ochiltree ;
When beggars o' the gangrel corps
    Are driven frae the hallan door,
'The gudewife cries, ' Come ye in owre,
    Auld Edie Ochiltree.' "

CONTEMPORARY BALLAD.

CHAPTER EIGHT   THE ANTIQUARY "EDIE OCHILTREE"

SCOTT'S ACCOUNT (INTRODUCTION TO THE novel) of the Original of Edie Ochiltree was borrowed from his own observation of the man in the days of his Border boyhood. Edie's archetype was too " kenspeckle " a figure to escape the attention of a schoolboy or even to be forgotten long after school-days were over. It was when Scott was living with his aunt at Garden Cottage, Kelso, when he was under the ferule of that " excellent classical scholar and humorist and worthy man," Lancelot Whale, that he made acquaintance with the picturesque and entertaining old worthy whom he afterwards immortalised in the pages of *The Antiquary*. Scott lived at a time when the land literally swarmed with members of the order of mendicants, and in the country he would have fuller scope than in the town for a study of the habits and ways of the tribe. The law favoured them exceedingly. No disgrace was then attaching to the beggar's profession, and the Blue-gown class, represented by Edie Ochiltree, was under express sanction of the State. The custom of legalising mendicity was a very old one, and the business of the mendicant was as profitable and lucrative as it was easy. Thus it was that the country became overrun by a race of strong and masterful beggars—sorners—to such an extent that an Act was passed permitting only the sick and impotent—those who were unable to earn a livelihood—to beg, and it was enacted that they

133

should receive a licence for that purpose in the shape of a badge.   By and by the begging area was set in limits, whilst an Act, passed in 1583, restricted the soliciting of charity to the mendicant's own parish. In 1625, and again in 1672, the Church, by a series of Acts, was brought into closer touch with the poor than it had hitherto been. Ministers and elders were enjoined to draw up lists of indigent persons within their jurisdictions, and being duly badged those were given so many miles as a circuit and so many days in the week in which to ply their vocation. This was done down to a date as late as the year 1824. The order of Blue-gowns was originated about the close of the fifteenth century. They derived their authority direct from the Sovereign, and the pewter badge which they wore bore the royal crown, and the words " Pass and Repass," giving them the privilege of wandering throughout the whole of Scotland, instead of being confined to a particular parish, or town, as were the holders of purely local badges or tokens.   Every Maundy Thursday they were given a fresh outfit, which included a cloak, or gown of coarse cloth of light blue colour, a wooden cup and platter, and a leathern purse containing as many shillings Scots as there were years in the king's life.

In 1832 there were sixty-eight bedesmen on the roll, though Scott, writing in 1829, said that few of them were seen on the streets of Edinburgh. They preferred the country, where they got better entertainment. The privilege, however, came to be abused, and it was ultimately determined to suppress the charity. The last survivor of this class of official almsmen died probably in 1863, for, though there is an item of £1 13s. 4d. in the estimates for 1864–65 for alms and a gown, there is no mention of its having been claimed. Scott was in doubt as to Edie Ochiltree's Original being a Blue-gown. More than likely he belonged to the order. Robert Chambers, a careful investigator, thought so, and if it affords any evidence, it may be remarked that upon Edie's rude effigy in Roxburgh Churchyard the bedesman's garb is a conspicuous adornment.

Of the early history of Andrew Gemmels, who was the individual Scott had in his eye in depicting the character of Edie Ochiltree, very little can be ascertained now. Andrew was an Ayrshire man. Scott may have been conversant with that circumstance, hence his adoption of the place-name Ochiltree. Gemmels, however, was not a native of Ochiltree, but of the adjacent parish of Old Cumnock. A fairly well-authenticated tradition points to Polquhap on its southern border as his birth-spot. The name Gemmel or Gemmels is still found in the locality. A Gemmel of Minshalt in Old Cumnock perished at Bothwell Bridge, and Wodrow mentions another of the name who was banished by command of Claverhouse. One of Joseph Train's intimates was Andrew Gemmels, a grandson of the Blue-gown. From being a farm-servant, this second Andrew reached the position of surgeon in the navy, attaining distinction in the Mediterranean Service under Lord Exmouth. He died at London in 1829.

All that can be learned about Andrew the proto-type is, that at some part of his career he was in the army.   Like Edie Ochiltree he fought at Fontenoy. Train says he was twenty years a soldier and twenty years a Blue-gown, but he must have held the latter post for a much longer period.   When his fighting days were done, Andrew, doubtless, drifted into that unsettled vagrant life which characterised his remain-ing years.   He was the best-known gaberlunzie on both sides of the Border. His stories of his campaigns and adventures in foreign countries, his flow of wit and drollery, his skill at the dambrod [draughts] and other agreeable qualities, rendered him a general favourite and secured him a cordial reception and free quarters in every shepherd's cottage and farm kitchen within the sphere of his peregrinations. Scott's description of him is that of a remarkably fine old fig-ure, very tall, and maintaining a soldier-like manner and address. He had intelligent features, with a power-ful expression of sarcasm. His motions were so grace-ful that he might almost have been suspected of having studied them.   He might have served as an artist's model, so wonderfully striking were his ordinary atti-tudes. He had little of the cant of his calling. His wants were food and shelter, or a trifle of money, which he always claimed, and seemed to receive as his due. He sang a good song, told a good story, was a fellow of infinite jest, and satirical to a degree. It was, to be sure, some fear of this latter propensity, as much as a feeling of kindness or charity, which won him the welcome he enjoyed everywhere. Unlike the Edie of fiction, Andrew was somewhat fond of "the siller," and was supposed to carry considerable sums about his person. He was said to be wealthy for one who was a waif of the road, and could change a pound note on occasion. At one time he rode his rounds on a good blood-mare. He was an inveterate better and gambler, and pocketed large amounts at the Border race meetings and fairs. Dr. Douglas of Galashiels told Scott that the last time he saw Andrew Gemmels he was engaged at a game of brag with the Laird of Gala, the latter sitting on a chair inside his domicile, the beggar on a stool in the yard. They played at the window-sill, and the stake was a moderately large parcel of silver. At Rutherford, close to Roxburgh, Andrew dropped a clew of yarn whose kernel was found to contain twenty guineas. In later life, however, he lamented that the Blue-gown's trade was £40 a year worse since he had first practised it. He declared that begging was no profession for a gentleman, and if he had twenty sons he could not be induced to breed any of them up in his own line. At his death Andrew was reputed to have left a small fortune to a nephew in Ayrshire.

It is curious that Scott was ignorant both of the time and the whereabouts of Gemmels's end. Quoting Burns, he hazards the likelihood of his having died

"A cadger powny's death at some dykeside."

But Andrew's demise was much more Christian-like, as was the wish of Edie, expressed to Miss Wardour : " Though I should die at the back of a dyke, they'll find as muckle quilted in this auld blue gown as will bury me like a Christian, and gie the lads and lasses a blythe lyke-wake too ; sae there's the gaberlunzie's burial provided for, and I need nae mair."

It was in the barn at the farm-steading of Roxburgh-Newtown, a favourite howf, that the redoubted Blue-gown closed his wanderings. A narrative of the circumstances from the pen of an eye-witness, a niece of the kindly tenant, has fortunately been preserved. In homely language she describes how Andrew came to Newtown in the year 1793, " in a very weakly condition, being, according to his own account, 105 years of age. The conduct of some of the country folks towards the poor man in his declining state was not what it should have been ; probably most of his old patrons had died out, and their more genteel descendants disliked to be fashed and burthened with a dying beggar ; so every one handed him over to his next neighbour ; and he was hurried from Selkirk to Newtown, a distance of sixteen miles, in three days. He was brought in a cart, and laid down at Mr. R[obertson]'s byre door, but we never knew by whom. He was taken in, and laid as usual on his truss of straw. When we spoke of making up a bed for him, he got into a rage, and swore (as well as he was able to speak) ' that many a clever fellow had died in the field with his hair frozen to the ground—and would he submit

to die in any of our beds?' He did not refuse a little
whisky, however, now and then; for it was cold in
the spring, lying in an outhouse among straw. A
friend who was along with me urged him to tell what
cash he had about him, 'As you know,' she said, 'it
has been reported that you have money.' Andrew
replied, with a look of derision, 'Bow, wow, wow,
woman! womenfolk are aye fashing theirsels aboot
what they hae nae business wi'.' He at length told
us he had changed a note at Selkirk, and paid six shillings for a pair of shoes which he had on him; but
not a silver coin was found in all his duddy doublets,
and many kinds of odd-like pouch he had: in one of
them was sixpence worth of halfpence, and two combs
for his silver locks, which were beautiful. The set
of teeth, which he had got in his one hundred and
first year, were very white. What was remarkable,
notwithstanding all the rags he had flapping about
him, he was particularly clean in his old healsome-
looking person. He at last allowed the servants to
strip off his rags and lay him on a bed, which was
made up for him in a cart in the byre. After he was
laid comfortably, he often prayed, and to good purpose; but if the servants did not feed him right (for
he could not lift a spoon to his mouth for several days
before his death) he would fire them a passing ban.
He lived nine days with us, and continued quite sensible until the hour of his decease. Mr. R[obertson] got
him decently buried. Old Jamie Jack, with his muckle
nose, got his shoes for digging his grave in Roxburgh

Kirkyard. Andrew was well known through all this county and a great part of Northumberland. I suppose he was originally from the West country, but cannot speak with certainty as to that ; it was, however, commonly reported that he had a nephew or some near relation in the West, who possessed a farm which Andrew had stocked for him from the profits of his begging.''*

The date of his death was 31st March 1793. More than half a century afterwards, William Thomson, tenant of Over-Roxburgh, at whose father's house Gemmels was a frequent and familiar guest, raised a plain but substantial memorial over his long disintegrated dust :

THE BODY OF THE
GENTLEMAN BEGGAR

ANDREW GEMMELS

ALIAS EDIE OCHILTREE

WAS INTERRED HERE

WHO DIED AT

ROXBURGH NEWTOWN

IN 1793

AGED 106 YEARS

✠　✠

ERECTED

BY W. THOMSON, FARMER

OVER-ROXBURGH

1849

* *The Scots Magazine*, September 1817.

CHAPTER NINE

THE BLACK DWARF

" He was so ugly and so grim
His shadow durst not follow him."

POPE.

THE *TALES OF MY LANDLORD*, OF WHICH
The Black Dwarf is the first, appeared in four series—
three between the years 1816 and 1819, the last in
1831. Scott represents them as the production of an
imaginary pedagogue, Peter Pattieson, and edited to
defray his funeral expenses by his mythical friend
and patron Jedediah Cleishbotham, schoolmaster and
parish-clerk of Gandercleugh. Gandercleugh is probably Galashiels, but Lasswade and Lesmahagow
claim the distinction. The Wallace Inn, Pattieson's
headquarters, may have been modelled from the old
" George " at Melrose. The cognomen Cleishbotham
was borrowed from James Broadfoot, dominie at the
clachan of Penninghame, who in a letter to Scott fa-
cetiously signed himself " Clashbotham "—to cleish,
or clash, in good Scots, meaning to flog. The real
venue of Broadfoot's revels was the Shoulder of Mut-
ton Inn at Newton-Stewart.

What were described as the weakest and the strongest of the Waverleys appeared in company—*The
Black Dwarf* and *Old Mortality*. The former the
critics have been accustomed to ban more or less.
The plot is thin, improbable, and none of the characters shine conspicuously. At the same time the
story is not devoid of merit. There are some passages which are simply admirable—the description of
the Elliot household, for instance, and the pictures of
143

Scottish rural life, as in *Guy Mannering*, are perfect. It is the conclusion, the *éclaircissement*, which is the disappointing part. We know the tone in which Scott resented Blackwood's kindly-intentioned criticism. 'Twere not for his temper, there should have been less " huddling up." Scott himself confessed that he began the tale well enough, but tired of it, not finding sufficient scope for his imagination, thereupon " bungling up a conclusion as a boarding-school miss finishes a task which she had commenced with great glee and accuracy."

There is no dominant character in the story. Ellieslaw is the rascal of the piece, one of Scott's few unnatural parents. The hero, Earnscliff, though spirited and sensible, is seldom seen. Isobel Vere is rather a "fusionless" heroine. Far the best-drawn figures are those of the Red Reiver of Westburnflat, "a picturesque savage," and honest Hobbie of the Heughfoot, types of men who follow in the wake of William of Deloraine and our old friends of the Poems. It is in the Black Dwarf,—Elshender the Recluse,—Sir Edwin Mauley,—that interest centres. Villainously misshapen, virulently misanthropic, he looks and speaks like an evil being incarnate, but is, in point of fact, the good genius of the story. He deplores his infirmity. The disgust and scorn inspired by his ogreish presence compel him to seek relief from the world's stare and (were it possible) from his own rebellious spirit. He retreats to the haunting solitariness of Mucklestane Moor. But even there he cannot es-

DAVID RITCHIE
"The Black Dwarf"

STATUE OF THE BLACK DWARF
Hallyards House, Manor

cape from himself nor from the process of heart-hardening. He is Misanthropos personified. Yet he is not all bad. At times kindlier touches reveal themselves. Spite of the cruel disparity that exists between him and other men, he cannot forget that he, too, is one of the humans : " Your deeds, Elshie, are better than your words," answered Earnscliff ; " you labour to preserve the race whom your misanthropy slanders." Professor Veitch's mother, who knew the Black Dwarf's Original, used to say there was " good in the body." In the novel, what fuming and storming at human nature ! For all that, Scott's Dwarf is not deaf to the call of distress, or blind to the consciousness of another's need. Even Westburn-flat—tough old sinner—he would win from his moral wanderings.

" So," said the Dwarf, " rapine and murder once more on horseback."

" On horseback ?" said the bandit; " ay, ay, Elshie, your leech-craft has set me on the bonny bay again."

" And all those promises of amendment which you made during your illness forgotten ? " continued Elshender.

" All passed clear away, with the water-saps and panada," returned the unabashed convalescent. " Ye ken, Elshie, for they say ye are well acquent wi' the gentleman—

'When the devil was sick, the devil a monk would be;
When the devil was well, the devil a monk was he.' "

" Thou say'st true," said the Solitary ; " as well divide a wolf from his appetite for carnage, or a raven
from her scent of slaughter, as thee from thy accursed
propensities."

To Miss Vere and the Elliot family the Dwarf was
a potent and gracious benefactor.

II

It was in the summer of 1797 that Scott met, for
the only time in his life, the archetype of his Black
Dwarf.* Of all his characters, none has been more
faithfully reproduced from the original, apart from
the idealisation necessary for the story. The occasion was a visit to Hallyards, in Peeblesshire, the home
of his boyhood's friend, Adam Ferguson, later his
bosom cronie at Huntlyburn. Scott was accompanied
by his brother, Captain John Scott. The pair were
making their way up the Tweed valley to Moffat and
Carlisle, *en route* for the English Lakes, a pilgrimage
fraught with romantic issues for the younger man.
He was then a briefless advocate of twenty-six, known
to a small Edinburgh coterie as a student of German
romantic ballads, the translator of Bürger's "Lenore"
and " Wild Huntsman." Hallyards is in the Manor
valley. It was occupied by Professor Ferguson, historian of the Roman Republic and author of an *Essay*

---

* Skene recalls a walk with Scott up Meggetdale and over the
Bitch Craig into Manor Water. While mention is made of Ritchie,
nothing is said as to a visit.

on Civil Society, one of the chief literary figures of his time. In earlier life, Ferguson served as chaplain to the Black Watch, in Flanders, and was present at Fontenoy, where his military ardour is said to have overcome his clerical decorum. It is interesting to recall that years afterwards, his son, Scott's friend, read aloud to his men in the lines at Torres Vedras the newly published *Lady of the Lake*.

On one of Scott's Hallyards' days, his host took him to see David Ritchie, known throughout the district as "Bowed Davie," and by those kindly disposed to and familiar with him as simply "Davie," or "Dauvit," or "Davie o' the Wuddus" [Woodhouse]. From Hallyards to Woodhouse is barely a mile. We can imagine the interest, the excitement, the feeling of curiosity, which such a visit would evoke on the part of Scott, who even then was living in a world of dreamland and of eld, the result of his German and Border studies. "We can picture the two," says Professor Veitch, "the venerable professor with his slim erect figure and flowing hair, and the young advocate, with his limping gait—making their way across the low-lying haughs by the stream in the quiet of the summer evening,—to be afterwards famous as Mucklestane Moor." It is William Chambers who gives the most graphic account of the interview : "At the first sight of Scott, the misanthrope seemed oppressed with a sentiment of extraordinary interest, which was either owing to the lameness of the stranger,—a circumstance throwing a narrower gulf between him and most other men,—or to some perception of an extraordinary mental character in this limping youth, which was then hid from other eyes. After grinning upon him for a moment with a smile less bitter than his wont, the Dwarf passed to the door, double-locked it, and then coming up to the stranger, seized him by the wrist with one of his iron hands and said : ' Man, hae ye ony poo'er ? ' By this he meant magical power, to which he had himself some vague pretensions, or which, at least, he had studied and reflected upon till it had become with him a kind of monomania. Scott disavowed the possession of any gifts of that kind, evidently to the great disappointment of the inquirer, who then turned round and gave a signal to a huge black cat, hitherto unobserved, which immediately jumped up to a shelf, where it perched itself, and seemed to the excited senses of the visitors as if it had really been the familiar spirit of the mansion. 'He has poo'er,' said the Dwarf, in a voice which made the flesh of the hearers thrill ; and Scott, in particular, looked as if he conceived himself to have actually got into the den of one of those magicians with whom his studies had rendered him familiar. 'Ay, *he* has poo'er,' repeated the Recluse ; and then, going to his usual seat, he sat for some minutes grinning horribly, as if enjoying the impression he had made, while not a word escaped from any of the party. Mr. Ferguson at length plucked up his spirits, and called to David to open the door, as they must now be going. The Dwarf slowly obeyed, and when they had got out, Mr. Ferguson observed that his friend was as pale as ashes, while his person was agitated in every limb." *

The Black Dwarf was not published for nineteen years afterwards, but how true to the facts was the novelist's reproduction of this scene in the cottage (chap. xvi.)—Isabella Vere's visit to the Solitary—and the almost exact description of the interior itself ! Indeed, so deep and strong must have been the impression made upon Scott that from the Dwarf of fiction there is hardly missing a characteristic belonging to the original, with the exception that in the story the Recluse is a personage of birth and quality, and that his motive in bidding adieu to the world was a reverse in love.

Ritchie was the queerest, most extraordinary-looking object imaginable—dwarf and giant in one. He was not more than three feet six inches in height, was oddly misshapen, preternaturally ugly, a shocking travesty of the human form divine, not bearing any likeness to anything in this upper world. Several sketches of him are extant, as well as a stone effigy in front of the modern Hallyards. The latter is, presumably, an imaginary representation. Two of the sketches are from memory ; the third (that reproduced), whilst the rudest and most repellent, may be regarded as a genuine likeness of the creature. The merit of this sketch lies in the fact that it was surreptitiously drawn from life by a tradesman (a mason) employed at Woodhouse during alterations

* *History of Peeblesshire*, pp. 403, 404.

about the year 1802. There is no reason to doubt the authenticity of the drawing.* As in other pictures of him, the Dwarf is shown wearing a cowl or nightcap, and carrying a long pole, a kind of alpenstock, which he called his kent, and without which he could not have moved but with great difficulty. His dress is hodden-grey, and a plaid is thrown over his right shoulder. Generally speaking, the sketch corroborates the careful pen-portrait given to Dr. " Rab " Brown by Robert Craig, a retired Peebles surgeon living at Hallmanor. Craig, it should be stated, had the best opportunities for learning all that could be known about the Solitary: " His forehead was very narrow and low, sloping upwards and backwards—something of the hatchet shape ; his eyes deep-set, small, and piercing ; his nose straight, thin as the end of a cut of cheese, sharp at the point, nearly touching his fearfully projecting chin ; and his mouth formed nearly a straight line ; his shoulders rather high, but his body otherwise the size of ordinary men ; his arms were remarkably strong." His legs were very short, and dreadfully deformed. Mungo Park, then a surgeon in Peebles, who attended him on one occasion, compared them to a pair of cork-screws. " The principal turn they took was from the knee outwards, so that he rested on his inner ankles and the lower part of his tibias. . . . The

---

* The sketch has come into the author's hands from a representative of the Ballantynes of Woodhouse, who many a time befriended the Dwarf.

thrawn twisted limbs must have crossed each other at the knees." *

Nothing, however, could be better than Scott's own description. This is how, in the early dawn, Elshie appeared to Earnscliff and Hobbie Elliot at the task of building his hut on Mucklestane Moor : " His head was of uncommon size, covered with a fell of shaggy hair, partly grizzled with age ; his eyebrows, shaggy and prominent, overhung a pair of small, dark, piercing eyes, set far back in their sockets. . . . The rest of his features were of the coarse, rough-hewn stamp, with which a painter would equip a giant in romance ; to which was added the wild, irregular, and peculiar expression, so often seen in the countenances of those whose persons are deformed. His body, thick and square, like that of a man of middle size, was mounted upon two large feet ; but nature seemed to have forgotten the legs and the thighs, or they were so very short as to be hidden by the dress which he wore. His arms were long and brawny, furnished with two muscular hands, and, where uncovered in the eagerness of his labour, were shagged with coarse black hair. It seemed as if nature had originally intended the separate parts of his body to be the members of a giant, but had afterwards capriciously assigned them to the person of a dwarf, so ill did the length of his arms and the iron strength of his frame correspond with the short-ness of his stature " (chap. **iv.**).

* *Horae Subsecivae.*

He never wore shoes, the extremities of his legs being wrapt in rags and old stockings, with the toes always exposed, even in the severest weather. There are curious stories of his extraordinary strength-of-arm and feats of heavyweight lifting. "Though ye may think him a lamiter," says Hobbie Elliot, "yet grippie for grippie, I'll wad a wether he'll make the bluid spin frae under yer nails. He is a teugh carle, Elshie! He grips like a smith's vice." With ease he could butt his head through a tar-barrel, or the panels of a door. On one occasion he overbalanced himself and fell over the steep Swire Bridge to the rocky bed of the Manor, without any apparent injury. His mode of locomotion was as peculiar as his shape. He placed his kent in front of him, rested his hands on its rounded top, then lifted one leg somewhat in the manner in which the oar of a boat is worked, and then the other, next advanced his staff, and repeated the operation, by diligently continuing which he was able to make not very slow progress. He frequently walked to Peebles—four miles—and back again in one day. Scott makes much of Elshie's strength in the manipulation of the boulders of his cottage. It was this feature which confirmed Hobbie's belief in his supernatural power. When Earnscliff and Elliot volunteered to help him in raising the rough walls of his dwelling the Dwarf stood aside and allowed them to proceed at his directions—but only that he might have his fling at the failure of ordinary capacity : " Elliot and Earnscliff placed the stone, by their joint efforts, upon the rising wall. The Dwarf watched them with the eye of a taskmaster, and testified, by peevish gestures, his impatience at the time which they took in adjusting the stone. He pointed to another—they raised it also; to a third, to a fourth—they continued to humour him, though with some trouble, for he assigned them, as if intentionally, the heaviest fragments which lay near. 'And now, friend,' said Elliot, as the unreasonable Dwarf indicated another stone larger than any they had moved, 'Earnscliff may do as he likes ; but be ye man or be ye waur, deil be in my fingers if I break my back wi' heaving thae stanes ony langer like a barrowman, without getting sae muckle as thanks for my pains.' "

Here is another story of the real Dwarf : " Near his cottage were some large trees to be dug up, one of which occupied two men for two days constant picking and undermining. The Dwarf happening to pass by, saw and taunted them with their weakness, telling them with his usual acrimony, 'that he would do in two minutes what had ta'en siccan twae whaesel-blawn creatures twae days to do without effect.' Then, setting his bull-like head and shoulders to the bottom of the tree, he gave it a push of so tremendous a force as fairly rooted it up from the foundation, to the astonishment of the men, who stared, thinking he was possessed of the powers of a giant. Davie marched off with all the

dignity of having done a great action, muttering :
' Brush o' Babel ! do that an' ye can.' "

The disposition of the misanthrope ran through
Ritchie's whole life, and it is that which is specially
emphasised in the character of the Black Dwarf. The
sense of his deformity haunted him like a spectre,
and the insults and abuse to which this exposed him,
had poisoned his heart with fierce and bitter feeling. He was not, as has already been said, wholly
given over to badness, or to an incarnate hatred of
the world in general. There were times when he mel-
lowed down, when the sentimental and emotional
element triumphed. He could be gentle on occasion. He had, for instance, a singular fondness for
children, notwithstanding William Chambers's statement to the contrary. He had a liking for good-
looking damsels, and was passionately attached to
all forms of animal life. He kept a cat and a dog,
a couple of goats, and was something of an apiarist.
His domestic pets and his bees he knew would not
mock him, or cast the torturing stigma in his teeth.
It is refreshing to find such traits in a character otherwise so unnatural and devoid of sympathy. Davie's
main hobby was his garden. He certainly bore no
grudge to Mother Nature in the generous moods with
which she had decked the green braes and haughs
of Manor. Long had he learned how true it is that
" Nature never did belie the heart that loved her."
His garden he planted and fashioned into a thing of
order and beauty, walling it round, digging it, stock-

ing it with incredible labour. " He had managed to collect flowers, fruit-trees, kitchen vegetables, and certain medicinal herbs known to the popular Scottish pharmacopœia. These he dried and dispensed to those who sought them. He planted willows and rowan trees. The rowan was his prophylactic against witches, whom he dreaded greatly. He stocked the place with bee-hives, until the garden became a model spot, quite unapproached by the plots of the peasantry of the district, whose highest ambition was cabbages. The hermit's garden thus grew to be the wonder of the countryside. It was the main delight and solace of his solitary life, and it pleased him greatly to show it to visitors, jealous and exacting as he was in regard to intercourse with strangers." *

Again, this characteristic is seen in the novel : " Next morning the heath was in its thickest and deepest bloom. The bees, which the Solitary had added to his rural establishment, were abroad and on the wing, and filled the air with the murmurs of their industry. As the old man crept out of his little hut, his two she-goats came to meet him, and licked his hands in gratitude for the vegetables with which he supplied them from his garden. ' You, at least,' he said, ' see no difference in form which can alter your feelings to a benefactor. . . . While I was in the world, did I ever meet with such a return of gratitude ? ' "

Nor was Ritchie altogether an ignoramus with re-

* Veitch's *Border Essays*, p. 44.

gard to life's deeper and weightier matters. He could read English fairly well, we are informed. He was fond of history and poetry. Shenstone's Pastorals fascinated him. He revelled in Allan Ramsay, though, curiously, Burns was one of his aversions. Scott heard him repeat Milton's description of Paradise in a vein of admirable appreciation. He paid some attention to Tooke's *Pantheon*, attracted, probably, by its mythologies, on which he descanted at every ingle-nook in the valley. Wallace and Bruce were his prime heroes, and his mind was stored with the traditionary lore of his native Tweeddale. He was supposed to have peculiar views on religious subjects, and was probably theistic in his belief. He seldom went to church, though there was a vein of real piety about the man. He left behind him a well-thumbed Bible—Kincaid's fine quarto edition—and he spoke of a future state with intense feeling, and even with tears. Scott's Recluse, notwithstanding his moods of despair, his fits of madness, never utterly forgets religion and God. Thus he exclaims : " All [mankind] are of a piece—one mass of wickedness, selfishness, and ingratitude—wretches who sin even in their devotions, and of such hardness of heart that they do not, without hypocrisy, even thank the Deity Himself for His warm sun and pure air."

In the main, however, we must not forget that David Ritchie was the jealous and irritable, the crabbed and surly dog depicted in the novel. His threats and the nature of his retorts on those who attacked him were not unfrequently of the coarsest character ; but we must keep in mind the circumstances. He had his tormentors and his persecutors, whose provocations were often far removed from the category of practical jokes. Take him all in all, Professor Ferguson's estimate is as sane and as charitable as any : " David Ritchie was a man of powerful capacity and original ideas, but whose mind was thrown off its just bias by a predominant degree of self-love and self-opinion, galled by the sense of ridicule and contempt, and avenging itself upon society, in idea at least, by a gloomy misanthropy."

As for the life-history of the Black Dwarf's Original there is not much to tell. Ritchie was born at Easter Happrew, in the parish of Stobo, in 1740, or 1741. His father, William Ritchie, was a labourer in the slate-quarries there. His mother was Annabel Niven, hence the Annaple of the novel—the nurse in Hobbie Elliot's family. Davie attributed his deformity to neglect in infancy, but he was doubtless misshapen and rickety from birth. He got very little schooling, for both parents died when he was young. By the time he was ten, he was at work at Broughton Mill, and at Lyne Mill, near his birth spot, stirring the husks of oats which were used in the process of corn-drying, an operation he could do sitting, and do well from his abnormal strength of arm. From Lyne, he was sent to Edinburgh to learn brush-making, and he averred to Scott that he wrought at the same trade in Dublin. But the annoyance to which he was sub-

jected by the street boys was more than he could
bear. Mortified and irritated, he found his way back
to Peeblesshire—to beautiful Manor, "that sweetest
vale of all the south," as Professor Veitch describes
it. His first cottage, on ground belonging to the farm
of Woodhouse, he built with his own hands, and there
he lived until 1802, when Sir James Naesmyth of
Posso, the laird, replaced it by one of stone and lime,
with a thatched roof. It is this house * which is
still standing,—modernised and slated, with another
dwelling tacked on to the west. The original doorway has been preserved, and the tiny window or bole
in the wall, through which, as the novel remarks, he
could see any one who approached it without the pos-
sibility of their seeing him.

If David Ritchie, on coming to Manor, began to receive assistance from the poor's fund administered
by the kirk-session, the date of his arrival was the
year 1762. In that year we find the first notice of
him in the parish records. For almost half a century
he was in receipt of a small half-yearly allowance.
The first entry, 28th February 1762, is as follows :
"To David Ritchie for cloathes £3 12s." There is a

* The height of the south or front wall is 8 feet 6 inches ; the
breadth 11 feet. Inside, the length of the area is 14 feet 10 inches ;
the breadth 7 feet 10 inches. The height of the roof is 7 feet 10
inches. The height of the Dwarf's doorway is exactly 3 feet 10
inches (Scott says 3 feet 6 inches). The window is, as from the first,
without glass ; it is 1 foot 4 inches in height, and 1 foot 5 inches in
breadth. There is also a small opening in the north wall of the
cottage, 1 foot 3 inches in breadth inside. A stone seat used by
Ritchie is exhibited in the back garden, the wall of which must
have been little altered since the Dwarf's day.

dole of five shillings on New Year's day 1764. On
13th September 1767 he gets another £3 12s. " for
cloathes." In 1769 he becomes the possessor of a
plaid. And so on, down to 1811, when he passed
beyond the need of human charity. About 1790,
David's sister, Agnes, came to reside with him in
the Woodhouse cottage. Agnes Ritchie had been
an out-worker, and in domestic service, but her
health had failed : there was some mental aberration.
Brother and sister lived in a state of perpetual feud.
To remedy matters, an apartment was partitioned
off for Agnes's use, with a separate, ordinary door
and window. After that, David dared her to darken
his door again. She survived the Dwarf ten years,
dying about the end of 1821. On 7th December
of that year, we find the following in the record :
" A coffin for the deceased Agnes Ritchie, £1," and
" for bread to persons at her death, £0 0s. 8d." A
touch of the miser as well as the misanthrope appears to have characterised David of Manor. At his
death he had accumulated upwards of £20, saved
chiefly from the charity of visitors, which he never
refused. From Dr. Craig's letter, we gather that he
had £4 2s. of gold in one bag, and £7 18s. in shillings
and half-crowns in another, besides a receipt for a
sum of £10 10s. 8d. deposited with James Brown, of
Peebles, by way of a banking transaction. All this
money, to the honour of the half-witted Agnes Ritchie, was returned to the poor's box. Here is the
minute attesting the same : "December 16th—After
159

prayer, sederunt—the Rev. William Marshall, Moderator, Dr. Robertson and Alex. Ker, Elders. The Moderator reported that he had received from James Brown, weaver in Peebles, on the fifth of December, Ten pounds sterling, which belonged to the late David Ritchie, Woodhouse : which money by his desire was lodged in the house of Sir Wm. Forbes and Co. As David Ritchie had received aliment money from the funds of the parish for many years, at his death his sister renounced all claim to the said ten pounds and requested the Moderator, as minister of the parish, to add to the poor's fund what was entrusted to the care of James Brown by her brother and lent out upon interest."

The exact date of the Dwarf's death was 6th December 1811. Once he had hoped—nay, implored—that he might not be buried among "the common brash" in Manor Kirkyard. As in life, so in death, the ruling passion was pre-eminent. He was eager to lie on the sun-lit top of the Woodhill, about the middle of the valley—a romantic, green little mount, crowned with an old fort and a cairn of stones. For such as he, it would have been the most fit place of sepulture. Unfortunately, Sir James Naesmyth who had promised to see Davie's desire carried into effect, was on the Continent at the time, and the Dwarf was interred in the ordinary way in the parish churchyard. A proposal to lift his remains and reinter them "where he longed to be" was abandoned. For many years a heavy whinstone slab kept guard

RELICS OF THE BLACK DWARF

over his gnarled and stunted bones. But on his sister's burial in 1821, the body of the brother was resurrected and his bones sent to Glasgow. The skull is said to have been replaced, but not the legs, which were at one time in the possession of Dr. John Brown.*

The Dwarf, says Professor Veitch, could repeat the lines attributed to Shakespeare regarding his remains, and wished them engraven on his own tomb :

> " Good friend ! for Jesus' sake forbear
> To dig the dust enclosèd here ;
> Blest be the man that spares these stones,
> And curst be he that moves my bones."

But the simple stone, erected by the brothers Chambers more than thirty years after Davie's death, expresses neither benediction nor malediction. If the latter has fallen, the circumstances have never come to light ;

IN

MEMORY

OF

DAVID RITCHIE

THE ORIGINAL OF THE

" BLACK DWARF."

DIED 1811.

ERECTED BY

W. AND R. CHAMBERS

1845

---

* See " The Black Dwarf's Bones " in *Horae Subsecivae*.

CHAPTER TEN

OLD MORTALITY

"Grand, pious sculptor of the tombs."

TODD.

WHATEVER THE DEMERITS OF *THE BLACK Dwarf*, there can be no question as to the excellence of its companion, *Old Mortality*. " If you could see me," John Murray wrote to Scott, " as the author's literary chamberlain, receiving the unanimous and vehement praises of those who have read it, and the curses of those whose needs my scanty supply could not satisfy, you may judge of the sincerity with which I now entreat you to assure the author of the most complete success." Lord Holland had said when asked his opinion : " Opinion ! We did not one of us go to bed last night,—nothing slept but my gout." It is curious to find Scott persisting in his equivocations. Affecting to deny the authorship, he reviewed *The Tales* in *The Quarterly*. In point of fact, he wanted an opportunity to rebut the charges which Dr. Thomas M'Crie, the biographer of Knox and Melville, had brought against him in the *Edinburgh Christian Instructor*. M'Crie had been criticising Scott's historical view of the Covenant. It is one of the lengthiest critiques on record. The critic's position was that the author of *Old Mortality* had perpetrated an attack in cold blood on the Covenanters, that he had aimed to belittle and to vilify them. No greater injustice could be done to Scott's always clean and manly motives. For Dr. M'Crie the novel was bristling with distorted representations, with the most grotesque caricatures of men who had carried their lives in their hands for conscience' sake, men who had been the sav-

165

iours of their country. He protests against the intolerable partisanship of the tale, and declares that its historical sense is false, narrow, outrageously unpatriotic. He falls foul of the earlier Waverley romances, pronouncing *The Antiquary* "tame and fatiguing," and so forth. He puts sentiments into Scott's lips which Scott never entertained in his life. He quotes the " Scripture-larded slang " of the most extravagant of the Cameronians as if the author intended it to be a sample of the whole Presbyterian sect. Scott's crowning sin is his characterisation of Claverhouse—a picture far removed from the " Bloody Claver'se " of rural tradition.

That *Old Mortality* contains exaggerations is undoubted. On a revision, there are some things which Scott would have amended. But as the novel stands, are not its " sins " those of omission rather than of commission ? No light is cast on affairs at the period of the story. No statement is made of the causes which drove the insurgents into the field in retaliation and self-defence. There is no hint of the dire oppression, or of the years of torture and despair preceding Drumclog and Bothwell Bridge. Worst blunder of all is the prominence given to the fanatical and disputative class among the Covenanters, and the almost total exclusion of those of them who had never a wish to overturn the king's civil authority but were only anxious for toleration to worship as conscience directed. At the same time, there exists evidence enough that Kettledrummle and his companions

(Mucklewrath excepted) were not without archetypes, whose extravagances equalled, if they did not surpass, anything that Scott had depicted.

Many of the names in *Old Mortality* were borrowed from that list of sufferers for the Covenant appended to *A Cloud of Witnesses*. The name of Habakkuk Mucklewrath is almost certainly derived from Matthew Micklewrath, or from Daniel Mickelwrick, victims both of the " saint-killing year." Maclure (the name borne by that most perfect heroine, Bessie Maclure) is Maclurg—improved. Scott himself says that the name of the mutinous and murderous trooper, black Frank Inglis, was taken from " Peter or Patrick Inglis who killed one James White, struck off his Head with an Ax, brought it home to Newmilns, and plaid at the Foot-ball with it." Gabriel Kettledrummle finds a precedent for his Christian name in Gabriel Thomson, who was executed at the age of eighteen. Halliday, Hunter, Wilson, are other names that appear on the *Cloud* list. As for Originals, Ephraim Macbriar, that fearless, radiant testifier (to whose heroism Scott does full justice), unquestionably stands for Hugh M'Kail, who, however, had run his brief race thirteen winters before Drumclog and Bothwell were fought. Goose Gibbie has his prototype in Willie Hawick, a silly, weak person about Kelso.* There were traits of Scott's old neighbour, " Nippy of the

* " I am confirmed in this opinion not only by the *vraisemblance* of the portrait, but by the circumstance that Scott frequently met Hawick at our cottage home in the days of his Kelso boyhood."—*Autobiography of William Jerdan.*

Peel," in the mean, close-fisted Laird Milnwood. John Balfour of Burley (properly " of Kinloch "), that Jehu of the Covenant, appears in a rather better light than he was in reality. A " little squint-eyed man, of a very fierce aspect," he was in actual life a conscience-less enthusiast, whose enthusiasm darkened into the bigotry of the fanatic, " who had never any great character for religion among those that knew him," and whom the ministers of the Scots congregation at Rotterdam would never allow to sit at Communion with them.*

Of Tillietudlem, Lady Bellenden's Castle, where Morton (one of the best of Scott's heroes) besieged his own lady-love, where Cuddie Headrigg was repulsed by Jenny Dennison's scalding brose, Scott wrote to Skene : " I did not think on Craignethan in writing about Tillietudlem, and I believe it differs in several respects from my *château en Espagne*. It is not on the Clyde in particular, and if I recollect, the view is limited and wooded, but there can be no objection to adopting it as that which public taste has adopted as coming nearest to the ideal of the place." Blackwood, near Lesmahagow, has been set down as Milnwood, and Crichope, in Closeburn, is as like the Black Linn of

* There is the curious tradition that Balfour actually returned to Scotland from Holland (instead of being drowned on the voyage). He is said to have settled at Rosneath under the name of Andrew Salter, where his descendants continued for generations. A small stone with the letters "A. S." rudely traced, and barely discernible in a corner of the churchyard, used to be pointed out as indicating the last resting-place of the terrible Burley. In the novel, of course, Balfour's end is entirely fictitious.

Linklater as any spot of the kind can be—"an awsome place as ever living creature took refuge in ; but he [Burley] loves it abune a' others ; and it's my belief he prefers it to a tapestried chamber and a bed o' down."

To Train the genesis of the novel is due. Calling on Scott at Castle Street one morning in May 1816, he brought with him some curios and a batch of gleanings from the realm of old-world story. In the *sanctum* the pair fell to discussing that portrait of Claverhouse which now hangs on the staircase of the study at Abbotsford. Scott expressed the Cavalier opinions about Dundee : "No character has been so foully traduced," he said. All this was new to Train, "who had been nurtured on the old beliefs." "Might he not," said Train, "be made, in good hands, the hero of a national romance as interesting as any about either Wallace or Prince Charlie ? " "He might," said Scott, "but your western zealots would require to be faithfully portrayed in order to bring him out with the right effect." " And what," replied Train, " if the story were to be delivered as if from the mouth of Old Mortality ? Would *he* not do as well as the Minstrel did in the *Lay* ? " "Old Mortality," said Scott, "who is he ? " " Never shall I forget," adds Train, " the eager interest with which he listened while I related to him what I knew of old Robert Paterson, the wandering inscription-cutter." On departing, Train promised that on his return to Galloway he would collect all particulars available respecting him. " Do so by all means," was Scott's reply; "I assure you I shall look with anxiety for your communication."

II

Robert * Paterson (not Patterson) was the youngest son of Walter Paterson and Margaret Scott. He was born at Burnflat, otherwise Haggisha', a little way out of Hawick. The statement that Closeburn was his birthplace is a mistake, arising probably from the fact that his wife was connected with that parish. The date of Robert's entry on the human stage has been variously recorded. At Haggisha', the Memorial Tablet gives the year 1712. A tombstone at Balmaclellan reads 1713, whilst Old Mortality's son Robert says 1715. This confliction is partly explained by the fact that there were two Roberts in old Walter Paterson's family, one born in 1713, the other, as we shall see, in 1716. The Hawick Registers may be quoted as authority for a circumstance of which the biographers, as well as the family of Old Mortality, do not seem to have been aware. On 14th July 1713 there is this entry: "Walter Paterson of Burnflat had a son baptized Robert before these witnesses—John Scott, *distinctionis causa* called John, the Souldier, and Henrie Paterson, Carrier in Hawick." Three years later, on 25th April 1716, we find the following: "Walter Paterson of Burnflat had a son baptized, called Robert, before these witnesses—Walter Paterson, in Hawick, and Walter Scott, Beddal."

* Lockhart, curiously, wrote "Peter" Paterson.

We may assume, therefore, that Robert the first had died some time previous to the birth of Robert the second. It will be remembered that, for the same reason, there were two Robert Scotts and two Walter Scotts in the family of the Edinburgh lawyer, and here we have two Robert Patersons.

In his thirteenth year, Robert Paterson was apprenticed to his brother Francis, tenant of Corncockle Quarry, Lochmaben. It was at Corncockle that Robert mastered the stone-craft which was to carry his name wherever the English language is spoken.

In the haunted Castle of Spedlins, close to Corncockle, lived Robert Gray, gardener to Sir John Jardine, and his daughter Elizabeth. Lizzie Gray went into the service of Sir Thomas Kirkpatrick of Closeburn, and about 1743 she became the wife of Robert Paterson, and brought him into Nithsdale. If the stone over her dust at Balmaclellan gives her age correctly at the time of her death, she must have been seventeen or eighteen when the wedding took place. No doubt it was the prospect of starting on his own account that led to the marriage, for immediately afterwards Robert Paterson obtained a lease of Gatelawbridge Quarry, in the parish of Morton, a mile east of Thornhill Station. There, in the words of a native, the surface beds of red freestone have been "tirled" for ages. In the meadow, young Paterson raised his cottage over a prehistoric hypocaust, unknown to him, but laid bare by the present lessee ; and by the brown stream of the Cample his family

171

increased. The couple sat in the old kirk of Morton, now wasted to the bell gable, and there, "before the congregation," John was baptized in 1747, and Walter in 1749. Robert was born in 1756, and there were two daughters, Margaret and Janet. It is Robert who narrates the story of his father's arrest by some of Prince Charlie's men retreating from England. The affair was trifling. All that the Highlanders wanted was to be shown the nearest smithy. That done, Paterson returned home nothing the worse for his adventure, though his wife had the fright of her life and thought she would never see her husband more.

When or how Robert Paterson blossomed into the Old Mortality immortalised by Scott we have no means of knowing. Our sources of information are confined to Joseph Train's statement and the narrative supplied by Old Mortality's son Robert. Train's account is to the effect that Paterson was a religious enthusiast who spent the best part of his life in a reparation of the tombstones over the graves of Covenanters in the South of Scotland. This good work he did without fee or reward, from sheer love of the thing, from a sense of the historic fitness of the task. All he asked was liberty to peacefully pursue his mission : if hospitality were proffered, he was glad to accept it; if not, he had means sufficient for his simple wants. Year by year he bent to his self-imposed labour. The marks of his chisel were to be seen in every kirkyard from Tweedsmuir to the Solway. And long had he lingered by lonely mounds on vacant wine-red moors.

The cause for which Christ's dead heroes surrendered their all was dear to his heart, and in such fashion as lay in his power to prevent it, their names at least should not be allowed to perish from the earth; their sleeping-places should still be pointed out—

> " Where hands were clasped, and the banner grasped,
>   When Covenant watchwords rang."

It was that aspect of Paterson's character which was poured into the ear of Scott, and it is that interpretation of Paterson's peregrinations which survives in the popular imagination.

In the statement furnished by the son, there is no reference whatever to his father's Covenanting propensities. According to Robert junior, Paterson the elder had " plenty of business as a builder and hewer, and gave employment to a number of men—occasionally at least." In the course of his business he made repeated trips into Kirkcudbrightshire for the purpose of erecting headstones, which he supplied from his quarry. " Galloway he found was a place destitute of freestone, and, as a consequence, of gravestones, or any to work them. After several trials of carrying gravestones into Galloway, and selling them, he saw that it answered his expectation of a profitable concern." To the graveyards of that locality he gave most of his attention, travelling from one hallowed spot to another, accompanied by James Rae, a young Highlander who became as adept as himself in the hewer's craft. Paterson's ordinary occupation of quarrying and mason-work was now entirely subordi-

173

nated to his newer employment. He became (to use a modernism) a tombstone specialist. The fashion for tombstones was on the increase. Formerly, it was only the better-off class who could indulge in the luxury of a headstone, but even the poorer people in Old Mortality's time were smitten with the wish to commemorate their departed by something more ornate than a grey slab from the hillside. Hence work such as Paterson could so well execute was in demand all over Nithsdale and throughout a great part of Kirkcudbright and Wigtown. Everywhere he was known as the Hewer or the Letterer or the Headstone-man, and latterly there was bestowed on him the waggish but immortal name of Old Mortality.

May we not trace the origin of his Covenanting proclivities to some of those churchyard visits ? Many of these God's acres were flowered with martyrs' graves—some with an appropriate memorial, others with nothing to show where the dear dust lay. May not the inspiration have come to him as he set himself—at a leisurely moment perhaps—to recut or deepen the epitaph on some rude block or a more ornamental " throuch " that proclaimed its brave tale to the passer-by—an inspiration which was destined to grow into a very obsession ? Nor must we forget that Old Mortality's epoch was not far removed from that of the Covenant. He was born within three decades of the memorable year 1685. In his boyhood at Hawick, as well as by the banks of the Carron and the Cample, he would hear many a rural hearth ring with

the exploits of the Hillfolk. He would be acquainted
with Andrew Ker of Shiel, one of the persecuted, who
still survived. And, indeed, his whole environment
would send him back in thought to the time

> "when kings
> Claimed right divine to murder honest men,
> And vassal bishops flapped their vulture wings
> O'er God's dear saints, hunted from glen to glen."

It is evident, therefore, that the restoration of
martyrs' monuments was not Robert Paterson's main
business to begin with. That is more than likely to
have been the work of his later life, after the Gatelawbridge tenancy ceased and his regular trade had
begun to diminish. The son's silence on the subject is
perplexing. It is not easy to see why he should fail to
mention the traditionary facts which were accepted
by everybody.

If the son has not chronicled traits commendable
and worthy in his father's character, he does not forget to tell of the less worthy and the unhappy things
which are associated with the name of Old Mortality.
For it is this same Robert who records that disagree-
able, that inexplicable episode in Old Mortality's
career—his ten years' desertion of wife and family.
All Robert Paterson's piety and zeal offer no atonement for an offence so scandalous. In 1758, Elizabeth
Paterson was thirty-two years old. Robert himself
was forty-two. Their children were all born. There
is no hint of domestic unpleasantness. Remittances
of money were frequent. Paterson was at Gatelawbridge every now and again. "But about the year

1758," says the son, " my father neglected to return to his family, and made few remittances." He ceased to communicate with them entirely. Explain it as we may (religious enthusiasm can hardly be set down as the reason), such conduct is rather an ugly blot on Old Mortality's scutcheon. Overtures were made to him to return. On one occasion Walter, his second son, a lad of eleven or twelve, set out, like another Japhet, in search of a father. He discovered him at work in the old churchyard at Kirkchrist, across the river from Kirkcudbright. The obdurate parent not only turned a deaf ear to the pleadings of his flesh and blood, but actually kept the boy from going home again. He put him to school, and taught him the trade of a stone-cutter, in which Walter Paterson more than literally made his mark. About 1768, Mrs. Paterson and her family, either on their own initiative or with the assistance of the father (as Robert reported), removed to the village of Balmaclellan, near New Galloway, and there Mrs. Paterson made a respectable livelihood by keeping a small school till her death in 1785. If Robert Paterson was the instrument of the removal to Balmaclellan, he must have returned to his old haunts soon afterwards, and it was then, probably, that his wandering life really began.

The circumstances that occasioned his meeting with Scott are these : In 1793 Scott was staying at Meigle, in Forfarshire, the seat of his friend Patrick Murray of Simprin. In the course of a trip to Stonehaven, to view the ruins of Dunnottar Castle, they stumbled

across the old man busy at his wonted occupation—
renovating the tombstone erected to the memory of
the captives who perished in the Whigs' Vault at
Dunnottar. Scott's pen-portrait (true to life, he says)
corresponds in detail with descriptions which have
come down from other quarters from contemporaries
who had often seen and talked with Robert Paterson :
" A blue bonnet of unusual dimensions covered the
grey hairs of the pious workman. His dress was a
large old-fashioned coat of the coarse cloth called
hoddin-grey, usually worn by the elder peasants, with
waistcoat and breeches of the same ; and the whole
suit, though still in decent repair, had obviously seen
a train of long service. Strong clouted shoes, studded
with hobnails, and *gramoches* or *leggins*, made of thick
black cloth, completed his equipment. Beside him,
fed among the graves a pony, the companion of his
journey, whose extreme whiteness, as well as its projecting bones and hollow eyes, indicated its antiquity.
It was harnessed in the most simple manner, with a
pair of branks, a hair tether, or halter, and a *sunk*, or
cushion of straw, instead of bridle and saddle. A
canvas pouch hung round the neck of the animal—
for the purpose, probably, of containing the rider's
tools, and anything else he might have occasion to
carry with him. Although I had never seen the old
man before, yet, from the singularity of his employment, and the style of his equipage, I had no
difficulty in recognising a religious itinerant, whom
I had often heard talked of, and who was known

in various parts of Scotland by the title of ' Old Mortality.' "

In Morton parish, writes Dr. King Hewison (a native), Paterson was remembered as a "little, bent, wizened old body of four-score years, and weird to look upon. Beneath his once blue Kilmarnock bonnet straggled bunches of long white hair over shrunken, rounded shoulders. His clothes of shepherd's hoddin were waulked and ' scaured ' by storm and sun, which did not add beauty to those baggy productions, ill-shapen by some Galloway ' whip-the-cat.' With him, sometimes ridden, anon riderless, journeyed his faithful old white horse, itself a scarred monument of antiquity, and very queer to behold with its wooden branks, bags suspended on either side (tools and victual) like Gilpin's bottles ' to keep the balance true,' and the hempen pad that counterfeited a saddle. ' A gey eerie pair,' said an eye-witness to the writer, and made more 'unco' when, with ' specs ' on, the grizzled sculptor lay chipping a green stone in a moorland."

Later in the day, Scott appears to have tried to get into conversation with Paterson at Dunnottar ; but even the glass of whisky in the manse, " to which he was supposed to have no objections," did not unlock his lips. He was dour and dull, and in a bad humour. " His spirit had been sorely vexed by hearing the psalmody directed by a pitch-pipe in some Aberdeen kirk ; and he had no freedom for conversation."

Scott says he met Old Mortality more than once

This, as we gather from Lockhart, is a mistake. The interview at Dunnottar was the only occasion on which Scott saw the great prototype. A few years afterwards, on St. Valentine's Day, in the opening year of the new century, Robert Paterson was making his way to Bankend, in the parish of Caerlaverock (not Bankhead of Lockerbie), when some people observed him approaching apparently in an uneasy posture. Whilst they were looking, he fell from his pony. He was carried to a house near by, spoke a few words, told who he was, where his sons lived, and in a short time all was over. Intimation was sent to Balmaclellan, but owing to the depth of snow at the time, none of his relatives were able to get forward to the funeral; nor in after years could the exact spot of sepulture be discovered either by Scott or Joseph Train. In 1855, his name was inscribed on the family tombstone at Balmaclellan.* A few years afterwards the firm of Adam and Charles Black, publishers of the Waverley Novels, considering that satisfactory evidence could

---

* To the Memory of

Robert Paterson, Stone-engraver, well known as "Old Mortality," who died at Bankend of Caerlaverock, 14th February, 1801, aged 88; also of Elizabeth Gray, his spouse, who died at Balmaclellan village, 5th May, 1785, aged 59; also of Robert, their son, who died 30th April, 1846, aged 90; also of Agnes M'Knight, his spouse, who died 5th August, 1818; also of John, their son, who died 29th January, 1810, aged 13; also of Alexander, who died at Wakefield, 26th October, 1837, aged 42; also of Robert, their son who died at Liverpool, 3rd February, 1865, aged 65—Erected by Thomas Paterson, 1855.

be shown of Paterson's having been interred in the churchyard of Caerlaverock, erected a plain, neat headstone with mallet and chisel over this inscription : *

ERECTED
To the Memory
of
ROBERT PATERSON
the
Old Mortality
of
Sir Walter Scott
Who was buried here
February, 1801.

> Why seeks he with unwearied toil,
>   Through Death's dim walks to urge his way,
> Reclaim his long-asserted spoil,
>   And lead oblivion into day ?

The remarkable story connected with Old Mortality's son, John, must be referred to, if only to set at rest once for all, statements that have absolutely no foundation in fact. It was (and still is) asserted that John Paterson, who is said to have emigrated to America between the years 1766 and 1776, was the Mr. Patterson, a wealthy Baltimore merchant, whose daughter, " the belle of Baltimore," became (in 1803) the wife of Jerome Bonaparte, Napoleon's youngest brother, and King of Westphalia. John Paterson, according to the story, had also a son, Robert, whose widow became Countess of Mornington, and Mar-

---

* Statues of Old Mortality and his pony have been erected in the Garpel Glen, Balmaclellan, and Maxwelltown, and in Laurel Hill Cemetery, Philadelphia, U.S.A.; in 1897, tablets were placed on his birth-cottage at Haggisha'.

chioness of Wellesley. It is a pretty tale—the descendants of Old Mortality linked to the conqueror of Europe and to the vanquisher of that conqueror. That Scott had doubts on the matter is seen from a letter to Train, who had furnished him with the tradition : " I shall hardly venture to mention the extraordinary connection between the Bonaparte family and that of Old Mortality till I learn from you how it is made out ; whether by continued correspondence between the families of the two brothers, or otherwise. A strain of genius (too highly toned in the old patriarch) seems to have run through the whole family."

The proof which Scott desired never existed. The matter seems to have originated in the mixing up of two families of the same name. In the latter part of the eighteenth century *William* Patterson, from the north of Ireland, settled in Philadelphia, and afterwards established himself in Baltimore, where he turned to business and became one of Baltimore's wealthiest citizens. In 1779 he married Dorcas Spear, the eighteen-year-old daughter of William Spear. By her he had thirteen children—eight sons and five daughters, among them a Robert and an Elizabeth. Robert, the second son, married Mary Caton, eldest daughter of Richard Caton. The husband died in 1822, and three years later Mrs. Patterson became the wife of the Marquis Wellesley, brother of the Duke of Wellington. Two of her sisters also allied themselves with the English aristocracy—Elizabeth Caton becoming Lady Stafford, and Louisa Caton, Duchess of Leeds. The lady with whom Jerome Bonaparte fell so deeply in love, and whom he married, but ultimately divorced, was Elizabeth, eldest daughter of William Patterson and Dorcas Spear. Elizabeth Bonaparte died at Baltimore in 1879, at the age of ninety-five. Her son, Jerome Napoleon, married an American lady, who had two sons, one of whom, Charles Joseph Bonaparte, was Attorney-General of the United States.

In an autobiographic note attached to the will of William Patterson, distinct mention is made of his ancestors and of his own birth-spot: "I was born on the first of November, old style, in the year 1752, at a place called Fanat, in the county of Donegal, Ireland." It has since been found that he was born at Rosgarrow, on the Fanad peninsula. To this place, and the neighbouring townlands of Urbleshinney and Glenkeen, the ancestors of William Patterson came from Newton-on-Ayr late in the seventeenth or early in the eighteenth century.

John Paterson, who was born in 1747 (parish register in General Register House), could *not* have been the grandfather of Elizabeth, as is suggested ; indeed there is no proof that John Paterson ever even emigrated to America. He *may* have done so ; but spite of the credence which still obtains amongst representatives of the families concerned, it must be said that there is not a shred of evidence to associate him with their very romantic story, much as one should desire to see it substantiated.

Old Mortality's descendants were destined to rise, not by any fortuitous circumstance of marriage or relationship, but by the slow recognition of worth and goodness. His grandson, Nathaniel Paterson (son of the lad Walter mentioned on page 176), became minister of Galashiels in 1821. A frequent visitor at Abbotsford, Scott speaks of him in the highest terms. Translated to St. Andrew's, Glasgow, he joined the Free Church, became D.D., and was Moderator of Assembly in 1850.

Nathaniel Paterson, who took considerable interest in mechanics, has been regarded as the inventor of a form of lifeboat. But he is best known as the author of *The Manse Garden.* That little work, written at Galashiels whilst an invalid, appeared anonymously (lest, as the preface quaintly puts it, the reverend writer should seem to be giving more thought to his own garden than to the Lord's vineyard), has passed through many editions, and is "still read for the sake of its poetry, and wisdom, and Christian kindness, where there are no gardens, and will be read for the sake of other days when there are no manses." A little volume of *Letters to his Family,* said to equal those of Cowper, was published after his death. Another grandson of Old Mortality, Walter Paterson, brother to Nathaniel, was at one time Professor of English at Jena. He became minister of Kirkurd, in Peeblesshire, and wrote what Christopher North has described as "that beautiful but neglected poem," *The Legend of Iona.* (Edinburgh 1814).

CHAPTER ELEVEN

ROB ROY

"The eagle he was lord above,
And Rob was lord below."
WORDSWORTH.

———————

"Do not Maister or Campbell me—my foot is on my native heath, and my name is MacGregor."—*Rob Roy*.

CHAPTER ELEVEN ROB ROY

ROB ROY WAS PLANNED IN THE SUMMER OF 1817, and published on the last day of the same year. To Constable is due the merit of the title, notwithstanding Scott's preference for another—unnamed. The novel received a welcome as warm as any of its predecessors. So great was the demand for copies that the entire cargo of a smack sailing from Leith to London consisted of an edition of ten thousand— an event unprecedented in the annals of literature, and in the history of the Custom House. When the novel was dramatised and acted at Edinburgh by William Murray's Company, it brought down the house. Along with the last proof-sheets, the author announced his satisfaction at being rid of the work :

> " Dear James [Ballantyne], with great joy
>   I send you Roy,
>   'Twas a tough job,
>   But we're done with Rob."

Rob was truly a " tough job." The novel was written *in tormentis*—amid a perfect tyranny of aches and pains. Scott suffered from an aggravated form of stomach cramp, the beginning of the illness which ultimately carried him off. He was obliged to swallow large doses of laudanum—a remedy almost certainly followed by intense lassitude and depression. Never given to voicing his melancholy moods in verse, it was at this time that he wrote the beautiful and touching poem :

187

" The sun upon the Weirdlaw Hill,
   In Ettrick's vale, is sinking sweet,
The westland wind is hush and still,
   The lake lies sleeping at my feet,"

"verses as sweet and sad as ever came from the broken heart of Byron, or from the lyre which Shelley flung aside, to lie down on the Bay of Naples, seeking, like a tired child, to weep away this life of care."

Calling one day for copy, Ballantyne found Scott sitting with a clean quill and blank sheet in front of him. Expressing surprise, Scott answered : " Ay, ay, Jamie, 'tis easy for you to bid me get on, but how the deuce can I make Rob Roy's wife speak with such a curmurring in my guts ? " The novel betrays none of this languorous feeling. The adventurous element is as strong, the humour as free, as unrestrained, and as sympathetic as ever. No novel of Scott's so charmingly depicts Scottish scenery, or gives more vivid glimpses of Scottish history, and it is but truth to say that seldom has any work of fiction so enriched the speech of the multitude. Ruskin's taunt that Scott never had a fit of the cramp without spoiling a chapter, is a curious commentary on the success of *Rob Roy* both as regards its popularity and as being perhaps the most perfect of the Waverley series. Rob, of course, is the central figure throughout,—ever a " bonnie fechter," no matter his occupation or situation—ordinary cattle-drover, or kilted chief on his native heath with his shaggy and adoring Highlanders around him. He has a hand in the fortunes of all the other characters in the story, whose affairs seem hopelessly tangled and involved. The end, however, brings its own adjustment ; difficulties vanish, the villains are killed off, the sun shines again for the virtuous and the brave.

How powerfully the subject appealed to Scott is seen in his very long-winded Preface. Scott's Prefaces have never been popular, notwithstanding the infinite pains he took with them. In his hands they acquired a dignity and an interest they never had before and have never since attained. To be sure, they are of use to the student more than to the casual reader of Scott. For those who wish to dig into the genesis of the story, ascertain what Scott himself has to say about Originals, gauge the author's mood and feeling at the moment, the "ravelling-out of his weaved-up follies "— the Preface—is indispensable. Where ordinary writers content themselves with expressing indebtedness to so-and-so, Scott gives us a delightful short story interspersed with wonderful pieces of descriptive writing which seem almost wasted upon Introductions so few people ever read.

As with the rest of the Waverleys, oral tradition and personal reminiscence contributed greatly to the making of *Rob Roy*. An old Lennoxer recounted his adventures as a lad of fifteen among the *herd-widdiefows* with Rob and his blackmailers. The story of the outlaw's escape at the Fords of Frew, Scott heard from the lips of a grandson of James Stewart, who was the actual liberator. Lockhart thinks that Rob's spleuchan (the gift of Joseph Train) was not without inspiration when the story was on the anvil. Another Abbotsford "gabion" was Rob's gun, a long-barrelled weapon of Spanish make, bearing the initials R. M. C. As for topographical details, Scott knew the Highlands well. In his teens (in 1790 or thereabouts) he was in charge of an expedition from the Court of Session with a Summons of Removal against Maclaren of Invernenty, in Balquhidder. After that, visits to Rob Roy's Country were frequent, and in the summer preceding the publication of the novel, the ground was again covered in the company of Adam Ferguson. It is the Rising of the Fifteen which is pictured in *Rob Roy*, not at such length or with such wealth of detail as the subsequent attempt of the Forty-five in *Waverley*. Alone of all the series, the hero himself narrates the story throughout—a literary accommodation run to seed by the modern school of romancers.

Frank Osbaldistone, the nominal hero, is in some ways a transcript of Scott himself. He is more staid than Waverley, more vivacious than Harry Bertram or Lovel. Bailie Nicol Jarvie is, of course, incomparable among the men characters. " He is, for all time, the classic figure of the pawky Lowland merchant—hard, but honest, natural and simply cynical, but kindly, good-natured, ever humorous—as true a being of flesh and blood as ever trod the ' Saut Market,' " in the words of Sir Leslie Stephen. There is no known Original, but Charles Mackay of the Edinburgh Theatre Royal acted the part to perfection on the occasion of

George the Fourth's first visit to Scotland in 1822. "Mackay is going up to London," wrote Scott to Joanna Baillie, "to play Bailie Nicol Jarvie for a single night at Covent Garden, and I beg you, of all dear loves, to go and see him; for, taking him in that single character, I am not sure I ever saw anything in my life possessing so much truth and comic effect at the same time; he is completely the personage of the drama, the purse-proud consequential magistrate, humane and irritable in the same moment, and the true Scotsman in every turn of thought and action; his variety of feelings towards Rob Roy, whom he likes, and fears, and despises, and admires, and pities all at once, is exceedingly well expressed. In short, I never saw a part better sustained, certainly; I pray you to collect a party of Scotch friends to see it."

Rashleigh, "whose game is man," is the scoundrel of the piece—that most difficult of characters to depict, plausible and talented, but an incarnation of baseness, the origin of all the mischief that happens in *Rob Roy*.

The canny gardener, "that flower of serving-men," Andrew Fairservice, is a deftly drawn figure, albeit a source of irritation at times.

Di (not Die) Vernon and Helen MacGregor are types which Scott can best describe—women in their more masculine moods. They have to thank their environment for their dispositions. Both are self-willed, high-spirited, hazarding. There is about the "divine Diana" a tender, quiet grace which offers an admirable foil to the intrepid, somewhat melodramatic tendency of the Amazonian chieftainess. Di Vernon is the first of Scott's heroines who has much character. In fascination and interest she ranks with the Rebeccas, the Lucy Ashtons, the Margaret Ramsays, and the Clara Mowbrays who followed.

Of descriptions in *Rob Roy*, the preaching in the High Kirk of Glasgow ; Fairservice's gallant apostrophe to the noble pile ; the midnight meeting at Glasgow Bridge ; and the Clachan of Aberfoyle on a harvest morning, are word-pictures couched in the highest art.

The fate of Morris, Rashleigh's tool, one of the few utter cowards in Scott, is a tragedy told in a few sentences, all the more impressive for its brevity.

II

Readers of the *Lady of the Lake* will recall the song (in the second Canto) which Scott puts into the mouths of the MacGregor boatmen with its wild cry of savagery :

> " Proudly our pibroch has thrill'd in Glen Fruin,
>   And Bannochar's groans to our slogan replied ;
> Glen Luss and Ross-dhu, they are smoking in ruin,
>   And the best of Loch Lomond lie dead on her side.
>   Widow and Saxon maid
>   Long shall lament our raid,
>   Think of Clan-Alpine with fear and with woe ;
>   Lennox and Leven-glen
>   Shake when they hear agen,
>   ' Roderigh Vich Alpine dhu, ho ! ieroe ! '
>
> Row, vassals, row, for the pride of the Highlands !
>   Stretch to your oars, for the ever-green Pine !
> O that the rose-bud that graces yon islands,
>   Were wreathed in a garland around him to twine !
>   O that some seedling gem
>   Worthy such noble stem,

ROB ROY

COUNTESS PURGSTALL
(Jane Anne Cranstoun—"Di Vernon")
with her husband and only son   [see page 209

Honour'd and bless'd in their shadow might grow !
    Loud should Clan-Alpine then
      Ring from his deepmost glen,
  ' Roderigh Vich Alpine dhu, ho ! ieroe ! ' "

The Alpines are better known as the MacGregors.
They claim to be the most ancient of Highland Clans,
boasting descent from Gregor, son of Alpin, King of
the Scots, who reigned A.D. 833. Their motto, *'S rio-
ghail mo dhream*—" My race is kingly,"—proclaimed their royal degree, and their badge was the pine of
their native hills.

They became a numerous and powerful sept,
especially in Perthshire, where they owned half the
county. From the Braes of Balquhidder they ruled in
their day of might, and they kept the central Highlands in awe for centuries. But gradually much of
their landed property found its way, mostly by royal
charters, into the possession of their more civilised
neighbours, the Campbells and others, until about the
middle of the sixteenth century they were reduced
pretty much to the position of a clan of Ishmaelites
whose hand was against every man's hand and every
man's hand against theirs. They acknowledged no
right but the *coir a glaive*—the right of the strongest
—and their constant attempts to recover their lost
territory, or avenge themselves on its new owners,
resulted in a long series of Acts of Parliament, and
of the Privy Council of Scotland, directed against
"the wicked clan Gregor, so long continuing in
blood, slaughter, hership [plundering], manifest reifts
and storths committed upon His Highness' peaceable

and good subjects." These Acts produced little effect: the MacGregor raids continued: horrid barbarities were practised.

It is Dugald Ciar Mohr, " the great mouse-coloured man," who divides with Rob Roy the reputation of the clan for feats of strength and skill in arms, and an absolutely fearless spirit. Dugald's is an unsavoury memory. It is one of his monstrous crimes which forms the groundwork of the incident detailed in *A Legend of Montrose*. Dugald's exploits were followed by an edict of the Privy Council (3rd April 1603) abolishing the very name of MacGregor, and ordering all who bore it to adopt another patronymic. They were not permitted to carry weapons beyond a blunt, pointless knife for their food. Not more than four might meet together at a time ; and there were other drastic enactments. The MacGregors obeyed to the extent of assuming other names, those chiefly of neighbouring families—Campbell, Graham, Drummond, Murray, Stewart,—but they were MacGregors still. Even if broken men, their unity as a clan remained, and spite of oppressions and persecutions they increased in numbers and influence. In the Great Rebellion they were loyal to the Crown, although that might have been an opportunity for retaliation. At the Restoration the various statutes against them were repealed. These were revived in full force after the Revolution, and it was not until 1784 that Parliament granted liberty to the MacGregors to resume their old cognomen, restoring them at the same time to the full enjoyment of British citizenship.

The plot of *Rob Roy* is concerned with the period when Jacobite agents were attempting to win the MacGregors for King James in the coming Rebellion of 1715. From both sides they had suffered : from both sides they had received favours, but by their best traditions, by the blood that tingled in their veins, they could not be other than thirled to the Stuarts.

III

Judged by Scott's novel, the biggest, bravest heart that ever beat beneath the MacGregor tartan was that of Rob Roy, so named from the colour of his hair and his fresh, ruddy complexion. Scott did not create the Rob Roy of romance. He idealises, no doubt, but his interpretation of the character of Rob rests mainly on the popular tradition of the man. A descendant of the blood-thirsty Dugald Ciar Mohr, Rob had all his ancestor's love of the sword and capacity for leadership, without his cruelty. His lot was cast in the most restless epoch of Scottish history. It was an age of semi-barbarism, when the passion for power was the main thing, when a pillaging of the industrious Saxon was considered the proof of manliness and bravery.

Rob was the third son of Donald MacGregor of Glengyle. The Clan History gives the year of his birth as 1660, while Scott, assuming him to have been twenty-five at the Hership, or Raid, of Kippen, in 1691, makes Rob born in 1666. An entry in the Register of Baptisms for the Parish of Buchanan will give us the correct date :

" On the 7 day of March, 1671, Donald M'Gregor in Glengill, pr. of Calender, upon testificat from the minr. yrof [and] Margaret Campbell—son baptized Robert. Witness, Mr. Wm. Andersone minr., and Johne M'Gregore."

It is reasonable to suppose that the baptism took place shortly after birth, according to the usage of the times. The statement that Rob, at the age of twenty, was leader in the Kippen foray is extremely doubtful. Like all his tribe, Rob MacGregor had to assume another name. He took his mother's, who was a Campbell of Glenfalloch, and he became Rob Roy MacGregor Campbell. Sometimes he signs himself " Robert Roy Campbell." In a document of 1711, he is " Robert Campbell." A letter to the Duke of Atholl written in the year 1713 bears the familiar name Rob Roy. Again, in 1714, he signs " Robert MacGregor," and " MacGregor of Cragrostan," and of " Inversnait "—a domain of rock and forest lying along the shore of Loch Lomond. Doubt has been cast on his position as a landowner, but it is certain he had a legal title both to Cragrostan and Inversnait. These properties may have been acquired by purchase, or, as seems more probable, by advancing money on mortgages. In Rob's more reputable epoch he was the occupant of grazing land in Balquhidder, a cattle-drover on a fairly extensive scale, doing business as far south as the Tweed and the Solway. It was a stroke of ill-luck which changed the whole current of Rob's career and made possible the Rob Roy of Highland legend and romance. Becoming involved in speculations, he not only lost his own savings but also considerable sums entrusted to him by the Duke of Montrose. Bankruptcy followed: Rob absconded. The warrant for his arrest can be read in the Appendix to the novel. A distraint was levied on his property, and Montrose's agents insulted Rob's wife in her husband's absence. To that incident is attributed the wild pipers' tune of "Rob Roy's Lament," in whose weird strains, one may almost say that something of the mournful beauty of the country has been incorporated. Rob now sought the protection of Argyll, the rival chief, and it was from this time that his life took on that new colour which characterised him ever afterwards.

What was the real character of this man whose name has been so enshrined in song and story? Was he the bad, villainous cateran fighting for his own hand, the "Highland Rogue," as Defoe has called him—crafty, quick to take an advantage, greedy, unscrupulous, carrying even murder in his heart to gain his ends? Or, instead of the red-haired, red-handed Tyrant of the Braes of Balquhidder, was he the friend of the poor and oppressed, as Robin Hood was, not given to wanton cruelty, not a monster thirsting for blood, but drawing the sword only when gener-

ous motives inspired him ? There can be little doubt
that Rob Roy had a large amount of that contemporary popularity which is reflected in the novel. Scott
had listened to Rob Roy's story from those who knew
Rob personally, and who gave him a high character
for beneficence and humanity. It was that aspect of
the freebooter's career which attracted both Scott
and Wordsworth, the latter of whom in his poem on
" Rob Roy's Grave " makes precisely the sort of defence which secured the respect of Bailie Nicol Jarvie:

> " The good old rule
> Sufficeth them ; the simple plan,—
> That they should take who have the power,
> And they should keep who can.
>
> A lesson which is quickly learned,
> A signal through which all can see :
> Thus, nothing here provokes the strong
> To wanton cruelty."

Little as the Bailie would approve of the first stanza, the spirit of the second appears in his own words :
" Set apart what he had done against the law of the
country, and the hership of the Lennox, and the misfortune o' some folk losing life by him, he was an hon-
ester man than stude on ony o' their shanks." " He
aye keepit his word—I canna deny but he keepit his
word.—A' men allow that Rob keeps his word."

As for Rob's manner of life, no one doubts that he
showed but little respect for what law and order there
was in the Highlands. Nay, as Stevenson puts it, he
" may many a time have been a kenning on the
wrong side of the law," but he was far from being the
terrible fellow portrayed in some of the biographies.

He is credited with, or blamed for, exploits performed by others more lawless than himself, and there has been much exaggeration of the misdemeanours of which he may have been really guilty.

The truth is that Rob Roy's cattle raids were confined almost exclusively to the Graham Country. Rob never forgave Montrose for having turned against him. He would, he said, "make His Grace rue the day on which he quarrelled with him," and he became the terror of Montrose's life to the end. But to many another he was a kind and gentle robber, who, while he took from the rich, was liberal in relieving the poor. He was not a plunderer for plundering's sake. He was not a robber, or a freebooter, in the Border acceptation. Freebooters are hardly chosen to settle disputes between neighbour tenants, but Rob is found to act in that capacity more than once. Nor must we conceive of him as ignorant and illiterate. He was not so. He possessed the accomplishment of being able to sign his name, which few Highlanders of that day could do, and his letters are couched in as good a style as the majority of his contemporaries.' His sons, also, were well educated, notwithstanding that to his kinsman, Professor Gregory of Aberdeen, Rob (banteringly) remarked that book-learning was but a useless art. Rob's own regard for letters is seen in the fact that his name, "Robert MacGregor, *alias* Rob Roy," appears in the list of subscribers to no less a work than Keith's *History of Affairs of Church and State in Scotland*, published at Edinburgh in 1734, the year of

Rob's death. Wordsworth is wrong, therefore, when he makes "generous Rob" exclaim:

> " What need of books ?
> Burn all the statutes and their shelves !
> They stir us up against our kind,
> And worse, against ourselves."

The time of Rob's death, says Scott, is not known with certainty. The date, however, as we learn from the *Caledonian Mercury* (9th January 1735), was 28th December 1734, and the place Inverlochlarig-beg, at the head of Loch Doine, in the parish of Balquhidder.*

The tradition which represents Rob as rising from his death-bed to receive the visit of one with whom he was at enmity is well known: "Raise me from my bed, throw my plaid round me, and bring me my claymore, dirk, and pistols; it shall never be said that a foeman saw Rob Roy MacGregor defenceless and unarmed." Shortly afterwards he said : " It is all over now ; put me to bed. Call in the piper. Let him play *Cha teill mi tuille* [I will never return] as long as I breathe." Another account of the closing scene has been handed down: " Before they parted, the priest arrived and conjured Rob, as he expected forgiveness from God, to bring his mind in the last moments to forgive all his enemies. Rob at first demurred at the expostulation, and the priest, to enforce it, quoted part of the Lord's Prayer. On hearing this,

* The house in which he died has been converted into a shepherd's house and bothy. By order of the Earl of Moray, the proprietor, a small part of Rob Roy's dwelling was preserved. Inverlochlarig-more and Inverlochlarig-beg now form an extensive sheep farm on the Moray estate.

Rob said, ' Ay, now ye ha'e gi'en me baith law and gospel for't. It's a hard law, but I ken it's gospel.' Then, turning to Rob Oig (young Rob), he addressed him thus : ' My sword and dirk lie there. Never draw them without reason, nor put them up without honour. I forgive my enemies ; but see you to them, or may——' and he expired." Both versions are likely to be pure inventions.

Rob died poor. The inventory of his personal estate, as recorded in the Register of Dunblane Testaments, gives a total value of £275, 13s. 4d. Scots. His wife was decerned sole executrix.

Rob Roy's wife, the Helen MacGregor of tale and tradition, was really christened Mary. Born a MacGregor of Comar, she was far from being the vengeance-loving virago of the novel, but is reputed to have been a woman of agreeable temper, domesticated, hospitable, musical, poetic. An error which has crept into all the genealogies may be corrected here : It is that Rob's wife bore her husband five sons instead of four. In the Introduction to the novel, Scott says : " Rob had five sons,—Coll, Ronald, James, Duncan, and Robert." Duncan, however, was not Rob's son. If he was, then he married his niece—Kate MacGregor, the daughter of his eldest brother. He is more likely to have been a cousin's son of Rob Roy, and may be identified with Duncan of Cuilt, author of a deeply-interesting *Journal of the Clan of MacGregor and Transactions of the Year 1745, from the Braes of Balquhidder till they returned.*

Rob's eldest son, Coll or Colin, a man of sterling upright life—in singular contrast to his brothers—died the year after his father at the age of thirty-one. James Mohr MacGregor, Rob's second son, is the best known of the four stalwarts. Like his brothers, he began life as a small farmer. It was the murder of Maclaren of Invernenty which brought him into notice and into trouble. Invernenty, a MacGregor holding for generations, had been let on lease to John Maclaren. The MacGregors refused to move, and the Maclarens appealed to the laird (Stewart of Appin) to support their claim. Appin marched into Balquhidder with two hundred men and there met Rob Roy, who, recognising the superior strength of his opponent, at once gave in and agreed to hand over Invernenty to the Maclarens. It was on this occasion that Rob sought a friendly bout with some of the Appin gentry when Invernahyle accepted—to Rob's humiliation. Following Rob's death in 1734, Maclaren of Invernenty * proposed to turn the widow out

* A brother of Maclaren's (Neil Maclaren) figures in *Redgauntlet* as Pate-in-Peril, the Laird of Summertrees. He had many adventures during the Forty-five, and was taken prisoner at Culloden. When on his way to Carlisle for trial, he managed to make his escape at the Devil's Beef Tub, between Tweedsmuir and Moffat. He darted over the steep side of the precipice and rolled down to the foot, where he concealed himself till nightfall. He returned to Balquhidder; escaping detection, dressed as a woman, for a year, when the Act of Indemnity relieved him from further danger. Invernenty was evidently a man of some culture, for "Ian Maclaren" (Dr. John Watson), his descendant, possessed his copy of Theophrastus, printed in Greek and Latin. This was probably the Maclaren mentioned at page 190, though Scott, writing thirty-four years later, had forgot his name.

of her farm, Inverlochlarig-beg, by offering a larger
rent. Whether at the instigation of Mary MacGregor
or not, Robin Oig (still in his teens) set out for
Invernenty armed with his father's famous gun.
John Maclaren was at the plough, and the words
that escaped his lips when he observed Robin, are
repeated in Balquhidder to this day : " What is that
snake doing round here ? " he remarked to his companion. Robin fired : Maclaren fell between the
plough-stilts mortally wounded. The youthful mur-
derer fled to France, but James Mohr and his brother
were arrested and indicted as accomplices. No Report
of the trial has been published, but from a perusal of
the Book of Adjournal it is evident that the charge
was not only unfounded, but had been literally
trumped up out of enmity to the MacGregors. Small
wonder that in the Forty-five the Gregarach were
ardent Jacobites, making full atonement for their
singular supineness in the Fifteen. Big James was an
energetic officer in the rebel army. At Prestonpans
he was wounded in the thigh, but he was *not* the
Captain MacGregor of whom it is related that after
receiving five wounds, he called out to his men : " My
lads, I'm not dead, and by God, I'll see if any of you
does not do his duty." *

After Culloden, James Mohr was attainted, but
evaded capture. He next comes into notice in con-

* The hero of the story was really Captain Malcolm MacGregor,
eldest son of Donald MacGregor of Craigruidhe in Balquhidder,
who was mortally wounded at Prestonpans.

nection with the abduction of Jean Key by Robin Oig, who, notwithstanding his outlawry, had returned home. (See Introduction to *Rob Roy.*) James, charged as accessary, was seized and thrown into prison. Stevenson has told how he escaped through his daughter Malie's wit, and once clear of Edinburgh, he took the road to England. Wearied out one night among the Cumberland fells, he sat down to rest, when the sound of voices reached his ears. He started to his feet, and by good fortune forgathered with Billy Marshall, the Galloway gypsy, who saw him embarked in safety for the Isle of Man. From thence he sailed to Ireland, and eventually to France. His melancholy end in Paris in 1754 readers of *Catriona* will recall, and his request for a set of pipes to while away his hours of sickness is the final and most pathetic passage in the life of James Mohr MacGregor.

Ronald MacGregor, Rob Roy's third son, lived to a great age on his farm, the Kirkton of Balquhidder, where he died about 1786. It is said that when the soldiers sent to watch the neighbourhood after the Forty-five became intoxicated and set fire to some houses, the people wished to rise and make an end of them. But Ronald, foreseeing the consequences, implored them for their lives to do nothing that would bring on them the fury of the Government; and so influential was he that they instantly relinquished their intention. The career of Robert or Robin Oig, the fourth son, has been referred to. Robin, having enlisted in the Forty-second Highlanders, then in France, fought at Fontenoy, lay in a French dungeon for a time, returned to England when the Forty-five broke out, and was posted with his regiment to defend the coast of Kent in case of invasion. The abduction of the young widow, Jean Key, took place in 1751, and in May 1753 Robin Oig was apprehended at Gartmore Fair, taken to Edinburgh, where he was tried 24th December 1753, and condemned to death. On 6th February 1754, he was hanged in the Grassmarket. In the words of the *Caledonian Mercury* of the 7th, " he was very genteelly dressed, behaved with great decency, and declared he died an unworthy member of the Church of Rome ; and further still, that he attributed all his misfortunes to his swerving two or three years ago from that communion." On his way to the scaffold he read from a volume of Gother's works. There is a tradition that when poor Rob's body was given over to his friends for burial, his niece, the redoubtable Malie, refused to let the executioner touch his body-clothes, which, according to custom, were a perquisite of the hangman. The story is that she seized his arm and swung him off to a distance, saying : " You've already done enough, and won't be allowed to touch any part of my uncle's dress." The body was conveyed to Balquhidder, and, clothed as it was, laid in the grave of his eldest brother Coll, to the melancholy wailing of the coronach.*

* The MacGregor graves are conspicuous objects in Balquhidder kirkyard. It should be noted that the flat stone covering Rob Roy's remains is of far older date than the " bold outlaw's " time.

CHAPTER TWELVE

ROB ROY
"DI VERNON"

"For you alone I ride the ring,
For you I wear the blue;
For you alone I strive to sing,
O tell me how to woo!"

GRAHAM OF GARTMORE.

SCOTT'S HEROES AND HEROINES ARE OFTEN
the dullest and most uninteresting of his characters.
Where they fail to interest their author, readers are
not likely to be ecstatic. Sir Walter, it has been
remarked, was the last man to saunter in the policies
with Miss Bertram and Miss Mannering and young
Hazlewood, when there was Dandie Dinmont ready
and able to discourse on the points of Dumple and
the pedigree of Pepper and Mustard. Why should he
linger in Miss Wardour's bower when he might take
the road with Edie Ochiltree? What he did not care
to do himself he would not inflict on his readers. Edith
Bellenden, Isabella Wardour, Rose Bradwardine,
Lucy Bertram, even dear, romantic Green Mantle
—mix them up and redistribute the rôles, and the
novels would remain practically unchanged. These
are the normal types of Scott's heroines. Listless,
insipid, mechanical, they maintain little hold on the
attention. Their sphere of action is limited, and
comparatively few are moved either by what they
say or do. Scott's female characters are unquestionably less excellent than his male characters. But
what of those abnormal types who carry their thrill
of life and interest into every chapter? Since Shakespeare's time no writer has given us so truly great
and superlative female creations as Scott has. He
reaches Himalaya height in such a character as Jeanie
Deans, for instance; or in Rebecca of York with

her peerless sacrifice; or in Diana Vernon and her sprightliness.

Di Vernon is the most fascinating of the trio just mentioned. She is *facile princeps* the ideal woman from the point of view of a man of the world, displaying that combination of qualities which he will most admire and desire. Diana is herself a woman of the world—a higher world than that with which the term is ordinarily associated. Her tastes, her interests, are far removed from the common sordidness, and when she loves, her passion is pure as a rose in June. She knows how to love. Among Scott's novels *Rob Roy* stands alone as regards its pictures of passionate love, yet how little of the really sentimental element there is in the story! Scott, unlike some writers—especially modern writers—handles the great theme with a "truly Greek reserve in his art." He "deals neither in analysis nor in rapturous effusions." Neither is he a cold, stolid delineator of the love-scene, but a very natural exponent of it. With Scott there is no stupid, often false, revelling in tears and kisses and caresses. He mentions the subject with a simple matter-of-fact directness. Indeed, the introduction of love affairs into any portion of Scott's works is, as a rule, accidental, and when introduced, is hurried over and dismissed as quickly as possible, in almost an impatient manner. The one occasion in which Scott allows himself to break his customary reserve in recording hypersentimental scenes between his heroes and heroines, is in the novel under notice. Barely two lines are occupied in describing the circumstances—that sad, quick embrace at the Fords of Frew when only the stars looked on (chap. xxxiii.).

" She extended her hand, but I clasped her to my bosom. She sighed as she extricated herself from the embrace which she permitted, escaped to the door which led to her own apartment, and I saw her no more." And so the days pass dolefully, for danger and intrigue are in the air, before the lovers meet again in the dusk and the solitude.

" 'Mr. Francis Osbaldistone,' cries a voice, the tone of which thrilled through every nerve of my body, ' should not whistle his favourite airs when he wishes to remain undiscovered.'

" And Diana Vernon—for she, wrapped in a horseman's cloak, was the last speaker—whistled in playful mimicry the second part of the tune which was on my lips when they came up."

Then it is that Diana says her farewell to Frank : " Her face touched mine. She pressed my hand, while the tear that trembled in her eye found its way to my cheek instead of her own. It was a moment never to be forgotten—inexpressibly bitter, yet mixed with a sensation of pleasure so deeply soothing and affecting as at once to unlock all the flood-gates of the heart." She rides into the night. " I felt the tightening of the throat and breast, the *hysterica passio* of poor Lear ; and, sitting down by the wayside, I shed a flood of the first and most bitter tears which had flowed from my eyes since childhood."

211

This is Diana Vernon, for whom, as says Andrew
Lang, all men who read *Rob Roy* are innocent rivals of
Frank Osbaldistone. Di Vernon is so utterly unlike
any other of the Waverley heroines. Rather does she
count cousin with the Rosalinds, the Portias, the
Beatrices, the Imogens—those " deathless daughters
of dreams." She has all their qualities. " Like them,
she is witty and loving; like them, she plays on every
note, passing from playful authority to serious heroism, and, like them, melting into womanly tenderness. She brightens the world as she passes, and our
own hearts tell us all the story when Osbaldistone
says, ' You know how I lamented her.' "

II

Captain Basil Hall, writing of events which happened in 1834, professed to have discovered the
Original of the divine Diana in the person of an old
Scottish gentlewoman of seventy-four, then on her
lonely death-bed in a great mediæval castle in Styria.
The circumstances are so romantic that it will be
necessary to tell the story from the beginning. It
was when Scott in his comely teens was attending the
Civil Law Classes at Edinburgh that he came under
the spell of Will Clerk. Through Clerk, Scott found
himself linked in close intimacy to a group of other
young men all high in birth and family connection,
and all remarkable in early life for the qualities which
afterwards led them to distinction in different spheres.
Among them was George Cranstoun (the Lord Core-

house to be), one of the best friends Scott ever had. Cranstoun lived in a modest flat in Frederick Street, where his sister Jane Anne * kept house and entertained the cronies—"the brotherhood of the Mountain," who made Cranstouns' their almost nightly howf. Dugald Stewart's was another of their meeting-places, the Professor's kind, romantic wife being Jane Anne's younger sister. In this way Scott and Miss Cranstoun came to see a great deal of each other. She was aware of his attachment to Miss Belsches, and she was among the first to divine his genius.

In the year 1796 Bürger's extraordinary ballad of "Lenore" (Taylor's translation) found its way to Scotland, when Miss Cranstoun heard Mrs. Barbauld recite it at her brother-in-law's. Hearing her describe the effect it had upon her, Scott's imagination became stirred and fired as never before, and he could not rest until he had mastered the poem in the original. Not only did he do that, but he dashed off a translation on his own account, which remains one of the best renderings of the poem in English. He tells us that he began the task one night after supper, and did not get to bed until he had finished it, having by that time worked himself into a state of excitement which set sleep at defiance. In the morning he carried his manuscript to Miss Cranstoun. It was as early as six o'clock, but Scott insisted upon seeing her. Miss

* The Cranstouns were the son and daughter of George Cranstoun, seventh son of the fifth Lord Cranstoun. Their mother was Maria Brisbane of Brisbane, in Ayrshire.

213

Cranstoun dressed in a hurry, and hastened downstairs wondering what Scott could want with her at such an untimely hour. He met her at the door. Holding up the result of his night's labour, he begged her to listen. She was all attention, praised the composition, sent Scott away happy, asking his permission, however, to retain the verses for a more leisurely perusal. Scott said he was going to the country—to Miss Belsches's home, and Miss Cranstoun was welcome to the ballad until he returned.

Now, as will have been guessed, Miss Cranstoun was Scott's confidante in his love-making. She was older by some years, and whether she suspected that the course of true love was not running as smoothly as it might, her quick brain conceived of a plan by which success might be hastened. If Scott could only be presented in the guise of an author, might not whatever lukewarmness was on Miss Belsches's part be removed? Will Erskine, that friendly critic of Scott's, was taken into confidence, and the plot perpetrated. They had "Lenore" printed, and bound in the most sumptuous fashion, and a copy of the little book dispatched to Scott, for presentation to the lady of his dreams. The stratagem succeeded well enough in a way. Scott was surprised, flattered. Miss Belsches was pleased, and the company, to whom the poem was read after dinner, no doubt regarded Scott as the hero of the hour. There is a scene in *Rob Roy* which this incident may have conjured up to the author's memory: Frank and Diana are sitting together in the library : Miss Vernon, in turning over a copy of the *Orlando Furioso*, shook a piece of written paper from between the leaves. "I hastened to lift it, but she prevented me :

"'It is verse,' she said, on glancing at the paper; and then unfolding it, but as if to wait my answer before proceeding—'May I take the liberty ?—Nay, nay, if you blush and stammer I must do violence to your modesty, and suppose that permission is granted.'

"'It is not worthy your perusal—a scrap of a translation. My dear Miss Vernon, it would be too severe a trial that you, who understand the original so well, should sit in judgment.'

"'Mine honest friend,' replied Diana, 'do not, if you will be guided by my advice, bait your hook with too much humility; for, ten to one, it will not catch a single compliment. You know I belong to the unpopular family of Tell-truths, and would not flatter Apollo for his lyre.'

"She proceeded to read the first stanza . . .

"'There is a great deal of it,' said she, glancing along the paper, and interrupting the sweetest sounds which mortal ears can drink in—those of a youthful poet's verses, namely, read by the lips which are dearest to him."

The frank criticism and the conversation which follow are probably a reminiscence of Miss Cranstoun. As for the "lips dearest" on which Scott's thoughts were running when he wrote this passage, these, as we know, were destined for another. In the autumn of 1796

215

Scott had his answer, and by the beginning of 1797 Williamina Belsches had become the wife of William Forbes, younger of Pitsligo, son of the banker. "Many an anxious thought I have of you," wrote the sympathetic Miss Cranstoun, on receipt of the tidings that the fateful monosyllable had been spoken to the lover at Fettercairn. She cloaks her solicitude with airy nonsense, and wonders why the rejected had not shaped his thought into song, "as Orlando would have done."

That same year, 1797, saw many changes in the circle of Scott's intimates. In June, Jane Anne Cranstoun had a love romance of her own. Count Wenzel Gottfried Purgstall, an Austrian nobleman of highest birth, visiting Scotland, fell in love with her, and carried her off to his princely old castle in Styria, where Scott might have seen in full swing that feudal system so dear to his imagination.

Miss Cranstoun was then thirty-seven. She lived to a green old age, and all her after life was spent out of Scotland, nor did she ever set foot on her native heath again. Scott and she corresponded occasionally. There is (or was) a bundle of her letters at Abbotsford. To Scott on his marriage she wrote in her lively way: "You can imagine how my heart burned within me, my dear, dear friend, while I read your thrice-welcome letter. . . . To have a conviction that those I love are happy and don't forget me!—I have no way to express my feelings—they come in a flood and destroy me." The letter throughout is an exile's lament. In the closing sentence her feelings overpower

her : " And is it then true, my God, that Earl Walter
is a Benedick, and that I am in Styria ? Well, bless
us all, prays the separated from her brethren, J. A. P."
Hers was a lonely life despite the splendour of its setting. She had all that wealth and position could give,
with several wonderful old crag-crowned castles to
call her own—one of which, Riegersburg, she likened
to Stirling Castle (it bears an even stronger resemblance to Edinburgh Castle), and regretted that it
did not look out on the Parliament Square of Edinburgh. Eventful, too, and ultimately tragic, was the
life of the brilliant Scottish Gräfinn. Goethe she
knew, and Schiller, and Kant, and Mozart, and all
who were worth knowing in Germany. But Napoleon
was the great harassing figure in Europe, and who-
ever were of the rank of the Purgstalls were faced
with peril and uncertainty. In 1809, Count Purgstall
was taken prisoner at Padua and sent to confinement
at Mantua. At immense risk, his brave wife travelled
to Vienna and procured his liberation. The hardships undergone had already sown the seeds of consumption, and his death took place at Florence, 22nd
March 1812. An only son, Wenzel Rafael, succeeded
to the vast estates, and to the position of the last of
the race of the once proud Purgstalls. It was his
mother's devotion which kept him alive to the age of
nineteen. Not all her care, not all his precociousness
could save him from the fate of his father, whom he
followed in a few years.

Her friends were anxious that the Countess should

now return to Scotland. She could not drag herself from the scene of so much happiness and sorrow. And had she not sworn to lay her dust beside her dear ones? Nor, so she thought, could the day be far distant. She, however, survived other seventeen years. On the 23rd March, 1835, she died at the Schloss Hainfeld, near Feldbach, forty miles from Graz, the Styrian capital.

Captain Basil Hall's association with Countess Purgstall is of singular interest. A mere chance put the Countess in the way of hearing about Scotland and of renewing acquaintance with "the language of her heart," which she had almost ceased to speak. Basil Hall was the son of old friends unseen for forty years. Whilst he and his family were travelling in Italy a beseeching invitation reached them to spend the winter with the Countess Purgstall at Hainfeld. Accordingly, they were there for four months—an infinitely happy season to the solitary chatelaine hungering and thirsting for a revival of the long ago. Her sparkling conversation and vivacity, notwithstanding age and approaching dissolution, the recital of old Frederick Street reminiscences, her playful allusions to her independent ways in young womanhood, her fondness for horseback, her talk of the days when she was Scott's confidante, forced Hall to the conclusion that she might have suggested the heroine of *Rob Roy*. Confirmations were not difficult to find. Amongst other things, though Scott had sent her each of the Waverleys as they had appeared, *Rob Roy* was wanting from her set. He had never sent it. Of course the novel was got, and the Captain read it aloud, watching narrowly the effect produced on his auditor. It interested her more than any of the other novels had done, especially the Cumberland part of the story. "Oh, I know that scene," she repeatedly exclaimed. "I remember describing it myself to Sir Walter. That anecdote he had from me—I know the man that character is taken from—" and so on through the greater part of the book. But what was more remarkable, though she discussed all the other characters and seemed to be aware of the identity of many of them, she was resolutely silent on the character of Diana Vernon, so much so that the Halls hesitated to say anything further on the subject. They dropped hints, and gave her openings, with no result. The evidence is meagre, but it is not convincing. While Lockhart will have none of Hall's theory, there is some probability in supposing that the Countess Purgstall had her own suspicion as to the Original of Di Vernon. She certainly answered to the part in a number of ways, and in her closing years she was, says Hall, "exactly like what we may suppose Di to have been in her old age," but this is all that can be said.

During Basil Hall's stay at Hainfeld he was the means of clearing up a misunderstanding, which for years had troubled and vexed Scott's old, warm-hearted friend. This was Scott's failure to acknowledge a little Memoir of her husband and son sent to Abbotsford as far back as 1821. In a letter to Hall,

Lockhart mentions finding among Scott's papers an undated letter thanking her for the book—her *Denkmal* or monument. The Countess was considerably agitated when the communication was read to her. She begged that the precious paper which Sir Walter had written, but evidently mislaid, should be immediately forwarded. Lockhart duly dispatched it. It succumbed to the uncertainties of the Continental Post Office. Fortunately Lockhart had made a copy of what is perhaps the most beautiful and touching epistle Scott ever penned. The only regret is that it never reached Hainfeld.

" MY DEAR AND MUCH-VALUED FRIEND,

" You cannot imagine how much I was interested and affected by receiving your token of your kind recollection, after the interval of so many years. Your brother Henry breakfasted with me yesterday, and gave me the letter and the book, which served me as a matter of much melancholy reflection for many hours.

" Hardly anything makes the mind recoil so much upon itself, as the being suddenly and strongly recalled to times long passed, and that by the voice of one whom we have so much loved and respected. Do not think I have ever forgotten you, or the many happy days I passed in Frederick Street, in society which fate has separated so far, and for so many years.

" The little volume was particularly acceptable to me, as it acquainted me with many circumstances, of which distance and imperfect communication had left me either entirely ignorant, or had transmitted only inaccurate information.

"Alas! my dear friend, what can the utmost efforts of friendship offer you, beyond the sympathy which, however sincere, must sound like an empty compliment in the ear of affliction. God knows with what willingness I would undertake anything which might afford you the melancholy consolation of knowing how much your old and early friend interests himself in the sad event which has so deeply wounded your peace of mind. The verses, therefore, which conclude this letter, must not be weighed according to their intrinsic value, for the more inadequate they are to express the feelings they would fain convey, the more they show the author's anxious wish to do what may be grateful to you.

"In truth, I have long given up poetry. I have had my day with the public; and being no great believer in poetical immortality, I was very well pleased to rise a winner, without continuing the game, till I was beggared of any credit I had acquired. Besides, I felt the prudence of giving way before the more forcible and powerful genius of Byron. If I were either greedy, or jealous of poetical fame—and both are strangers to my nature—I might comfort myself with the thought, that I would hesitate to strip myself to the contest so fearlessly as Byron does; or to command the wonder and terror of the public, by exhibiting, in my own person, the sublime attitude of the dying gladiator. But with the old frankness of twenty years since, I will fairly own, that this same delicacy of mine may arise more from conscious want of vigour and inferiority, than from a delicate dislike to the nature of the conflict. At any rate, there is a time for everything, and without swearing oaths to it, I think my time for poetry has gone by.

"My health suffered horridly last year, I think from overlabour and excitation ; and though it is now apparently restored to its usual tone, yet during the long and painful disorder (spasms in the stomach), and the frightful process of cure, by a prolonged use of calomel, I learned that my frame was made of flesh, and not of iron, a conviction which I will long keep in remembrance, and avoid any occupation so laborious and agitating, as poetry must be, to be worth anything.

"In this humour, I often think of passing a few weeks on the Continent—a summer vacation if I can —and of course my attraction to Gratz would be very strong. I fear this is the only chance of our meeting in this world, we, who once saw each other daily ! For I understand from George and Henry, that there is little chance of your coming here. And when I look around me, and consider how many changes you will see in feature, form and fashion, amongst all you knew and loved ; and how much, no sudden squall, or violent tempest, but the slow and gradual progress of life's long voyage, has severed all the gallant fellowships whom you left spreading their sails to the morning breeze, I really am not sure that you would have much pleasure.

"The gay and wild romance of life is over with all of us. The real, dull, and stern history of humanity has made a far greater progress over our heads ; and age, dark and unlovely, has laid his crutch over the stoutest fellow's shoulders. One thing your old society may boast, that they have all run their course with honour, and almost all with distinction ; and the brother suppers of Frederick Street have certainly made a very considerable figure in the world, as was to be expected, from her talents under whose auspices they were assembled.

"One of the most pleasant sights which you would see in Scotland, as it now stands, would be your brother George in possession of the most beautiful and romantic place in Clydesdale—Corehouse. I have promised often to go out with him, and assist him with my deep experience as a planter and landscape gardener. I promise you my oaks will outlast my laurels ; and I pique myself more upon my compositions for manure than on any other compositions whatsoever to which I was ever accessary. But so much does business of one sort or other engage us both, that we never have been able to fix a time which suited us both ; and with the utmost wish to make out the party, perhaps we never may.

"This is a melancholy letter, but it is chiefly so from the sad tone of yours, who have had such real disasters to lament—while mine is only the humorous sadness, which a retrospect on human life is sure to produce on the most prosperous. For my own course of life, I have only to be ashamed of its prosperity, and afraid of its termination ; for I have little reason, arguing on the doctrine of chances, to hope that the same good fortune will attend me for ever. I have had an affectionate and promising family, many friends, few unfriends, and, I think, no enemies—and more of fame and fortune than mere literature ever procured for a man before.

" I dwell among my own people, and have many whose happiness is dependent on me, and which I study to the best of my power. I trust my temper, which you know is by nature good and easy, has not been spoiled by flattery or prosperity ; and therefore I have escaped entirely that irritability of disposition which I think is planted, like the slave in the poet's chariot, to prevent his enjoying his triumph.

" Should things, therefore, change with me—and in these times, or indeed in any times, such change is to be apprehended—I trust I shall be able to surrender these adventitious advantages, as I would my upper dress, as something extremely comfortable, but which I can make shift to do without." *

* The verses alluded to have never been found and may never have been written. It was probably owing to this circumstance that the letter was not sent. Since this chapter was written, the author has paid a visit to Schloss Hainfeld. Following a search amongst its archives (including the Countess's papers), he is inclined to discredit much of Hall's story. No presentation Waverleys are in the library, which remains as it was in Jane Anne's time. Her correspondence with Scott was destroyed in accordance with her last will and testament. The only things connected with him now existing at Hainfeld are an autographed copy of *The Lay of the Last Minstrel*, and, in " Earl Walter's " (so it is inscribed) handwriting, what appears to be an original draft of " The Eve of St. John." For fascinating accounts of Riegersburg and its parish church (the Purgstall burial-place) see *Die Riegersburg in Wort und Bild* (Franz Stallinger) and Basil Hall's *Schloss Hainfeld* (1836).

CHAPTER THIRTEEN

THE HEART OF MIDLOTHIAN
"JEANIE DEANS"

P

> " She has no birth,
> No dowry, graces ; no accomplishments,
> Save a pure cheek, a fearless innocent brow,
> And a true-beating heart."
>
> ALEXANDER SMITH.

CHAPTER THIRTEEN: THE HEART OF MIDLOTHIAN "JEANIE DEANS"

WITH *ROB ROY* IN SIGHT OF COMPLETION Scott had begun to work on *The Heart of Midlothian*. Comprised in four volumes, its publication was arranged for the King's birthday, 4th June 1818, on which date it appeared. The reception given to the novel in Edinburgh was enthusiastic beyond precedent, "such as I never witnessed there on the appearance of any other literary novelty," says Lockhart. People were beginning to say the author would soon wear himself out, that public interest was on the wane, and so forth, "Yet I am in a house where everybody is tearing it out of each other's hands and talking about nothing else," wrote Lady Louisa Stuart in August. By the critics the tale was received no less cordially. Walter Savage Landor, who had little good to say of Scott's poetry, declared that in itself the authorship of *The Heart of Midlothian* was sufficient to stamp Scott the most illustrious author of the age.

In apportioning the Waverley order of merit, so far as that can be done, it is possible to put the novel, as Edward FitzGerald has put it, in the very first place. A criterion as sane as any is that adopted by Professor Grant of Leeds: Scott's work is at its best, first, when it deals with Scottish life ; second, when it brings public and private life into relation with one another ; and third, when the lives of the poor play an important part. Judged by this, or by any other lofty standard, the palm may well be given to *The Heart of Mid-lothian.*

The charm of the story is the simple, intense pathos that runs through the whole of it. Its crowning glory is the delineation of the Deans family—the pious, practical, heroic peasant household crossed by the tragedy of the erring daughter. One trembles to think how such a tragedy would have fared in other hands than Scott's. " Had the story," says Lady Louisa Stuart (whose criticism is the last word on the subject), " been conducted by other hands, Effie Deans would have attracted all our concern and sympathy, Jeanie only quiet approbation. Whereas Jeanie, without youth, beauty, genius, warm passions, or any other novel-perfection, is here our object from beginning to end." In fiction was there ever (of her class) a purer or a more innocent-minded damsel than Jeanie Deans, or heroine so utterly unconscious of her heroism ? While she lives and moves and has her being amid life's lowlier walks, there is not one of Scott's women who so merits the old-fashioned and all but obsolete title of "gentlewoman." Jeanie is the essence of honesty and nobility. Her absolute naturalness is the grace that beautifies her. She is without charms and accomplishments in the ordinary meaning of the words. The most she prides herself on is her capable housekeeping. To have given the premier place to integrity, unaccompanied by beauty and fine words, is a proof of Scott's power, and of his right to

228

be ranked in the category of great and unselfish souls.

Scott's women are mostly of the pretty, somewhat vapid type. This was due, we are told, to the novelist's inherent chivalry—a chivalry which would not permit him to vivisect womankind—an operation of interest to the heart of Thackeray. For women in general, and particularly of his own class, Scott entertained a very high opinion. He was content, however, to admire rather than to analyse. The result is that he gives us a fair face, and nothing more. A few there are, to be sure, who stand out pre-eminently from the rank and file of colourless amiability, and they are either of the peasantry or royalty. Jeanie Deans is as striking a figure with Sir Walter as Queen Elizabeth is; and Meg Merrilies and Madge Wildfire are as supreme in their own sphere as Rebecca or Rowena are in theirs. As has been already said, Scott was always happiest in painting human nature from the side of the poor. That dash of originality which is to be found chiefly amongst them he never allowed himself to be insensible of. Hence the firm and the kindly grip with which the world of common men and women has welcomed Sir Walter's work, nor ever let it slip away from them.

One is not surprised to know that of all his heroines Jeanie Deans (by his own confession) was Scott's favourite : " The lass kept tugging at my heartstrings." Than that, Jeanie could not have a greater compliment paid her. Indirectly, Scott did a real service to religion in his characterisation of Jeanie Deans. She is the type of the Scot of both sexes with whom faith in the Unseen is the driving force. The Scot says little on the subject of religion, even to his dearest ones. But it is often his dominating passion, lying at the root of everything else. Jeanie's religious aspirations are never a theme of talk and publicity on her own part, but that she is deeply, reverently devout, the outside world realises. She is a doer, and not a mere hearer of the Word. In her conduct towards father and mother, towards friend and lover, towards even the ill-disposed and the uncharitable, she approaches as near the ideal standard as human nature is capable of.

Of the other characters in the story, Reuben Butler (said to be modelled from John Ramsay, schoolmaster of Liberton), a quiet, sensible country dominie who blossoms into the minister of Knocktarlitie, is, of course, entirely fictitious, as the real Jeanie never married. Jeanie's father, David Deans, exhibits many of the traits of Patrick Walker, Cameronian, and biographer of the Saints of the Covenant. Both avowedly and unavowedly, Scott borrowed incidents from him, and has frequently appropriated his language and phraseology. The tirade against dancing, for instance (chap. x.), occurs in Patrick's "Vindication of Cameron's Name," and in a note to the novel, the two paragraphs from Patrick are quoted *in extenso*: "I bless the Lord that ordered my lot so in my dancing days, that made the fear of the bloody rope and bullets to my neck

and head, the pain of boots, thumbikins, and irons, cold
and hunger, wetness and weariness, to stop the light-
ness of my head and the wantonness of my feet."

There is the sheepish Dumbiedykes, and Rory Bean,
and the quasi-lawyer, Bartoline Saddletree, that
prince of "bores." Daddy Ratcliffe (not all a degenerate), Robertson, and Wilson, were borrowed from
the incident of the Porteous Mob, the narrative of which
the novelist must not be held as rehearsing with historical exactitude. The real Robertson was no disguised aristocrat, but a common "stabler in Bristo,
indicted and accused together with Andrew Wilson of
Pathhead, and William Hall, indweller in Edinburgh,
at the instance of Duncan Forbes of Culloden, His Majesty's Advocate, for the crimes of Stouthrieff, House-
breaking, and Robbery." It was hardly a happy expedient to evolve a baronetcy from so unexpected a
quarter as that of a Bristo innkeeper. And, indeed,
the whole part of George Robertson, or Staunton, is
extravagant and unreal, whilst the dénouement, as almost every reader is agreed, well-nigh spoils the story.

II

For thirteen years—from 1814 to 1827—anony-
mity put an embargo on Scott. So long as he remained behind the scenes, acknowledgment of literary
indebtedness was impossible. But the moment the
curtain was lifted, obligations were pleasantly paid.
First and foremost (see Introduction to *Chronicles of
the Canongate*) the unwearied industry of Joseph Train

was handsomely acknowledged. Next, followed a tribute of gratitude to the lady who sent Scott the information about Jeanie Deans's prototype. The particulars were furnished anonymously, and made a deep impression on Scott. Pleased with the reception given to Jeanie's portraiture, he tells us how much of its success was owing to the truth and force of the original sketch, which " I regret I am unable to present to the public, as it was written with much feeling and spirit." In the *magnum opus*, however, Scott was able to reveal the name of his " obliging correspondent," and to print her communication. She was the wife (maiden name, Helen Lawson, Girthhead) of Thomas Goldie of Craigmuie, Commissary of Dumfries. Mrs. Goldie's narrative may be thus summarised : In the year 1790 she was spending a holiday near Lincluden Abbey. Whilst there, acquaintance was made with a little, stoutish woman called Helen Walker, respecting whose earlier history Mrs. Goldie was afterwards made aware of some interesting and striking facts. Helen lived alone, eking out a slender livelihood by knitting stockings and keeping poultry. She is said to have taught a side-school at one time. Helen was now old and frail, her long life approaching its close. More than fifty years previous to Mrs. Goldie's narrative, Helen's sister, Isobel, had been tried for the crime of child-murder, and Helen was chief witness in the case. Counsel for the defence did his utmost to impress upon her the necessity of affirming that she had been in Isobel's confidence. But

232

M.S. of "The Heart of Midlothian"—

Jeanie's Interview with
Queen Caroline.

all to no purpose.   Helen pleaded entire ignorance
of the affair, and asserted that it was impossible for
her to swear falsely.   Be the consequences what they
might, she could not give her oath against her conscience.   The trial came on: Isobel Walker was found
guilty, and condemned.   Immediately afterwards
Helen got a petition drawn up in her sister's behalf,
and set out on foot for London (a more formidable
venture then than going to America is to-day).   She
reached the metropolis within a fortnight or so, where
she made appeal to John, Duke of Argyll, through
whose instrumentality the prayer of the petition was
granted.   Helen returned home, arriving in the nick
of time to save her sister's life.   About the whole
circumstances Helen was singularly reticent.   The
subject was distasteful.   "None of the neighbours
durst question her about it."   Mrs. Goldie inquired of
an old woman who lived at the other end of Helen's
cottage if Helen ever spoke of the incident.   "No,"
said she, "she aye turned the conversation if ever any
o' the neebours happened to mention it."

From M'Diarmid's " The Real History of Jeanie
Deans " in *Sketches from Nature* (1830), we learn that
Helen Walker was the daughter of [William] Walker,
a day-labourer at Cluden, in the Covenanting parish
of Kirkpatrick-Irongray, Kirkcudbrightshire.   Scott
says (Postcript following Introduction) that she was
" the daughter of the farmer of Dalwhairn," but that
is a mistake, the result of a careless reading of M'Diarmid's statement.   M'Diarmid does not say that *Helen*

233

resided at Dalwhairn, but that Elizabeth Grierson, his informant, resided there, who in her girlhood was well acquainted with Helen.

The sisters Walker (there is no mention of brothers) with their mother, a widow, and delicate, lived together at Cluden. Helen and Isobel were out- or field-workers. There is no tradition of domestic service for either of them. All accounts agree in describing Helen, who was considerably the elder of the two, as a woman of strong, even remarkable character for one in her so humble position. M'Diarmid says that " her conversational powers were of a high order, her language most correct, ornate and pointed, her deportment sedate and dignified in the extreme." To some, indeed, she was "a *pensy* body," that is, conceited or proud ; but her shy, retiring disposition may have led to that idea. She was a deeply religious woman, a diligent student of the Scriptures, and a devout and regular worshipper in the parish kirk.

It was about the end of 1736 that the terrible blow fell on the Walker family. Isobel, a girl barely out of her teens, was betrayed by a youth named Waugh, and denied to the last the rumour as to her condition. The neighbours, however, suspected that a child had been born. Isobel was deaf to all entreaties to confess, though she was confronted with the body of a dead infant found shortly afterwards by the bank of the Cluden Water. She was remitted to the authorities for trial—a trial which, under the circumstances, could have but one ending.

It is in the dénouement that interest centres, and this, with embellishing differences, is powerfully depicted in the novel. There is no reason to doubt the authenticity of the story. That Helen Walker embarked on her voluntary mission of mercy to London town—tramping all the way—seems as true to the facts of tradition as that a person bearing her name was buried beneath the shadow of Irongray Kirk, or that Irongray Kirk rears its head above the clear stream of the Cluden. The details of Helen's interview with Argyll and the petition itself have not been forthcoming. But the Report embodied in the Records of Justiciary appears to corroborate the main facts of the case. One must, of course, read between the lines. The chief trouble is with the trial itself. The popular imagination (based on the novel) has raised Jeanie Deans to the most conspicuous place in that memorable and moving spectacle. Upon Jeanie is laid the burden, not so much of disproving Effie's guilt as of being able to present a palliation for the offence with which she stood indicted. And though in the romance Jeanie goes into the witness-box, there is no lifting of the shadow from her unhappy sister's fate.

Now in the Report of the trial of Isobel Walker contained in the Book of Adjournal no light whatever is cast upon Helen's position. Helen does not appear on the scene at all. There is no witness of that name, unless she is the *Emelia* Walker* who advances speci-

---

* Jeanie had an aunt so named. Could she have been the witness ? Her descendants are in Canada.

ally strong evidence against Isobel, a supposition which is untenable. The probability is that in the course of the precognitions, the friends of Isobel had completely failed to win Helen to their view of the situation. Only one thing could save their client—the establishment of a case of concealment. But to that, Helen, who alone could be of service, would not consent. Thus Helen Walker had no summons to the witness-box. The invalid state of the mother (who is referred to by witnesses) may possibly explain *her* absence. That appears to be the only explanation of the serious discrepancy between Mrs. Goldie's narrative and the authoritative account of the proceedings at Dumfries. It is curious to find a considerable interval intervening between Isobel's first appearance at Dumfries and her last. The first date given is 2nd May 1737. The child's body had been washed up by the Cluden in October 1736, and the trial (see Appendix) took place 1st May 1738, more than a year and a half after the discovery of the crime—an extraordinary travesty of justice, it must be allowed.

Of Isobel Walker's subsequent career little is known. She married Waugh, and spent the remainder of her life at Whitehaven. Helen clung to sweet and pastoral Irongray. She resumed her quiet, rural employments, and after a life of "unsullied integrity," died in a cottage known as Knowehead (now extinct) about the end of 1791, having entered her eighty-first year. Mrs. Goldie, profoundly touched with the story, and the sterling character of the woman, resolved to erect a stone to her memory in Irongray churchyard, but died before her wish could be accomplished. Her daughter, Miss Jean Goldie, invited Scott to write the inscription, and offered to collect money to carry out her mother's intention. Scott intimated that he would do it all himself. He arranged with William Burn, an Edinburgh architect, as to the most suitable kind of monument * and the inscription is in his own noble and deathless words:

THIS STONE WAS ERECTED
BY THE AUTHOR OF WAVERLEY
TO THE MEMORY
OF
HELEN WALKER,
WHO DIED IN THE YEAR OF GOD 1791
THIS HUMBLE INDIVIDUAL
PRACTISED IN REAL LIFE
THE VIRTUES
WITH WHICH FICTION HAS INVESTED
THE IMAGINARY CHARACTER OF
JEANIE DEANS:
REFUSING THE SLIGHTEST DEPARTURE
FROM VERACITY,
EVEN TO SAVE THE LIFE OF A SISTER,
SHE NEVERTHELESS SHOWED HER
KINDNESS AND FORTITUDE,
IN RESCUING HER
FROM THE SEVERITY OF THE LAW,
AT THE EXPENSE OF PERSONAL EXERTIONS
WHICH THE TIME RENDERED AS DIFFICULT
AS THE MOTIVE WAS LAUDABLE.

RESPECT THE GRAVE OF POVERTY
WHEN COMBINED WITH LOVE OF TRUTH
AND DEAR AFFECTION.

---

* The monument is a handsome table stone, not a "little pillar" as Lockhart has it.

Three letters of Scott's (hitherto unpublished) on the subject of Jeanie Deans, bear further testimony to the courteous, generous character of Jeanie's creator :

To Walter Dickson, Esq., W.S.

DEAR SIR,—I learned from Mr. Gibson that it was from your mother-in-law, Mrs. Goldie, that I received the very interesting anonymous favour which enabled me to produce to the public the efficient and interesting character of Jeanie Deans, as I have christened her most respectable friend Helen Walker. I would have taken the liberty to publish her very interesting and simple narrative—for I have it by me—but I make it a kind of rule not to publish even anonymous letters for fear of giving offence. I hope Mrs. Goldie will add to the great favour she has done me by permitting me, when time and opportunity occur, to publish her own simple narrative, with anything concerning the history of Helen Walker which can yet be procured. I would have addressed my personal thanks and request to Mrs. Goldie herself, and still hope to do so. But I wished to transfer them, in the first instance to you, mainly to show you that I have been sorry for having shown some ill-humour when we last met, which I am sure you will excuse, under the circumstances of my situation, which were irritating for the moment and no longer.

As I sometimes go to Dumfriesshire, I hope to make Mrs. Goldie's personal acquaintance and thank her in person for the favour she conferred on me. Had I known where to address my acknowledgments, they would not have been so long due.

> I am, Dear Sir,
>> Your obedient servant,
>>> WALTER SCOTT.

27th October 1827.

> To the Rev. David Dow, minister of
> Kirkpatrick-Irongray.

REVEREND SIR,

Begging your excuse for the intrusion, I am about to request your permission and that of your Kirk Session to erect a simple monument in the Church-yard of Kirkpatrick-Irongray to a poor woman of the name of Walker respectable in her time for an act of great worth and fortitude. The late Mrs. Goldie, wife of the Commissary of Dumfries, sent me the anecdote for the purpose of its being used in a fictitious composition named [termed?] the Heart of Mid Lothian and as it was her peculiar wish that Helen Walker's grave should be marked by a tomb-stone I conceive I shall but show my respect to her memory by discharging the duty which she earnestly desired. I hope, Revd. Sir, you will be pleased to grant your consent to what is proposed. I propose a sarcophagus as the shape of the monument which shall be begun so soon as I have received your answer [&] Mr. Burn architect draws the plan. If your register affords the date of Helen

Walker's interment perhaps you will have the goodness to mention it.   I am Reverend Sir,

> With respect,
>> Your obedient servant,
>>> WALTER SCOTT.

Edinburgh, 5*th March* 1830.

My address is Sir Walter Scott, Bart., Shandwick Place, Edinburgh.

> To William Burn, Architect.

MY DEAR SIR,

I enclose the inscription intended for Helen Walker, which you will be so good as to commit to Mr. Ramsay's care. Mr. Cadell will pay him all expenses whenever he reports that the monument is complete and place it to my accompt :

I entreat your kind attention to this if you think any moral is necessary.

> Respect the grave of Poverty
> when combined with the
> Love of Truth and Dear Affection.

> [best]

This just as you think [but] having no time to correct it as I expect to set sail on Tuesday. I have written Mr. Cadell on the subject.   Mr. Walter Dickson took some share in erection of the monument and I dare say would give a look at the work.

> I am always yours,
>> With best wishes,
>>> WALTER SCOTT.

London, 13*th October* 1831.

CHAPTER FOURTEEN

THE HEART OF MIDLOTHIAN
"MADGE WILDFIRE"

Q

" There Madness enters; and the dim-ey'd Fiend,
  Sour Melancholy, night and day provokes
  Her own eternal wound."

ARMSTRONG.

IN *THE HEART OF MIDLOTHIAN*, MADGE Wildfire was Meg Murdockson's insane daughter— "a tall, strapping wench of eighteen or twenty, dressed fantastically in a sort of blue riding-coat with tarnished lace, her hair clubbed like that of a man; a Highland bonnet and a bunch of broken feathers; a riding-skirt or petticoat of scarlet camlet embroidered with tarnished flowers. Her features were coarse and masculine, yet at a little distance, by dint of very bright, wild-looking black eyes, an aquiline nose and a commanding profile, appeared rather handsome." Her cognomen was derived from the song so frequently on her lips :

> " I glance like the wildfire through country and town,
> I'm seen on the causeway—I'm seen on the down;
> The lightning that flashes so bright and so free,
> Is scarcely so blithe or so bonny as me."

Madge is one of the most original of Scott's characters. Coleridge pronounced her *"the* most original." She is a sort of Scottish Ophelia. Indeed the part played by this dreamy and liberty-loving child of nature, this loquacious and melodramatic waif of the dews and night-winds, is just what Shakespeare might have conceived, or Goethe, in whose Margaret the madness of Madge Wildfire has its parallel, both of them lamenting the lost bairn. Madge's death-scene is indescribably touching, and the words with which she

243

sings life away are among the finest things Scott ever wrote, the sweetest and wildest of his lyrics :

> " Proud Maisie is in the wood,
>   Walking so early ;
> Sweet Robin sits on the bush,
>   Singing so rarely.
>
> ' Tell me, thou bonny bird,
>   When shall I marry me ? '
> ' When six braw gentlemen
>   Kirkward shall carry ye.'
>
> ' Who makes the bridal bed,
>   Birdie, say truly ? '—
> ' The grey-headed sexton
>   That delves the grave duly.'
>
> The glow-worm o'er grave and stone
>   Shall light thee steady ;
> The owl from the steeple sing,
>   ' Welcome, proud lady.' "

Probably all that can be known of Madge's story will be found in the author's notes appended to the novel.   Madge was modelled (with differences) from Feckless Fannie (*i.e.* feeble or weak-minded Fannie), a curious, crazed, pathetic figure who wandered the country far and near about the end of the eighteenth century.   Joseph Train collected all the available information about her.   Wherever she went she was known as the " wife with the sheep " from being accompanied by a number of sheep, whose faculties seemed to be much superior to those of their kind. Each member of the flock went by its own name, to which it answered and obeyed in the most surprising manner the command of its mistress.   Eastern-like, Fannie's sheep followed her footsteps, and her nights were spent in the open, surrounded by her strange charge. She had her favourite resting-places which even the sheep knew as well as she; at Cumnock and Moffat these are still pointed out. In person she was about the middle height, her features were sharp and thin, and about her eyes there was a wild unnatural gleam when provoked. When treated kindly, she was gentle and docile. Unlike other demented creatures Fannie was not fond of finery (though Madge Wildfire was). On her head she wore an old slouch hat, over her shoulders was an old plaid, and the shepherd's crook was constantly in her hand. She was said to be the only daughter of a rich squire in the North of England. Having fallen in love with a shepherd of the district she incurred the anger of her parent, who drew his pistol and shot dead the unfortunate herds-man. The shock unhinged the girl's mind, and taking up the crook, plaid and hat of her hapless lover, along with a few of his sheep, she proceeded to move about from place to place, nor could she be persuaded to return to her friends or avail herself of the shelter of a home during her peregrinations. Fannie is said to have been done to death by a crowd of Glasgow youths, but there is no mention of any Trial, which, as Scott says, would certainly have taken place had her death occurred in the manner indicated.

In the Melrose district, Whirlybet Meg (Betty Grahamslaw), a harmless maniac who lived in the locality, has been mentioned as a possible Original of Madge Wildfire.

CHAPTER FIFTEEN

THE BRIDE OF LAMMERMOOR
"LUCY ASHTON"

"Love had, like the canker-worm,
     Consumed her early prime:
The rose grew pale, and left her cheek—
     She died before her time."

MALLET.

CHAPTER FIFTEEN: THE BRIDE OF LAMMERMOOR "LUCY ASHTON"

THE GENESIS OF THAT FINEST OF TRAGIC tales, *The Bride of Lammermoor*, presents an interesting psychological problem. When it was written, Scott was supposed to be dying. He suffered from a form of illness which allowed him little or no rest the twenty-four hours through. He was obliged to fall back on opiates, in copious doses every two or three hours, and it was whilst practically under the influence of these that the whole of *The Bride* was penned. That is to say, Laidlaw and John Ballantyne took the chapters down from Scott's dictation—a literary feat without parallel, in the circumstances. Here is proof of the great modern doctrine that mind is everything—that mind and spirit may triumph over the weakest frame, over the severest bodily torture. Scott declared to Ballantyne that he did not recollect a single incident, or character, or conversation the novel contained, and when he saw the first copies he feared to read lest something grotesque and stupid should meet his eye. But to many *The Bride* is the best of Scott's romances, notwithstanding the almost absolute melancholy which hovers around it from first to last. In style it is the most finished, most emotional, most Homeric of the series; and dramatised as in Donizetti's great opera, none has been more popular.

In fiction there are few better-known plots than that of *The Bride of Lammermoor*. Scott tells us he heard the story from friends of his own who lived very near the period, and were closely related to the family of the Bride. He heard the story from Anne Murray Keith, and from Will Clerk, who was great-grand-nephew of the Bride, and himself one of Scott's numerous Scotch cousins. It was from his own mother, however, that Scott listened, not once nor twice, to a recital of the ever-moving tragedy. She lived just long enough to discuss upon her death-bed the difference between her son's fiction and the tale as she knew it. He was reluctant, he says, "to disclose the origin of the unhappy incident from a fear of offending the descendants of the parties." It was probably for the like reason that he transferred the scene to the east of Scotland from the south-west, where the events are said to have occurred. Some time, however, previous to the appearance of the novel, attention had been drawn to the affair in one of Kirkpatrick Sharpe's notes to the Rev. Robert Law's quaint *Memorials of the Memorable Things that fell out within this Island of Britain from 1638 to 1684*. And in Symson of Kirkinner's Poems there is a somewhat cryptic reference to the tragedy. So that when Scott wrote the Introduction to the *Chronicles of the Canongate* (1827), in which he deprecates publicity for the family's sake, the story was well enough known. Wide credence had been given to it not only in Wigtownshire but throughout Scotland. Like most tales of mystery, in which the circumstances have never clearly been brought to light, this Bride's tragedy has been the subject of many variations. What was its precise nature has not and cannot be expiscated now. It is unlikely that it followed, even approximately, the particular line taken in the novel. Indeed, very strong evidence exists against the probability of the whole story, which may never have rested on anything more substantial than gossip's airy asseverations :

> " The flying rumour gathered as it rolled,
>   And all who told it added something new,
>   And all who heard it made enlargements too."

In Paterson's *Lands and their Owners in Galloway* and Murray's *Literary History of Galloway* the affair is regarded as purely fabulous ; and, as we shall see, there is no contemporary corroboration for the facts as alleged.

The title of the novel connects itself with the counties of Berwick and Haddington. Attempts have been made to identify actual scenes and localities with those described in the story. This, of course, is hopeless and unprofitable guess-work. Such was Scott's use of poetic licence that the *locale* was only a secondary arrangement. All through the Waverleys, Scott plays ducks and drakes with history, with locality and scenery alike, just as in these chapters we see the composite character of his portraiture with regard to individuals. Nevertheless, there is no end to the identifying process. Winton House, in Haddingtonshire, is confidently spoken of as the Ravenswood of *The Bride of Lammermoor*. A wood close by is pointed to as the spot where fate brought Lucy Ashton and the Master so dramatically together. A site has been found for the Tod's Den, where Bucklaw and Craigengelt waited Edgar's return. Pencaitland Kirk becomes the scene of the wedding and burial of the poor, distracted Bride. Another set of identifiers incline to the belief that Cranshaws Castle in the heart of the Lammermoors is the true original of the ancient seat of the Ravenswoods. The very name is suggestive—Cranshaws (Cranewoods). Here, too, is the Ravens' Scaur, and does not the little Inn at Ellem approximate to the Tod's Den? A further resemblance is seen in the broken fortunes of the Swinton family, which forced them to part with Cranshaws, their ancestral property. Others, with equal certainty, regard Cockburnspath Tower, Yester House, Garvald Tower, Spott House, and Crichton Castle, as Ravenswood. Some curious coincidences may be observed respecting Wedderlie House at the base of the Lammermoors, on the Berwickshire side. The Laird of Wedderlie was an Edgar. Against the Wolf's Crag may be put Wolfstruther (now Westruther), the parish in which Wedderlie is situated. Edgar of Ravenswood was related to the Humes, the Douglases, and the Swintons, as was Edgar of Wedderlie. Still more remarkable, the families were connected with that of Chiesley, and at the same period. The Ravenswoods were involved in a litigation in which Chiesley was implicated, while from the Court of Session's Decisions at the time of the tale, Edgar of Wedderlie had a bitter law-suit with Chiesley the tutor of his father's younger children.

Edgar of Wedderlie was impoverished by his opposition to the Presbyterian Church. Edgar Ravenswood opposed its minister at his father's funeral. Both families were turbulent, and both were brought to ruin by espousing the losing cause. Scott himself is all but silent as to identifications. The most he is willing to admit is a likeness between Fast Castle and the imaginary Wolf's Crag. "But fortalices of this description are common to the eastern coast of Scotland": elsewhere he states that the Kaim of Urie suggested an idea "for the tower called Wolf's Crag, which the public more generally identified with the ancient tower of Fast Castle."

Coming to the romance itself, the venue of the grim tragedy on which it rests is the county of Wigtown. Once on a time the Kennedys were the great masters and lords of the shire :

> " 'Twixt Wigtown and the toun of Ayr,
> Portpatrick and the Cruives of Cree,
> No man need think for to bide there
> Unless he court with Kennedie."

When the reign of the Kennedys was at an end they were followed by the scarcely less influential sept of the Dalrymples, Earls of Stair, " whose family history," says Lord Macaulay, " has furnished poets and novelists with material for the darkest and most heart-rending tales." This was specially true of Viscount Stair's family, the lawyer whose *Institutes* remained for more than two centuries the standard work on Scottish Jurisprudence. Born in 1619, James Dalrymple was the eldest son of the Laird of Drummurchie and Stair, the original Ayrshire seats of the Dalrymples. He studied at Glasgow University, was M.A. in 1637, and the first graduate of his time. He accepted a commission in the Earl of Glencairn's regiment supporting the Covenant. In passing through Glasgow, he found that the Chair of Philosophy was vacant and open to public competition. He became a candidate, and without doffing his regimentals sat for the examination and was successful. The art of war he forsook for the study of philosophy—Mars for Minerva. He took up his abode in Glasgow, and married Margaret Ross of Balniel. On the death of his father-in-law in 1655, he and his wife were served heir to the adjoining estates of Balniel and Carscreugh, and thus it was that the Dalrymples first became connected with Wigtownshire. In 1648, James Dalrymple was admitted a member of the Faculty of Advocates. He quickly attained honours in his profession. Within nine years he was a Lord of Session, and in 1671 became President of the Court. He was a Knight, a Baronet, and, in 1690, a Viscount. His death took place on 23rd November 1695. By Margaret Ross he had a numerous family. Interest centres on his eldest daughter, Janet Dalrymple, the Original of Scott's Bride, who, according to the popular tradition, stabbed her bridegroom on their wedding night and died a few days afterwards, a grinning maniac.

Such is the story embodied in Scott's romance. It is curious to find so exact a historian as Macaulay reporting as a fact of history an episode which never occurred. In blackest colours he paints the character of Stair, and says "one of his daughters poinarded her bridegroom on their wedding night." *

The suggestion that Stair's daughter murdered her husband is contrary to the facts of the case. It is more than likely, however, that something untoward did happen in connection with the marriage, for Scott's and Macaulay's is not the sole tradition, and traditions more or less similar could hardly have originated without cause unless, indeed, we are to discern a clue in the fierce antagonism to the Dalrymples which obtained in some quarters. What of truth is in the matter it is difficult now to say. Stair's old pupil Law, the minister of Inchinnan (already mentioned), declares in his *Memorials*—a hair-raising record of supernatural occurrences—that the "President had a daughter who, being married, the night she was bride in, was taken from her bridegroom and harled [tossed about] through the house [by spirits we are to suppose], and soon afterwards died." Kirkpatrick Sharpe, the Jacobite editor of Law's book, gives two versions of the tale which contradict each other in the material point—who was the actor in the tragedy. In the first of these, it was the *bridegroom* who wounded the bride —the bridegroom who was "found in a state of idiocy." The marriage had been against the mother's inclination, whose consent was given with the omin-

* Macaulay apparently borrowed from Scott's fiction : " The fatal weapon was found in the chamber smeared with blood. It was the same poinard which Henry should have worn on the wedding day."

ous words, " Well, ye may marry him, but sair will ye repent it." In the second account, the parts are reversed. It was the *bride* " who attacked the bridegroom furiously with a knife, dreadfully injuring him before any one could gain admittance to the nuptial chamber. When entrance was effected, the youth was found half-dead upon the floor, and his wife in a state of wildest madness exclaiming, ' Take up your bonnie bridegroom.' " It is added that she never regained her senses, that her husband, who recovered his wounds, would tolerate no remark on the subject, taking even the slightest hint as a mortal affront. As readers are aware, Scott follows this second version. According to still another tradition—the tradition favoured by the Dalrymple family—the disappointed suitor concealed in the bridal chamber becomes the attacking party, and a window found open was said to substantiate that belief.*

* " Sir Walter seems to have assumed as a fact that the forlorn and distracted victim, seeing no other means of escaping from a fate which she held with disgust and abhorrence, had in a fit of desperation inflicted the fatal wound upon her selfish and unfeeling husband. But in justice to the memory of our unhappy relative, we may be permitted to regret Sir Walter's not having been made acquainted with a tradition long current in the part of the country where the tragical event took place—namely, that, from the window having been found open, it was conjectured that the lover had, during the bustle and confusion occasioned by the preparations for the marriage feast, and perhaps by the connivance of some servant of the family, contrived to gain admission and to secrete himself in the bridal chamber, whence he had made his escape into the garden after having fought with and severely wounded his successful rival—a conclusion strengthened by other concurring circumstances, and rendered more probable by the fact of young Baldoon having, to his latest breath, ob-

BALDOON CASTLE

At the Conference the twentie nynth daye of Maye Jai vjc flfteen scoir nyne yeiris the ... and articles of the Contract of Marriage nowe....

...

Gordoune witnes   Da: Dunbar

William md graffock witnes   James Dalrymple

James Dalrymple witnes   Ja: Dalrymple

M Speddan witnes

In Scott's Introduction, which, by the way, is the most interesting and readable of all his Prefaces, mention is made of Hamilton of Whitelaw, who had never a good word to say of the Dalrymples. A bitter feud existed between him and Lord Stair. Stair's family misfortunes are the theme of his most malignant satire, and nothing less than the intervention of the Evil One himself could be held responsible for the catastrophe:

> " Nick did Baldoon's posterior right decide
> And, as first substitute, did seize the bride ;
> Whate'er he to his mistress did or said,
> He threw the bridegroom from the nuptial bed,
> Into the chimney did so his rival maul,
> His bruised bones ne'er were cured but by the fall."

Having said so much, it is time to look at what are probably the true facts of the case. They appear to be these: Janet Dalrymple and Archibald, third Lord Rutherfurd, an impecunious Scottish peer, had plighted their troth together. Her parents disapproved of the match. The mother, a proud dame, possessed of an iron will and an ungovernable temper, did all she could to break the engagement and to foster instead an alliance between her daughter and David Dunbar, heir of Sir David Dunbar of Baldoon, and nephew to Rutherfurd. Lady Dalrymple is said to have worked on her unfortunate child by insisting on observance of the Levitical Law (Num. chap. xxx.) which declares that a woman shall be free of a

stinately refused to give any explanation on the subject. . . . The unfortunate lover was said to have disappeared immediately after the catastrophe in a manner somewhat mysterious ; but this part of the story has escaped my recollection."—*Letter from Sir Robert Dalrymple Horn Elphinstone, Bart.* (1823).

257   R

vow which she has made, " if her father disallow her in the day that he heareth." Janet at length gave in and agreed to marry Dunbar. The wedding took place on 12th August 1669, at the Kirk of Glenluce, two miles from her home, Carscreugh. The Bride rode to church behind one of her younger brothers who long afterwards spoke of the marble coldness of her hand as it touched his when holding by his waist. This tradition seems well authenticated—a lady who had conversed with young Dalrymple repeated her story to Scott, so that only one link lay between him and the Bride. The bridal party remained about a fortnight at Carscreugh, and on the 24th August the Bride went to her new home at Baldoon, in Kirkinner Parish, near the town of Wigtown. A gallantly-attired troop of friends accompanied the married pair, and a dramatic entertainment, or masque, was prepared. But to the consternation and grief of all, the bride suddenly sickened and died within a month of her marriage-day, 12th September 1669.

The sole contemporary evidence is contained in an "Elegy" by the Rev. Andrew Symson, Episcopal minister of Kirkinner, bearing to be written on the day of the lady's funeral. Symson makes no suggestion of any such sinister event as that which the popular imagination has succeeded in handing down. Did he deliberately draw a veil over the actual facts ? He was the parish clergyman, the personal friend of the bridegroom. He would be familiar with every detail of the story ; would take part in the wedding ceremony, and in the welcome-home rejoicings. It is incredible that Symson would put his verses together in such a fashion, if the circumstances were as the traditions allege. The "Elegy" is one of a group of thirteen which appeared at the end of *Tripatriarchicon* (The lives of the Patriarchs), a series of religious poems, printed at Edinburgh in 1705 by Symson himself, who turned printer after his ministering days were over at the Revolution. The title of the poem is as follows :

" ON THE UNEXPECTED DEATH OF THE VERTUOUS LADY, MRS. JANET DALRYMPLE, LADY BALDONE, YOUNGER.

Nupta, Aug. 12 ; *Domum ducta*, Aug. 24 ; *Obiit*, Sept. 12 : *Sepult.* Sept. 30, 1669." *

The composition is in the form of a dialogue between a stranger and a domestic servant at Baldoon. So excessively rare is the little volume that the entire "Elegy" may be quoted :

Dialogus inter advenam et servum domesticum

Stranger.

" ' What means this sudden unexpected change ?
This mourning Company ? Sure, sure some strange
And uncouth thing hath happen'd. *Phœbus's* Head
Hath not been resting on the wat'ry bed

---

* The Bride's remains are said to have been removed from Kirkinner to Kirkliston Church, Linlithgowshire, by her brother, the first Earl of Stair, who had his principal residence in the parish. The Bride's mother was interred here in 1692. The story of the old lady's coffin having been set in an upright position as a charm to ensure the prosperity of her family, is in all probability a myth. No such coffin was seen there more than eighty years ago.

Of *Sea-green Thetis* fourty times, since I
In transitu did cast my tender Eye
Upon this very place, and here did view
A Troop of Gallants : *Iris* never knew
The various colours which they did imploy
To manifest and represent their joy.
Yea more ; Methinks I saw this very Wall
Adorn'd with Emblems Hieroglyphicall.
As first ; The glorious *Sun* in lustre shine :
Next unto it, A young and tender *Vine*
Surround a stately *Elm*, whose tops were crown'd
With wreaths of *Bay-tree* reaching to the Ground :
And, to be short, methinks I did espy
A pleasant, harmless, joyfull Comedy.
But now (sad change, I'm sure,) they all are clad
In deepest Sable, and their Faces sad.
The *Sun's* o'erclouded and the *Vine's* away,
The Elm is drooping, and the wreaths of Bay
Are chang'd to Cypress, and the Comedie
Is metamorphos'd to a Tragedie.
I do desire you, Friend, for to unfold
This matter to me.'

Servant.

'Sir, 'tis truth you've told.
We did enjoy great mirth, but now, ah me !
Our joyful Song's turned to an Elegie.
A vertuous Lady, not long since a Bride,
Was to a hopeful plant by Marriage ty'd,
And brought home hither. We did all rejoyce,
Even for her sake. But presently our voice
Was turned to mourning, for that little time
That she'd enjoy : She wained in her prime.
For Atropus, with her impartial Knife,
Soon cut her Thread, and therewithall her Life.
And for the time, we may it well remember,
It being in unfortunate September,
Just at the *Æquinox* : She was cut down
In th' harvest, and this day she's to be sown,
Where we must leave her till the Resurrection ;
'Tis then the Saints enjoy their full perfection.' "

In these lines there is nothing of poetical moment, but they are written with feeling and delicacy of taste by one who was a contemporary of the parties, and who may be regarded as having knowledge of the facts as well as any one. The " Elegy " points distinctly to rapid decline occasioned by the operation of an unseen cause, but which may be surmised from the circumstances already mentioned of the lady's affections having been blighted, whilst not the most distant allusion is made to any such harrowing catastrophe as that on which the novel is based. This, at all events, seems a plausible solution of the matter. It *may* have had its origin in grim fact, or it may be one of those accretions curiously common that later years have gathered around this old Wigtownshire legend as around many others everywhere. As for the bridegroom, Dunbar bore little likeness to Bucklaw, but was " a cultivated gentleman of unimpeachable honour." He married a second time (before 1679) Helenor, daughter of Hugh, seventh Earl of Eglinton. She died at Kilwinning in September 1687. Dunbar's death was brought about by a fall from his horse " at the Quarrel Holes," Edinburgh, in 1682. His rival, Lord Rutherfurd, died unmarried, 11th March 1685. The only child of David Dunbar's second marriage became the wife of Lord Basil Hamilton and was ancestress of the late Captain Hope of St. Mary's Isle, in whose charter chest the Marriage Contract of the Bride of Baldoon was discovered in 1869. It is dated 29th May 1669, and a most handsome provision was made by Sir David Dunbar, father of the bridegroom, a man rich in lands and money. There are eight signatures, the parties and their witnesses, as under :

" H. Gordon, *witness*   " Da: Dunbar
" William McGuffock, *witness* " Janet Dalrymple
" James Dalrymple, *witness*   " Ja: Dalrymple
" Thomas McGraddon, *witness* " Baldone."

The signature of the Bride is large and distinct. A little tremulousness appears at some of the letters. The capital D is so written that the first stroke is made across within three parts of an O. The boldest signature is that of Sir David Dunbar, the bridegroom's father, who simply gives his territorial designation of Baldone or Baldoon. Sir James Dalrymple gives his name and surname. The witnesses are Hugh Gordon of Grange of Cree, parish of Penninghame ; William McGuffock of Alticry, parish of Mochrum, and afterwards of Rusco, parish of Anwoth ; James Dalrymple was the second son of Sir James and brother of the Bride. Thomas McGraddon was the solicitor to Sir James Dalrymple.

Scott, of course, could not have seen the Marriage Settlement, even though in the novel there occur these words : " I have myself seen the fatal Deed." That is the romancer who is speaking. The Introduction of 1830 would certainly have mentioned it as a fact, but there is no notice of the Document having been seen earlier than 1869. Minus the Deed in front of

him, how wonderfully has Scott delineated the movements of the chief actor in that agonising signature
scene! "It was now Miss Ashton's turn to sign the
writings, and she was guided by her watchful mother
to the table for that purpose. At her first attempt, she
began to write with a dry pen, and when the circumstance was pointed out, seemed unable, after several
attempts, to dip it in the massive silver ink-standish,
which stood full before her. Lady Ashton's vigilance
hastened to supply the deficiency. I have myself seen
the fatal Deed, and in the distinct characters in which
the name of Lucy Ashton is traced on each page, there
is only a very slight tremulous irregularity, indicative
of her state of mind at the time of the subscription.
But the last signature is incomplete, defaced and blotted ; for, while her hand was employed in tracing it,
the hasty tramp of a horse was heard at the gate, succeeded by a step in the outer gallery, and a voice,
which, in a commanding tone, bore down the opposition of the menials. The pen dropped from Lucy's
fingers, as she exclaimed with a faint shriek : 'He is
come—he is come!'"

Scott is careful to disclaim any intention of "tracing
the portrait of the first Lord Stair in the tricky and
mean-spirited Sir William Ashton," but he virtually admits the close resemblance between Lady Ashton, the
ambitious, shrewd, but hard-hearted, vindictive mother of the Bride, and the wife of the Viscount. "Lady
Ashton was of a family more distinguished than that
of her lord, an advantage which she did not fail to use

263

to the uttermost, in maintaining and extending her husband's influence over others, and, unless she was greatly belied, her own over him. She had been beautiful, and was stately and majestic in her appearance. Endowed by nature with strong powers and violent passions, experience had taught her to employ the one, and to conceal, if not to moderate, the other. She was a severe and strict observer of the external forms, at least, of devotion ; her hospitality was splendid, even to ostentation ; her address and manners, agreeable to the pattern most valued in Scotland at the period, were grave, dignified, and severely regulated by the rules of etiquette. Her character had always been beyond the breath of slander. And yet, with all these qualities to excite respect, Lady Ashton was seldom mentioned in the terms of love or affection. Interest—the interest of her family, if not her own—seemed too obviously the motive of her actions ; and where this is the case, the sharp-judging and malignant public are not easily imposed upon by outward show. It was seen and ascertained that, in her most graceful courtesies and compliments, Lady Ashton no more lost sight of her object than the falcon in his airy wheel turns his quick eyes from his destined quarry ; and hence, something of doubt and suspicion qualified the feelings with which her equals received her attentions. With her inferiors these feelings were mingled with fear : an impression useful to her purposes, so far as it enforced ready compliance with her requests and implicit obedience to her com-

mands, but detrimental, because it cannot exist with
with affection or regard." *

Another of Symson's panegyrics contained in the
Tripatriarchicon is entitled : " A Funeral Elegie occasioned by the sad and much lamented Death of that
worthily respected and very much accomplished Gentleman, David Dunbar, Younger of Baldone, only
son and apparent Heir to the Right Worshipful Sir
David Dunbar of Baldone, Knight Baronet. He departed this life on March 21, 1682, having received a
bruise by a Fall, as he was riding the day preceding
betwixt Leith and Holyroodhouse ; and was honour-
ably interred in the Abbey Church of Holyroodhouse, on April 4, 1682." The intimate relationship
between minister and parishioner is rendered a more
amusing circumstance in that Dunbar seems to have
been his solitary hearer. Kirkinner Parish was an
absolutely Whiggish one. That notwithstanding,
Symson got on well with the people and was obliged
to leave only with the increasing persecution of the
Covenanters in 1685–86. He had been minister for
twenty-three years. His *Description of Galloway in the
Seventeenth Century* is an invaluable epitome of information. It is thus that he writes of his faithful Baldoon:

* In the satires of the day Lady Stair was described as the
Witch of Endor. For examples of her witchcraft and of the fear
in which she was held by the common people, see Mackay's
Memoir of Sir James Dalrymple. It was this Lady Stair who
observed to Claverhouse when inveighing against John Knox:
"There is not, after all, so much difference between you and
him ; only he gained his point by 'clavers,' you gain yours by
'knocks.'"

" Men might, and very justly too, conclude
Me guilty of the worst ingratitude,
Should I be silent, or should I forbear
At this sad accident to shed a Tear—
A Tear, said I ? Ah ! that's a petit thing,
A very lean, slight, slender Offering,
Too mean, I'm sure for me, wherewith t' attend
The unexpected Funerals of my Friend.
A Glass of briny tears charg'd up to th' brim
Would be too few for me to shed for him—
For him my noble, constant, only Friend.
That's a proud word you'll say, yet ere I end
I'll make it evident, I nothing doubt,
Ere I conclude to make it fully out.
In th' late Rebellion, that unhappy time
When Loyalty was looked on as a Crime,
And Royalists were hooted at like Owls,
Esteemed deserving nought but Scoffs and Scowls,
Frowns, Mocks and Taunts, of which he had his share
(And 'twas my daily bread and constant fare)—
In that unhappy time, I say, when I
Was almost drown'd in deep perplexity,
When many persons would no longer stay
And all my Summer Birds fled quite away ;
Yet He (brave soul !) did always constant prove,
My change of Fortune never changed his Love,
For change who lik'd, he ever was the same ;
In nothing chang'd, save that he chang'd his name.
His name was only changed, but not the man ;
I was the David, he the Jonathan.
He was no *Schismatick*, he ne'er withdrew
Himself from th' House of God ; he with a few
(Some two or three) came constantly to pray
For such as had withdrawn themselves away,
Nor did he come by fits,—foul day or fair,
I, being in the church, was sure to see him there.
Had he withdrawn, 'tis like these two or three,
Being thus discouraged, had deserted me ;
So that my Muse, 'gainst *Priscian*, averrs,
He, HE alone, WERE my Parishioners,
Yea, and my constant Hearers. O that I
Had pow'r to enternize his Memory ;

Then (though my joy, my glory, and my crown,
By this unhappy fall be thus fall'n down,)
I'd rear an everlasting monument,
A curious structure of a large extent,—
A brave and stately pile, that should outbid
Ægyptian Cheops's costly Pyramid,
A Monument that should outlive the blast
Of Time, and Malice too,—a pile should last
Longer than hardest Marble, and surpass
The bright and durable *Corinthian Brass* !
He was my bosom friend, I us'd to enshrine
My secrets in his breast : he his in mine.
His House was as my Home, and 'tis well known
He look'd upon my Chamber as his own,
As being so often there, where he and I
Delighted in each others Company,
And (through some secret Sympathetick Art)
When ere we met, we still were loathe to part.
His Body, though not very large or tall,
Was sprightly, active, yea and strong withall ;
His constitution was, if right I've guessed,
Blood mixed with Choler, said to be the best.
In's gesture, converse, speech, discourse, attire,
He practis'd that which wise men still admire,
Commend, or recommend, what's that you'll say :
'Tis this : He ever choos'd the middle way
'Twixt both th' extremes.   Almost in every thing
He did the like, 'tis worth our noticing :
Sparing yet not a Niggard, liberal
And yet not lavish or a prodigal,
And knowing when to spend and when to spare,
And that's a Lesson which not many are
Acquainted with.   He bashfull was, yet daring
When he saw cause, and yet therein but sparing.
Familiar, yet not common, for he knew
To condescend, and keep his distance too.
He used, and that most commonly, to go
On foot : I wish that he had still done so."

For seventy-eight lines more the poem goes on to speak
of his attainments in learning and his great accomplishments, and then ends as follows :

THE SCOTT ORIGINALS

" When five or six months since I play'd the Poet
(And 'twas his proper motion made me do it),
And having done, he read my Lines, commended
The same, but chiefly two wherewith they ended.
O God Almighty, grant when Death shall seize us
We may not dy, but only sleep in Jesus.
This distich he read o'er and o'er again
And from his very heart subjoyn'd *Amen,*
And truly I have ground of hope that he
Reap'd good thereby in his Catastrophe.
For though, alas ! he rode but too too fast,
Yet, death pursu'd, and seized him at the last.
And like a surly messenger he came
Abruptly in, devoid of fear or shame,
Selecting this our Friend from all the rest
In furious manner, smote him on the breast,
Would hardly be intreated to delay
His final stroke, to the succeeding day.
His Death doth grieve us, but the very chief
Ingredient that aggravates our grief
Is the sad accident, this sudden fall ;
Oh ! that's the very Wormwood and the Gall.
Yet this should mitigate our grief and ease us,
In hopes that now he sweetly sleeps in Jesus."

[No portrait of Janet Dalrymple appears to be in existence.]

CHAPTER SIXTEEN

A LEGEND OF MONTROSE
"DUGALD DALGETTY"

"Such as do build their faith upon
The holy text of pike and gun."

BUTLER.

CHAPTER SIXTEEN : A LEGEND OF MONTROSE "DUGALD DALGETTY"

THAT MOST EXCITING OF THE WAVERLEYS, *A Legend of Montrose*, appeared in company with *The Bride of Lammermoor*. Both novels were the fruit of the most gloomy period in Scott's career, bating that which followed the death of Lady Scott. It is curious to find Scott, despite sufferings which would have quelled the stoutest soul, giving us in the *Legend* some of the finest delineations in fiction, and creating that most comically-refreshing of his characters, the redoubted Dalgetty. "Never," says Andrew Lang (to repeat what was said of *The Bride*), " was a more signal triumph of mind over body : never a more convincing disproof of the strange theory that Scott's genius was subdued by the tribulations of the flesh." His physical prostrations seemed rather to quicken and intensify the mental moods. The *Legend* exhibits some of *The Bride's* sad and distressing elements, and both stories end dismally.

Montrose was a figure who was sure to appeal to Scott's sentiment both from a historical and a romantic standpoint. In him were fulfilled all the conditions for a really powerful romance. Montrose's espousal of the Covenant and sudden abandonment of the same ; the splendid loyalty of him whose motto was " I live and die for loyaltye " ; his remarkable adventures, hair-breadth escapes, exhibitions of consummate bravery, his sweeping tides of victory ; and finally, his rout, and flight, and death were pulsat-

ing with dramatic possibilities. Scott does not carry
Montrose down to the bitter end, and he is not the
leading character in the novel. By this it is not to be
inferred that his exploits do not give body to the book,
or that the Great Marquis himself is not finely described. He appears often enough throughout the
story, but there is no towering grandeur about him.
He might perfectly well change places with Menteith
and we should scarcely see the difference.

A lesser theme contented Scott. The fate of
Lord Kilpont, who takes his father's title of Earl of
Menteith, and the strange history of James Stewart
of Ardvoirlich, who becomes the half-crazed deutero-
scopic, Allan M'Aulay of Darnlinvarach, were the
topics on which Scott chose to work. Nor, as he confessed, could he resist the temptation to follow that
" wandering knight so fair," Dalgetty, " over hill and
corrie, in prison and in camp and field." That was
the temptation of the *Legend*. It is the great Dugald
Dalgetty of Drumthwacket—most perfect type of
the wandering Scot of a bygone age, conceited, prag-
matic, garrulous,—that dauntless soldier of fortune,
who monopolises the interest of the tale. Strictly
speaking, he has nothing to do with the story, and was
originally introduced as " a personage proper to the
time and country," who might serve as a foil " to
enliven the tragedy of the tale." The truth is, he
ends by absorbing the attention of author and reader
alike. We cannot have too much of him, spite of
Jeffrey's protest. How Scott loved to mould his men

IN THIS AISLE ARE INTERRED
THE REMAINS OF MARGARET
ROSS OF BALNIEL WIFE OF
JAMES VISCOUNT STAIR LORD
PRESIDENT OF THE SESSION
WHO DIED 1692; OF JOHN 2ND
EARL OF STAIR K.T. AND P.C.
FIELD MARSHAL AND COMMAN
DER IN CHIEF AMBASSADOR TO
FRANCE POLAND AND THE STATES
GENERAL OF HOLLAND COLONEL
OF THE SCOTS GREY DRAGOONS
VICE ADMIRAL OF SCOTLAND
&c. &c. BORN 1673 DIED 1747
AND OTHER MEMBERS OF THE
FAMILY OF DALRYMPLE OF STAIR

BURIAL VAULT OF THE BRIDE OF LAMMERMOOR
Kirkliston Church [see page 265

SIR JAMES TURNER
"Dugald Dalgetty"

of the Dalgetty stamp! Once on their track, restraint was hopeless: "I think there is a demon," he says (in the Introductory Epistle to *The Fortunes of Nigel*), "who seats himself on the feather of my pen, when I begin to write, and leads it away from the purpose. When I light on such a character as Bailie Jarvie, or Dalgetty, my imagination brightens, and my conception becomes clearer at every step which I take in his company, although it leads me many a mile away from the regular road, and forces me to leap hedges and ditches to get back into the route again. If I resist the temptation, as you advise me, my thoughts become prosy, flat, and dull; I write painfully to myself, and under a consciousness of flagging which makes me flag still more; the sunshine with which fancy had invested the incidents departs from them, and leaves everything dull and gloomy. . . . In short, sir, on such occasions I think I am bewitched."

The minor characters, including the nominal hero and heroine—Menteith and Annot Lyle—occupy only a trifling place in the novel, and there is no special interest attaching to them.

II

There is good warrant for the character of Dalgetty. The name itself was borrowed from that old acquaintance of Scott's boyhood, Captain Dalgetty of Prestonpans, "who had fought in all the German wars, but found very few to listen to his tales of military feats." "He formed," says Scott, "a sort of alli-

s

ance with me, and I used invariably to attend him for the pleasure of hearing these communications." The real antecedents, however, out of which grew the Dalgetty as we know him, are to be found in the memoirs of the Scottish mercenaries of the period. Travel and adventure and the love of fighting had ever distinguished the Scots, and they had always been poor. As early as 1578 Scottish soldiers gave gallant and memorable service at the Battle of Mechlin, where they fought the Spaniards in their shirts like Montrose's men at Kilsyth. The great war which for thirty years desolated Europe was the epoch *par excellence* of the Scottish soldiers of fortune. They disdained no service, but the name of Gustavus Adolphus was one to conjure with, for the noble spirit displayed by the Swedes and their sovereign in their championship of the liberties of Protestant Europe. A large national brigade fought for the "invincible Gustavus," and their numbers, Scott says, may be guessed from those of the superior officers, which amounted to thirty-four colonels and fifty lieutenant-colonels. But " the taste for foreign service was so universal that young gentlemen of family, who wished to see the world, used to travel on the Continent from place to place, and from state to state, and defray their expenses by engaging for a few weeks or months in military service in the garrison or guards of the state in which they made their temporary residence."

Scott has been accused of injustice to the spirit and bearing of the Scottish mercenaries in his picture of

Dalgetty. But the very qualities of courage, and military skill, and the queer notions of fidelity which characterised the mercenaries, are qualities the Rittmaster possesses in a remarkable degree. He is *soldado* and student, as were many of the mercenaries—as Le Balafrè and Bradwardine. As for the principles on which he regulated his frequent choice of sides, the condition of the times rendered that almost inevitable. Sir John Urrie (who figures in the *Legend*), "changed sides twice during the Civil War and was destined to turn his coat a third time before it ended," without damaging his reputation in the least. Scott styles him " a brave and good partisan."

Of memoirs of the mercenaries, two, in particular, were used by Scott, both of them written, he remarks, very much in the humour of the doughty Captain : the Memoirs of Lieutenant-Colonel Robert Munro, and of Sir James Turner. Annotations on the margin of Munro's closely-printed black-letter folio of *Expeditions and Observations*, preserved in the National Library of Scotland, have a suspicious resemblance to Scott's handwriting. This was probably the copy he used in gathering materials for *A Legend of Montrose*, and evolving the immortal personality of Dalgetty. Hints in several of the novels—in *Old Mortality*, for instance (in the remarks of Bothwell and Major Bellenden)—show that Scott was familiar with both books, and had carefully studied them.

It was, however, the Memoirs of Sir James Turner to which Scott was most indebted for many touches of the portraiture of the intrepid Dugald, and of the scenes in which he is made to figure. Turner was a son of the manse; born in 1615, under the shadow of Borthwick Castle, of which parish his father, Patrick Turner, was minister from 1604 to 1629. His mother was Margaret Law. At Glasgow (Dalgetty was a Marischal College man) Turner ruefully pursued his studies, and took his degree sorely against his will. Not in books but in battles was the young heart of him. His dream was to handle the pike instead of to wag his head in a pulpit. "A restless desire entered my mind to be, if not an actor, at least a spectator of those warrs which made so much noyse over all the world." He had friends, and an ensigncy was found for him in the regiment Sir James Lumsdale—the "stout Lumsdale" of Dalgetty's "intake" of Frankfort—was then raising for the service of the Lion of the North. Turner's apprenticeship to campaigning was a rough one. He had many "a lamentable cold, wet, and rainie march." In winter, he lay in the open with no covering but his plaid. His fare was poor : bread and water, "little of the first, but an abundance of the latter." But "I was so hardened with fatigue and so well inured to toyle that I fully resolved to go on in that course of life of which I had made choice." At Oldendorf, and Hamelin, the town of the Pied Piper, he drew first blood, blossoming into an apt pupil in all that pertained to the art of self-help (not in Dr. Smiles' sense) "I had got so much cunning and became so vigilant to lay hold on opportunities that I wanted for nothing, horses, clothes, meate, nor money, and made so good use of what I had learned that the whole time I served in Germanie I suffered no such miserie as I had done." There is an amusingly frank passage in the memoirs as to a cavalier of fortune's code of morality—Dalgetty's very sentiments : " I had swallowed without chewing in Germanie a very dangerous maxime, which military men there too much follow : which was, that so we serve our master honestlie, it is no matter what master we serve." He had, for example, the chance of a couple of ships sailing from Gothenburg—an Englishman bound for Hull, a Dane for Leith. It was a toss-up which he should take : if he went to the Humber, he would be for the King ; if to the Forth, for the Covenant. An accident " deemed providential " decided the matter, and he arrived at Leith. From Edinburgh he followed General Alexander Leslie to his leaguer on the Tyne, where, on the recommendation of the " dissolute Rothes," he became Major in Lord Kirkcudbright's regiment of Galwegians—" a people fatale to me." Turner never took the Covenant. A Royalist at heart, he had never any liking for it. But, indeed, it mattered not what side he served. King's man or Covenanter, for Montrose or the Solemn Leaguers, for Prelacy or Presbytery, he could be either ; " for I had a principle, having not yet studied a better one, that I wronged not my conscience in doeing anything I was commanded to doe by those I served." He served in Ireland with the Ulster Scots against the Irish rebels, in all that " war of ambushes and surprises, of desultory fighting through swamps and wood-lands, of lining hedgerows with musketry, and meet-ing pikes, scythes, and bludgeons with desultory volleys ": at Newark, where he plotted for the King's escape : with Leslie's expedition into Kintyre, " not, of course, for base considerations of pay, but because I thought it dutie to fight against those men who first had deserted their Generall Montrose, when he stood most in need of them." Turner confirms all that Scott says in the *Legend* about the formidable passes leading into Argyll's country, traversed only by the hunters and shepherds. Had Colkitto but secured them " with his thousand of brave foot," Leslie could never have entered Kintyre " but by a miracle."

In 1648, Turner was all in all for Royalty, full of the Duke of Hamilton's ill-timed project in aid of the English Royalists and for the rescue of Charles. Never a more foolish enterprise ! With Cromwell hard at their heels the dénouement came in the heart of Staf-fordshire. Hamilton, like his royal master, went to the block, Turner to a twelvemonth's captivity at Hull. Released, he crossed to Hamburg, where he found him-self " among a number of penniless compatriots atten-ding the orders and motions of Montrose." Want of money, he tells us, prevented him from joining Mon-trose's final attempt in January 1650. But he made his way to Scotland, landing near Aberdeen on the very eve of the Battle of Dunbar. Again his services were in demand. As Adjutant-General he marched into England, to be taken prisoner at Worcester. He escaped, and reached London, where he concealed himself for a time, then joined Charles II. at Paris. Greatly daring, he landed in Fife in 1654, to inquire as to the chances of a fresh Royalist rising. Everything was discouraging: he got safely out of the country, and for the next two or three years " danced attendance on the impecunious Charles, whose Court was agitated by alternate hopes and fears," according to the news from England.

At the Restoration, Turner (like Dalgetty) received the accolade of knighthood, by which he set small store, as it was promotion without pay. In 1663 he became commander of the forces in the south-west of Scotland, endeavouring to crush the Covenanters. There we see him in his true colours as Bite-the-Sheep Turner, " a merciless brigand, wherever there was a house to harry or a fatted calf to kill." A lust for loot possessed him, and hundreds of families were beggared by his fines. Given a free hand, to one of his kidney the opportunities for feathering his nest were irresistible. Even such a friendly Court as the Privy Council saw fit to interpose; but all his protestations of clemency could not save him from losing his place as an officer and a soldier. Still, bad as Turner was—a hard drinker, an unscrupulous mercenary, a " booted Apostle of Prelacy " of the most tyrannical and dragooning type—some better traits must have been left in the man. Cruel and bloodthirsty in the Claverhouse sense he does not seem to have been, despite Defoe's epithet of "butcher," or he would not have fared so mercifully when the Whigs took him in his lodgings at Dumfries. Lang declares that Turner was "infinitely more of a Christian than the Saints of the Covenant." A coarse Christian, then! Even Scott speaks of him with some harshness. Any inner light that he possessed must have been faint enough. His was not a nature sensitive to the highest and holiest things. In Walter Smith's lines (applied to Burley) we may hear him speak in his own tongue:

> "Bah! give me a conscience that rules with a will,
> Or one that can hold its peace and be still;
> But neither the Lord nor the devil will care
> For your conscience that scruples and splits on a hair."

Turner's last days were spent at Glasgow, and at his place at Craig, in Ayrshire, where he busied himself with literature, writing his *Memoirs* and *Pallas Armata*—Essays on the Art of War, and even courting the Muses. He died probably soon after 1685. His wife, Mary White, "a good beautie," whom he met "at the Neurie," survived him till about the year 1716.*

* Skene, curiously—but "Sir Walter himself told me,"—finds a prototype of Dalgetty in "an ancestor of mine in the military annals of Holland—the General Martin Skene [Maarten Schenk] who, in command of the Dutch army at the siege of Namur, was killed [1589] in forcing the passage of the river. His body floated down to the island, on which he had constructed a strong fort, which still bears his name" [Schenkenschans, near Nymegen— not Namur].—*Memories of Sir Walter Scott.*

CHAPTER SEVENTEEN

IVANHOE
"REBECCA"

" She moves a goddess and she looks a queen.'
POPE'S *Homer*.

JUDGED BY SUCH MUNDANE THINGS as book-selling returns, *Ivanhoe* is far and away the most popular of Scott's romances. In many respects it is more adapted to the taste of boyhood than any of the others. Boys do not relish the vernacular, and *Ivanhoe* is splendidly free from " the dialect "—that great stumbling-block to English readers of Scott. And what, from a boy's point of view, shall be said of the fights in *Ivanhoe*, the crowded lists, the flashing lances, the terrible storming of Front-de-Bœuf's Castle— that happy company of knights, ladies, dragons, en-chanters, of the world of Ariosto? Here is enough and more to seal the heart of youth for ever to this grand-est essay in historical fiction. In *Ivanhoe*, Scott pass-ed from scenes familiar on his native heath to a less known arena, and to times historically earlier than those he had yet delineated. He crossed the Border, let his fancy run riot in the realm of Southern story and tradition, and won several of his noblest tri-umphhs. The first of these, *Ivanhoe*, was also the most notable. The novel was received throughout England with a more clamorous delight than any of its Scottish predecessors had been. Twelve thousand copies were sold almost at once, notwithstanding the higher price. It had been a question in Scott's mind whether he could with success pass into the untried field, but the reception given to the new romance re-vealed the marvellous adaptability of the man. *Ivan-*

hoe was, as Lockhart remarks, the flood-tide of Scott's popularity as an author. It was written at the pinnacle of his fame. He was a newly-fledged baronet, and had just declined the laureateship. It was written when his health was so poor that he hardly expected to live to see it completed. The greater part, indeed, was dictated. He had at this time also a spate of domestic afflictions. Worst sorrow of all, his mother died a week after *Ivanhoe* had been published and was setting the Thames on fire.

The name Ivanhoe was suggested by an old rhyme in which mention is made of the manors forfeited by one of John Hampden's ancestors :

> " Tring, Wing, and Ivinghoe,
> For striking of a blow,
> Hampden did forego,
> And glad he had escaped so." *

The word, Scott says, suited his purpose, first for its ancient English sound ; and second, because (disliking to " write up " to a name) Ivanhoe conveyed no indication as to the nature of the story.

The period of the narrative is the reign of Richard I., when Norman and Saxon had scarcely begun to fuse, and it abounds with characters whose names are sure to attract attention. The plain, blunt Saxon, the refined, elegant Norman, the wealthy but despised Jew, the faithful serf, are each portrayed in successful contrast to one another. The result is an

* Ivinghoe is in Buckinghamshire. The story goes that a Hampden struck the Black Prince a blow with his racket when they quarrelled at tennis. It appears, however, that neither of the three manors mentioned ever belonged to the Hampdens.

authentic and fascinating picture of Old English manners and romance. Lockhart says that the group of Jews originated in a conversation between Scott and Skene of Rubislaw. Skene visited Sir Walter when his agony was at its worst, and tried to amuse him by an account of the Jews as he had seen them in the German ghettos, suggesting the introduction of types of this race into his next novel. Lockhart, apparently, knew nothing of the Washington Irving episode to be referred to. The tragic death of the Templar was founded on the sudden demise of Mr. Elphinstone of Glack, which happened in the Edinburgh Parliament House in Scott's presence. An after-dinner conversation with Will Clerk supplied the materials for one of the most amusing chapters in the story—the talk of the wise fool Wamba (one of Scott's finest creations) and Gurth on English calf and Norman veal. The formidable name of Front-de-Bœuf was borrowed from a roll of Norman warriors occurring in the Auchinleck Manuscript. As for the historicity of *Ivanhoe*, Freeman carries his cavilling rather far. No doubt there are anachronisms. In the matter of historical correctness Scott did not profess to be immaculate. Besides, *Ivanhoe* is romance, not history. But every available source of information was ransacked. More " reading-up " was spent over this novel than on any others. The facts of English mediæval life Scott set out to master, with one result, that the putting together of the story was accomplished with unconscionable rapidity, illness and all. The resuscitation of Athelstane (derived from Lindsay of Covington's trance), Scott admitted, was a "botch" (Letter to Ballantyne, 1828); and somewhere else he pleads guilty of writing Cedric for Cerdic, the true form.

II

Laidlaw tells how interested he was (in the course of dictation) in the character of Rebecca. The amanuensis repeatedly exclaimed: "That is fine. That is fine. Get on, Mr. Scott. Get on!"* Scott, himself highly pleased with the character, laughed and replied: "Softly, Willie; recollect I have to make the story—I shall make something of my Rebecca."

It is Rebecca who is the triumph of *Ivanhoe*. More than in the Cœur de Lion himself, or in the Knight of Ivanhoe, or in any of the haughty templars and barons so prominent in this romance, its strength and charm lie in the sad, devoted and unrequited tenderness of the Jewish damsel. In almost every one of Scott's works there is a poetical, may we not say an impossible, character—some one too good and enchanting to be believed in—yet so identified with our nature as to pass for a reality. Rebecca is the angelic being in *Ivanhoe*, and at the last engrosses all the interest. She is the noblest of all the daughters of Israel who have appeared on the page of fiction. Among Scott's women characters of her class none

* Laidlaw abjured with some warmth the old-wife exclamations which Lockhart ascribes to him—as, "Gude keep us a'!"—"The like o' that!"—"Eh, sirs! eh, sirs!" etc.

has been more admired. Her beauty, her grace, her
devotion to her father, her sacrifices for her faith,
and the sweetness of her heroic nature constitute a
picture of Jewish womanhood which no Christian
writer has surpassed in its delicate but enduring
charm.

Curiously, in the almost inexhaustible mass of literature which clusters around Scott and his work, we
have no hint of an Original for this so winsome, this
so peerless of his creations. Rebecca has her prototype, nevertheless. This is perhaps the only instance
in which Scott went far afield for the model of one
of his great characters. For Rebecca's *alter ego* belongs to America, a country but seldom mentioned
in the Waverleys. Except, indeed, for Major Bridge-
north's reminiscences of New England life in *Peveril*
there is scarcely another reference to the land of
the Stars and Stripes. No nation in the world has
taken Scott to its heart as America has done. In
his lifetime many transatlantic visitors found their
way to Abbotsford, and several well-known Americans Scott counted among his lifelong friends. But
America itself does not seem to have appealed to him.
How surprised, how overwhelmed would he now be
at the extraordinary homage which thousands of admirers from over the sea pay, as it were, to his very
footsteps year by year! The bulk of those who flock
to the Scott Country every summer are Americans ;
and in their own country, whatever the case in ours
may be, Scott's place as the mightiest of the magici-

ans is unassailable. In the leading libraries of the United States it is Scott who heads the fiction-lists. He has become a widely-adopted school classic ; and everywhere there is the keenest appreciation of even the most trifling circumstance over which the glamour of his name is cast.

It was, then, from an American man of letters, come of good Scots blood, that Scott heard the story of the real Rebecca. To those who knew her, the identification in *Ivanhoe* presented small difficulty. Scott and Washington Irving met for the first time in the autumn of 1817. Irving came to Abbotsford armed with a letter of introduction from Tom Campbell, who was aware of Scott's high estimate of Irving's genius. He was most cordially received and welcomed by Scott himself, who came limping to the gate followed by Maida. Scott grasped the hand of the stranger in a way which made Irving feel as if they were already old friends. At Abbotsford, Irving spent several of the most delightful days of his life, rambling from morn till night about the hills and streams ; listening to old tales told as no one but Scott could tell them ; and charmed by the storied and poetical associations of the Tweed. A warm, mutual attachment ensued. Scott was forty-six, and in the brilliancy of his early fame. Irving was thirty-four, and just rising in literary reputation by the favourable reception of his *Salmagundi* and the Knickerbocker *History of New York*. Scott's opinion of Irving is expressed in a letter to John Richardson of

REBECCA GRATZ
" Rebecca "

MARGARET SCOTT OF DELORAINE
"Brenda"   [see page 304

" REBECCA "

Kirklands : " When you see Tom Campbell, tell him
with my love that I have to thank him for making me
known to Mr. Washington Irving, who is one of the
best and pleasantest acquaintances I have made this
many a day." Irving's opinion of Scott is given in a
letter to James K. Paulding : " I cannot express my
delight at his character and manners. He is a sterling
golden-hearted old worthy, full of the joyousness of
youth, with a charming simplicity of manner that
puts you at ease in a moment."

To this friendship we owe the character of Rebecca
in *Ivanhoe*. During one of their many conversations,
when personal and family affairs were the topics,
Irving confided to Scott an account of the great
tragedy of his life—the death of his fiancée, Mathilda
Hoffman, and the beautiful devotion of her friend,
Rebecca Gratz, of Philadelphia. Miss Hoffman was
the daughter of Josiah Ogden Hoffman of New York.
To her Irving formed an attachment which was re-
ciprocated. Both were handsome and engaging figures
in the social circles of New York and Philadelphia,
and they were equally attractive in the strength and
beauty of their intellectual qualities. But in the midst
of his dreams of future bliss, the blow fell like a bolt
from the blue which reduced Irving's world to chaos
and all but distracted him. Mathilda Hoffman was
seized with consumption. She faded away in a single
winter, dying in 1809 at the age of eighteen :

> " A saint though but a child in years,
>   Older in goodness than her grey compeers."

T

Irving was then twenty-six. He lived forty-four years longer, treasuring to the end (like Scott) the memory of his lost and only true love. He slept with her Bible and Prayer Book beneath his pillow, and when he passed away, there was found in his home at Sunnyside a little repository of which no one but himself knew the secret. It was opened; a memorandum told the story of his sorrow, and there lay the picture of his betrothed, a braid of her golden hair, and a slip of paper, on which he had written " Mathilda Hoffman." In his notebook he wrote : " She died in the beauty of her youth, and in my memory she will ever be young and beautiful." In " St. Mark's Eve " in *Bracebridge Hall*, Irving was thinking of the vanished " light of his eyes " when he says : " There are departed beings that I have loved as I shall never love again in this world—that have loved me as I never again shall be loved." In " Rural Funerals " in the *Sketch Book*, the same tinge of quiet sadness is apparent.

Now Miss Hoffman had a friend who was almost as dear to her as Irving himself. When sufferings came, and the last shadows stole round the sick-bed, it was that friend who was the best of ministering angels. As has been said, she was Rebecca Gratz. Scott also heard *her* story from the lips of Washington Irving ; and it was the recital of Rebecca's love romance and sacrifice which captured Scott's imagination. Miss Gratz had experienced a noble affection for one of the many suitors who sighed for her hand, but her religion rose up an insuperable barrier between her and every boon that the world could bestow. Loyal to the ancestral faith, she could not conscientiously take the step of uniting with one of a different creed. Had she mingled only with her own people her position had been easier to understand. But accustomed to the society of Christians, loving them, and beloved by them, her attachment to the beliefs and hopes of Israel is rendered more conspicuous, and her firmness in the struggle between inclination and duty may be considered an index of the exalted character of the woman. Like Irving, Rebecca Gratz lived the life of a celibate. She wedded herself to the most varied acts of philanthropy, and the rest of her career became one long chain of golden deeds. In the last chapter of *Ivanhoe* the whole spirit of the life of Rebecca Gratz is summed up in the words of Isaac's daughter when she bade farewell to Rowena, who had asked if there were a convent of her sect to which she could retire: " No, lady," said the Jewess, " but among our people since the time of Abraham have been women who contributed their thoughts to Heaven and their actions to works of kindness to men, tending the sick, feeding the hungry, and relieving the distressed. Among these will Rebecca be numbered. Say this to thy lord should he chance to inquire after the fate of her whose life he saved." Thus it came about that in the streets of Philadelphia Rebecca Gratz was hardly less known as " the good Jewess " than as " the beautiful Jewess." As for her personal appearance, her admirers were wont to say that when she was

young she needed only the Eastern attire to have sat
for the study of Scott's mediæval Jewess. Had Sir
Walter met her he could not have given a more finished description of the New World's lovely daughter of
Zion : "The figure of Rebecca might indeed have compared with the proudest beauties of England, even
though it had been judged by as shrewd a connoisseur
as Prince John. Her form was exquisitely symmet-
rical, and was shown to advantage by a sort of Eastern dress, which she wore according to the fashion of
the females of her nation. Her turban of yellow silk
suited well with the darkness of her complexion. The
brilliancy of her eyes, the superb arch of her eyebrows,
her well-formed aquiline nose, her teeth as white as
pearl, and the profusion of her sable tresses, which,
each arranged in its own little spiral of twisted curls,
fell down upon as much of a lovely neck and bosom as
a simarre of the richest Persian silk, exhibiting flowers
in their natural colours embossed upon a purple
ground, permitted to be visible—all these constituted
a combination of loveliness which yielded not to the
most beautiful of the maidens who surrounded her.
It is true, that of the golden and pearl-studded clasps,
which closed her vest from the throat to the waist,
the three uppermost were left unfastened on account
of the heat, which something enlarged the prospect to
which we allude. A diamond necklace, with pend-
ants of inestimable value, were by this means also
made more conspicuous. The feather of an ostrich,
fastened in her turban by an agraffe set with bril-

liants, was another distinction of the beautiful Jewess, scoffed and sneered at by the proud dames who sat above her, but secretly envied by those who affected to deride them."

Miss Gratz's portrait was painted by Malbone, and by Thomas Sully, an English artist who had studied in Philadelphia. The latter declared that he had never seen a more striking Hebraic face. The easy pose, suggestive of perfect health, the delicately turned neck and shoulders with the firmly poised head and its profusion of dark, curling hair, large, clear black eyes, the contour of the face, the fine white skin, the expressive mouth and the firmly chiselled nose, with its strength of character, left no doubt as to the race from which she had sprung. Possessed of an elegant bearing, a melodiously sympathetic voice, a simple and frank and gracious womanliness, there was about Rebecca Gratz all that a princess of the blood Royal might have coveted.

Michael Gratz, her father, was a native of Langer-dorff in Upper Silesia, the family name being derived from the town of Gratz in Styria. When a mere youth he emigrated to America, and engaged in the business of supplying Indian traders with merchandise. He grew wealthy, married Miriam Symons of Lancaster, Pa., and of his eleven children Rebecca was born on 4th March 1781, and lived to complete her 87th year, a charming woman to the end. She died 29th August 1869. " I commend my spirit to the God who gave it," she said, " believing with firm faith in the religion of my fathers : " Hear, O Israel, the Lord our God is one Lord." Her dust reposes in a graveyard which the Jews of Philadelphia used more than a century and a half ago and the gates of which were violated by the British as the place of execution for their deserters.

Scott finished *Ivanhoe* in 1819, two years after Irving's visit. One of the first copies was dispatched to Irving along with a letter in which the question was put, " How do you like your Rebecca ? Does the Rebecca I have pictured, compare well with the pattern given ? "

Scott has been censured for not ultimately uniting Wilfrid to Rebecca rather than to the less interesting Rowena. He defended himself by declaring that the prejudices of the age made such a union almost impossible, while he thought that a character so highly virtuous and lofty would have been degraded rather than exalted in the attempt to reward virtue with temporal prosperity. " Such," he said, " was not the recompense which Providence usually deemed worthy of suffering merit. In a word," he observed, " if a virtuous and self-denying character is dismissed with temporal wealth, happiness, rank, and the indulgence of such a rashly-formed and ill-assorted passion as that of Rebecca for Ivanhoe, the reader will be apt to say, ' Verily, virtue has had its reward.' But a glance on the great picture of life will show that the duties of self-denial and the sacrifice of passion to principle are seldom thus remunerated ; and that the internal consciousness of their high-minded discharge of duty produced on their own reflections a more adequate recompense in the form of that peace which the world cannot give or take away."

The Letters of Rebecca Gratz, edited by Rabbi David Philipson, D.D. (Philadelphia, 1929), contain interesting references to Sir Walter and the Waverleys. Everywhere Miss Gratz was declaimed as " Rebecca's " prototype, and she herself rejoiced greatly in the honour. Scott's novels she read with delight, commending them to all her friends. America recognised her as the foremost Jewess of her time, and one of the noblest women in the country. " Her place," says Dr. Philipson, " is secure among the exalted spirits that glorify American womanhood."

CHAPTER EIGHTEEN

THE PIRATE
"CAPTAIN CLEVELAND"

" Robin Rover said to his crew,
  ' Up with the black flag,
  Down with the blue.' "

Scott.

CHAPTER EIGHTEEN   THE PIRATE   "CAPTAIN CLEVELAND"

CHIEFSWOOD, ON THE ABBOTSFORD ESTATE, was the birthplace of *The Pirate*. There, in the summer of 1821, Scott spent some of the pleasantest hours of his life. In the early morning he walked or rode over from his own home, about a couple of miles off. After breakfast he busied himself with his chapter, prepared his packet (the previous day's work) for " The Blücher " (the Edinburgh and Melrose Mail-coach), and then, for the rest of the day, he was his " own man," as he was fond of saying. Lockhart (who never wore his heart on his sleeve) confesses, with some emotion, that the years at Chiefswood were the high-water mark of his own happiness. Thither he brought his bride, Sophia Scott, for " the first of several seasons which will ever dwell in my memory as the happiest of my life. We were near enough Abbotsford to partake as often as we liked of its brilliant society ; yet could do so without being exposed to the worry and exhaustion of spirit which the daily reception of new comers entailed upon all the family except Sir Walter himself. But, in truth, even he was not always proof against the annoyances connected with such a style of open housekeeping. Even his temper sunk sometimes under the solemn applauses of learned dulness, the vapid raptures of painted and periwigged dowagers, the horse-leech avidity with which underbred foreigners urged their questions, and the pompous simpers of condescending magnates. When

299

sore beset at home in this way, he would every now and then discover that he had some very particular business to attend to on an outlying part of his estate, and craving the indulgence of his guests overnight, appear at the cabin in the glen before its inhabitants were astir in the morning. The clatter of Sibyl Grey's hoofs, the yelping of Mustard and Spice, with his own joyous shout of réveillé under our windows, were the signal that he had burst his toils, and meant for that day to 'take his ease in his inn.' On descending, he was to be found seated with all his dogs and ours about him, under a spreading ash that overshadowed half the bank between the cottage and the brook, pointing the edge of his woodman's axe, and listening to Tom Purdie's lecture touching the plantation that most needed thinning. . . . He would take possession of a dressing-room upstairs, write a chapter of *The Pirate*; and then . . . away to join Purdie . . . until it was time either to rejoin his own party at Abbotsford, or the quiet circle of the cottage."

Lockhart describes the progress of *The Pirate*, the " constant and eager delight " taken in the tale by that dearest, most intimate of all Sir Walter's friends— William Erskine. Erskine was Sheriff of the Orkneys —land of the *roost* and the *voe*, towards which Scott had turned in search of further conquests. " Under our favourite tree " Erskine read aloud the MS. of *The Pirate*, " and I can never open the book," says Lockhart, " without thinking I hear his voice." Pathetic it is to recall that Erskine (a six-months' Lord of

Session, Lord Kinnedder) died only the next August, when (as Skene tells us) at his funeral Scott "wept like a child."

The years have wrought little change on Chiefswood. A couple of gabled wings have been added in the red stone of the original. The dressing-room of *The Pirate* is the same as it was a hundred years since, but the bureau at which Scott worked (seen here not so long ago) has been removed. In the grounds, the tiny well (Scott's wine-cooler) is to the fore, and Lockhart's tree is living yet. A luxuriance almost tropical-looking clothes that once bare Dick's Cleugh, which Scott in his esctasy rechristened the Rhymer's Glen, appropriating for the haunts of True Thomas a spot which had not the most distant connection with the Seer of Ercildoune.

It was at this place, then, that the novel of the wind-swept Orcades took shape. Scott had visited the islands during a cruise with the Northern Lighthouse Commissioners, in 1814, immediately after the publication of *Waverley*. Abundant material lay to his hand, not only in the "five little paper books" which comprised his diary of the trip, but his prodigious memory must also have served him in good stead, so magically does he describe all that he had heard and seen of the people, the natural features, the customs and superstitions of Ultima Thule:

> " Land of the dark, the Runic rhyme,
>   The mystic ring, the cavern hoar,
>   The Scandinavian seer, sublime
>   In legendary lore."

Scott made the most of his tour. He climbed Sumburgh Head, and "e'en slid down a few hundred feet" to the beach where Mordaunt rescues Cleveland from the waves, where Norna protects his property from the wreckers. He examined the broch of Mousa, model of Norna's lair. Excursions to the Dwarfie Stone; to Stennis—the Scottish Stonehenge; to Kirkwall Cathedral, " the wonder and glory of all the North," are each reflected in the story. Scott missed nothing, and forgot nothing—not even the curiously absurd little corn-mills of the islands, and the stupid one-stilted ploughs only passing out of use at the time of his visit.

It is in the characteristic vividness of its scenic descriptions that the charm of *The Pirate* is found. But many of the characters, if somewhat strained, are admirable. Nothing could be finer than the hospitable old Udaller (a sort of Cedric) and his household. Perhaps the best of the male characters is the missionary agriculturist Yellowley (did Scott borrow the name from Will Yellowlees of Mellerstain ?). The equestrian adventures of Babby and himself on their way to the Troil feast are considered to equal anything in Fielding or Smollett. Claud Halcro (gay *scald*) " bores " with his catchwords but compensates with his songs. Cleveland, pirate more of the heart than of the sea, is surely the most inconsistent figure in Scott, and therefore a failure. Even Norna, sovereign of the elements, devotee of the dead deities and broken faiths of Thule, is not a happily-conceived character. It is Minna and Brenda, that matchless pair, who shine in the story. Nothing can be more beautiful than the description of those winsome sisters and the gentle and innocent affection that continues to unite them, even after love has come to divide their interests and wishes. Never was there a perfecter study in womanly contrasts — temperament, depth of passion, personal appearance—Minna, "dark and stormy as an Oriental night; Brenda, serene and lustrous as a Shetland summer day." " Like Mordaunt in early years, we know not to which of them our hearts are given." *

II

It was from Bessie Millie, the Stromness sibyl, that Scott heard the story of John Gow the pirate, on whose brief, inglorious career he founded his Captain Cleveland. Bessie herself was Norna's prototype, answering well to the picture of the hag in the novel. She made her living by selling winds to the

* Originals (in externals only) have been found for Minna and Brenda in the Scotts of Scalloway; in the daughters of William Roy of Nenthorn; in the Scotts of Deloraine; and in Catherine and Anne Morritt of Rokeby. The latter (nieces of Scott's friend) were known in their family circle by the names in the novel, and "no doubt was ever expressed on the subject" of identity. The claim is equally persistent and strong for the daughters of Henry Scott of Deloraine, Sir Walter himself "having said as much." Margaret, the eldest (afterwards wife of Dr. Thomas Anderson of Selkirk), is said to have stood for Brenda; and Eliza, the youngest (afterwards wife of the Rev. William Berry Shaw of Langholm), for Minna.

sailors—favourable winds which were sure to come—
in time. Nearly a hundred years old, she was "withered and dried up like a mummy. A clay-coloured
kerchief folded round her head corresponded in
colour to her corpse-like complexion. Two light-
blue eyes that gleamed with a lustre like that of insanity, a nose and chin that almost met together, and
a ghastly expression of cunning gave her the effect of
Hecate."

Gow's story can be told in few words. He was a
native either of Scrabster, near Thurso, or of Claistron, on the other side of Cairston Roads. About
1716 his father, William Gow, settled in Stromness, where he built a house, Gowsness, on " ane
piece of wast land lying on the shoar of Hammin-
gar, upon the neck of the poynt called Ramsness."
A sasine in favour of himself, his wife—Margaret
Calder, and John, his eldest son, is still extant. Leaving school, young Gow went to sea. We have no
further mention of him until the year 1724—the
date at which he appears in the pages of Defoe's
narrative.* Gow was then a full-blown pirate,
whose flying of the " Jolly Roger " was destined
to be as short and swift as it was bold and venture-
some.

Gow had been boatswain on an English sloop, ply-

* It is not a little singular that the career of John Gow should
have engaged the attention of two of the world's greatest story-
tellers—the author of *Robinson Crusoe* and the author of *Waverley*.
Of Daniel Defoe's account of Gow (printed in 1725) only one copy
is known to exist—that in the British Museum Library.

ELIZA SCOTT OF DELORAINE
"Minna"

REV. ALEXANDER DUNCAN, D.D.

"Josiah Cargill"   [see page 325

ing between Lisbon and London. He proposed to the crew to seize the vessel, and to work it for their own profit—a suggestion scouted by every man of them. Arrived in the Thames, the captain was informed of the matter, and an attempt to arrest Gow failed. He escaped to Holland, and after a time shipped at Amsterdam as a fore-mast hand on board the *George*, an English galley, 200 tons burden, carrying eight guns, and captained by a Guernsey man, Oliver Ferneau. During that summer the Dutch were at war with the Dey of Algiers, and were glad to avail themselves of the help of neutral bottoms for the prosecution of their Mediterranean trade. The *George* was chartered to proceed to Santa Cruz on the Barbary Coast to load up with a cargo of beeswax for Genoa. On the return voyage Gow, a most competent seaman, was appointed second mate, a post which did not prevent him fomenting a plot to take possession of the ship. He was overheard and reproved. He attained his object not many days afterwards. The crew mutinied, murdered the chief officers, put Gow at their head, and changed the name of the *George* into the *Revenge*. Williams, who acted as Gow's lieutenant, may be regarded as the Goffe of *The Pirate*—Cleveland's rival. A sloop, bound with a cargo of fish to Cadiz, was their first prize. Having taken what they wanted, they sunk her. After that, they seized several vessels of various nationalities, until finally, in the middle of January 1725, they found themselves in Cairston Roads close to Gow's reputed birthplace. Their intention was to plunder on land as well as on sea, and raids were proposed to be made on certain houses which stood unguarded by the shore. One of Gow's men had been permitted to land, and without any suspicion to be absent from the ship for hours at a time. He gave his comrades the slip, escaped to Kirkwall, surrendered to the authorities, and told everything. Kirkwall was only about twelve miles from where the *Revenge* lay at anchor. It was resolved to take instant action. Other ten of Gow's men now deserted him in the longboat, making for the Caithness coast. But "hardened for his own destruction," Gow grew bolder, and "notwithstanding that the Country was alarm'd, and that he was fully discover'd, instead of making a timely Escape," he determined to put his project into execution, whatever the cost. "In Order to this, he sent the Boatswain and 10 Men on Shore the very same Night, very well Arm'd, directing them to go to the House of Mr. Honnyman of Grahamsey, Sheriff of the County, and who was himself at that Time, to his great good Fortune, from Home. The People of the House had not the least Notice of their coming, so that when they knock'd at the Door, it was immediately open'd; upon when they all enter'd the House at once, except one Panton, whom they set Centinel, and order'd him to stand at the Door to secure their Retreat, and to secure any from coming in after them.

"Mrs. Honnyman and her Daughter were extremely

Frighted at the sight of so many Armed Men com'ng into the House, and ran screaming about like People Distracted, while the Pirates, not regarding them, were looking about for Chests and Trunks, where they might expect to find some Plunder. And Mrs. Honnyman, in her Fright, coming to the Door, ask'd Panton what the meaning of it all was? And he told her freely they were Pirates, and that they came to plunder the House. At this she recovered some Courage, and ran back into the House immediately; and knowing, to be sure, where her Money lay, which was very considerable, and all in gold, she put the Bags in her Lap, and boldly rushing by Panton, who thought she was only running from them in a Fright, carryed it all off, and so made her Escape with the Treasure. The Boatswain being inform'd that the Money was carryed off, resolved to revenge himself by burning the Writings and Papers, which they call there the Charter of their Estates; but the young Lady, Mr. Honnyman's Daughter, hearing them threaten to burn the Writings, watch'd her Opportunity, and running to the Charter Room, where they lay, and tying the most considerable of them in a Napkin, threw them out of the Window, jumpt after them herself, and Escaped without Damage; though the Window was one Story high at least. However, the Pirates had the Plundering of all the rest of the House, and carryed off a great deal of Plate and Things of Value; and forced one of the Servants, who played very well on the Bagpipe, to march along,

Piping before them, when they carryed them off to the Ship." *

Gow now purposed to plunder the house of his old schoolfellow, Fea of Claistron. Fea had, however, been laying plans for the capture of the *Revenge*. And on 13th Febuary 1725, he succeeded, through a stratagem, in taking Gow and most of his men, at a public-house hard by his own home. The pirates were conveyed to London. At the trial Gow refused to plead, but the threat of squeezing his thumbs with a whipcord (technically called " pressing to death ") took all the bravado out of him. He pled to the indictment, was found guilty, and executed 11th June 1725. When he had hung four m'nutes the rope snapped, but the unhappy wretch mounted the ladder a second time "with very little concern." As Defoe quaintly says: "It was as if Providence had directed that he should be twice hang'd, his crimes being of a twofold nature, and both capital."

Love plays its part in the tale. Cleveland loved Minna and the real buccaneer had his love-romance too. At the Stone of Odin—that northern stone of Destiny where thousand hearts Orcadian vowed to be true till death—John Gow and Katherine Gordon †

* Defoe's Narrative.

† Not Katherine Gordon, but Katherine Rorieson, was the lady's name. Her father, Bailie Rorieson of Thurso, disapproved of the pirate for a son-in-law. Katherine married George Gibson, schoolmaster of the island of Stroma. Gow is said to have attempted to carry off his betrothed by force from Stroma.—*Caithness Family History.*

plighted their troth. That lady travelled to London for a last meeting with her lover—but Gow had passed his agony before she could arrive. She sought a sight of his dead body, took the cold responseless hand in her own, and formally revoked the Odin promise.

> "Give me my faith and troth, Margaret,
>   As I gave it to thee."*

* For the complete story of John Gow, see Allan Fea's *The Real Captain Cleveland*, (London 1912).

CHAPTER NINETEEN

ST. RONAN'S WELL
"MEG DODS"

"She speaks poinards, and every word stabs."

SHAKESPEARE.

IN *ST. RONAN'S WELL* WE HAVE SCOTT'S
solitary essay in contemporary fiction. Scott wrote
of this work that it was " upon a plan different from
any other that the author has ever written," and he
declares that it was an attempt to imitate the subject and style of the novels of Miss Edgeworth, Miss
Ferrier, and Miss Austen. He determined to turn
aside from public life and the higher topics which had
hitherto occupied his pen and make his story turn
upon the gossip and the petty intrigues of an unimport-
ant Scottish watering-place.

The novel was published before Christmas, 1823,
and was coldly enough received by English readers, a
judgment from which Scott's own countrymen stoutly dissented. There are characters and passages in
the story which may be set alongside any of Scott's
previous work. The novel does not reach the pinnacle
height of *The Antiquary* or *Guy Mannering*. It does
not rank even as high as *The Monastery* and *Peveril*,
but it possesses extraordinary interest, and apart
from the unfortunate conclusion, it is as high as any
novel of its class. Balzac, curiously, considered *St.
Ronan's Well* the " most finished " of all Scott's productions. There is general unanimity as to Scott's
blunder in submitting to Ballantyne's " Philistine
prudery " in protesting against the original story,
in which Clara did not discover the cheat put on her
until a later period than the mock marriage. There

313

was really no occasion for Aldiborontiphoscophornio's supersensitive interference. But what *is* all the pother about? As Professor Saintsbury has pointed out, no law and no church in Christendom would have hesitated to declare the nullity of a marriage which had never been consummated, and which was celebrated while one of the parties took the other for some one else. Clara Mowbray is clearly innocent. Her brain must have been shaken by some undescribed trouble. Lockhart hints what it was, but the "catastrophe" is fully explained by Mr. J. M. Colly's note to the *Athenæum* of 4th February 1893, in which extracts are printed from the original proof-sheets. The truth is Clara had compromised with Tyrell, her real lover, and on the head of this and the affront of the false marriage, her mental balance became overthrown. Her tragedy is one of the highest efforts in romance.

Of the other characters, that meddlesome, but well-meaning old Nabob, Mr. Peregrine Touchwood, is a thoroughly original figure, and Meg Dods, pearl of alehouse-keepers, "the modern and more than Mrs. Quickly," deserves a place, as Lockhart says, beside Monkbarns, the Bailie, and the inimitable Dalgetty. The widow, Mrs. Blower, afterwards Mrs. Quackleben, is one of Scott's very best characters.

As to the genesis of the novel, while Scott, Laidlaw, and Lockhart were riding along the brow of the Eildons, Scott mentioned the "row" (as he called it) which was going on in Paris over *Quentin Durward*, meaning *Quentin's* rousing reception by the Parisians:

" I can't but think I could make better play still with
something German," Scott said. Laidlaw protested :
" You are always best, like Helen MacGregor, when
your foot is on your native heath, and I have often
thought if you were to write a novel and lay the
scene *here*, in the very year you are writing it, you
would exceed yourself." " Hame's hame," quoth
Scott, smiling, " be it ever sae hamely," and Laidlaw bade him " stick to Melrose in 1823." But in
the next fiction there is never a hint of Melrose.
Scott laid his scene elsewhere. Lockhart and Laidlaw believed that this conversation on the hill overlooking Melrose and Gattonside suggested *St. Ronan's Well*, the locale of which, Innerleithen, a mere
village, at once assumed to itself. It is possible that
Scott *had* Innerleithen in view, or was it Peebles ?
Marchthorn may be Peebles, the Earl of March (now
Wemyss) being its principal landowner, and in Peebles,
according to William Chambers, dwelt Miss Ritchie,
the true Original of the termagant landlady of the
Cleikum Inn,* which, as the Cross Keys, still exists.
There are indications, however, that Gilsland, where
Charlotte Carpenter was wooed and won twenty-five
years before, was the locality of the new tale, or had
at least contributed to it. Shaws Castle may stand
for Traquair House, or Neidpath Castle, as some say,
but the name is more suggestive of Shaws Hotel at

---

* Andrew Lang thought that The Crook Inn, in
Tweedsmuir parish, may have suggested the name "Cleikum."
In Scots, the crook or cleek is the hook on which pots over a
fire are hung.

315

Gilsland, where Scott stayed during his sojourn in 1797. Much of the scenery of the novel harmonises with that of the little Cumberland watering-place, and the setting of the story in some respects is more English than Scottish.

As for Innerleithen, Scott knew the place well. One of his intimates, Dr. Wilkie, was surgeon there; and with Peebles he was as familiar. In the one place he would be aware of its mineral spring, then rising into fame; in the other, he may have encountered his paragon of despotic landladies. Innerleithen in Scott's day was a characteristically primitive hamlet, having a population less than six hundred. Its Spa, known as the Doo's Well, from the flocks of pigeons which made it their haunt, was a very uninviting spot. The first visitors drank the waters at the source, standing amid spongy grass and wet clay, there being but a plain wooden bench for the aged and infirm. By and by, Lord Traquair (the laird) had suitable accommodation erected. The mineral properties of the fountain were not discovered till near the end of the eighteenth century, and not for many years afterwards did the Well really come to its own. The publication of Scott's novel ushered in the period of its greatest glory, and visitors were further attracted by an annual festival established by an association known as the St. Ronan's Border Club. Amongst those who countenanced, or took part in the proceedings, were Scott and Adam Ferguson, Christopher North and the Ettrick Shepherd, Sheriff Glassford Bell, and others. It was under the patronage of these notables that the famous Border Games which Lockhart describes in the Biography came into being. Hogg was generally the presiding genius on these occasions, and it was the greatest evening of his year when, supported by Scott and his friends, he filled the president's chair at the distribution of the prizes, some of which were gained by himself, even after he had reached years three-score. The Games are still held, though shorn of their original character, and possessing a mere remnant of their ancient glory.

II

Meg Dods is incomparably the best Scottish character in *St. Ronan's Well*. Scott borrowed the name from Mrs. Margaret Dods, at whose little inn at Howgate, among the Moorfoots, with Will Clerk, and John Irving, and George Abercromby, he spent a night during a fishing excursion in their student days. When the novel was published, Clerk met Scott in the street, and observed, " That's an odd name ; surely I have met with it somewhere before." Scott smilingly replied, " Don't you remember Howgate," and passed on. The name alone, however, was taken from the Howgate hostess.

According to a well-grounded tradition of the town of Peebles, it was Miss Marion Ritchie who was the prototype of Scott's landlady of the olden time, his " lady of Luckies," as Gilfillan styles her. There are resemblances in their family history. Miss Ritchie succeeded her father in the business of inn-keeper or vintner ; so did the redoubted Meg. Miss Ritchie's father, Walter Ritchie, who was Provost of Peebles, died reasonably wealthy ; so did Meg Dods's parent. Miss Ritchie abode in single-blessedness ; Meg " had the honour of refusing three topping farmers, two bonnet-lairds, and a horse-couper who successively made proposals to her."

The Cleikum Inn was formerly a mansion of the Mowbray family. The Cross Keys, in the Peebles Northgate, was the town-house of the Williamsons of Cardrona. The court and the garden are still existent, but other parts of the description of Meg's hostelry scarcely tally with the modern building, or even as it was a century ago. It seems likely, however, that the essential features were derived from the quondam Cardrona domicile.

As for Meg's characteristics, these agree tolerably well (with exaggerations) with the traits ascribed to Marion Ritchie. Scott's portrait is, of course, a caricature. " She had hair of a brindled colour, betwixt black and grey, which was apt to escape in elf-locks from under her mutch when she was thrown into violent agitation ; long skinny hands, terminated by stout talons ; grey eyes, thin lips, a robust person, a broad though flat chest, capital wind, and a voice that could match a choir of fish-women." The real trouble lay in Meg's mannerisms, her treatment of chance customers, and the woman's habitual ill-nature—qualities in which she was akin to her Tweedside copy. The following account of Miss Ritchie, from the pen of one who knew her well, seems to exhaust all that can be said on the subject : "The characteristic features of Miss Ritchie were so nearly the same as those described in Meg Dods, that it is not easy, without a repetition of these, to say anything respecting her. She was more of a gentlewoman than Meg, being well connected, considering her position in life. Her abilities, too, were of no mean order. The great leading point of resemblance between the fiction and the reality was that tone of independence, approaching to rudeness, which is ascribed to Meg even in her days of greatest adversity. Miss Ritchie, though invariably civil when treated with due respect, had an outspoken way with her, and could never conceal her real sentiments when either provoked, or, as she thought, injured. She rather appeared as the obliging than as the obliged party in her transactions ; and if any indulgence or comfort was expected in her house, it was necessary, in the first place, to use all soothing terms of speech. No doubt much of this arose from natural character ; yet it was fostered in a great measure by the circumstances in which she was placed. Previous to 1808, when a good hotel of the modern fashion (the Tontine—Meg's "Tamteen") was erected in Peebles by the gentlemen of the county, she reigned without a rival ; and as there was no tolerable house within perhaps twenty miles of her in all directions, it is easy to conceive that travellers must have felt some little deference to their hostess to be quite indispensable. When the hotel was set up, she growled like a lioness deprived of her whelps. Yet she would not give in. She was too old to learn new tricks of civility, and too independent in her circumstances to require to put them in practice. Accordingly, when any one came to her house, who, she learned, was in the habit of going to the hotel, she never hesitated to break out upon him in a tone of indignation and sarcasm, which was not always very easily borne. ' Troop aff wi' ye to another public.' Sometimes she would absolutely refuse, at first, to send to such individuals the liquors or refreshments which were wanted. The setting up of the hotel was, to Miss Ritchie, what the erection of the new Well and its inn was to the acrid mistress of The Cleikum.''

" One instance of the manner of mine hostess of the Northgate may be narrated. In the year 1810, a detachment of French officers came to reside at Peebles, as prisoners on parole ; and a party of about twenty called, immediately on their arrival, to take dinner at Miss Ritchie's. They were speedily set down to a large preparation of ordinary barley-broth, which, on tasting, they declared to be ' *bon, bon !* ' Miss Ritchie, overhearing this expression, immediately burst out with—' *Banes* ! d'ye say there's *banes* in *my* kail ? Get out o' my house, ye hallan-shaker-lookin' scoundrels ! Gae wa wi' ye back to Penicuik, and see what ye'll get there. They're owre gude for you, or ony like you. *Banes* in my kail ! My certy ! ' And it was not without some difficulty that the hostess and her guests were brought to a right understanding, and the unfortunate gentlemen permitted to proceed with their dinner." *

Marion's brusquerie withal, there was the beating of a kind heart within. Like Meg Dods, her severe, her almost despotic government was exercised, upon the whole, for the good of the subject. In her house she tolerated no excess. Her clients were dismissed at her discretion. If any young man was tempted to linger over his cups, there was the invariable refusal to supply another drop, the firm and honest rebuke : " You have had plenty now. Gae awa hame to your mother." †

* *Chambers's Journal*, June 1833.

† A curious difficulty emerges with regard to Meg's prototype. Provost Ritchie had two daughters, Marion and Wilhelmina, both of whom succeeded him in the business of Innkeeper. (In the novel, Meg Dods is an only daughter.) Marion, according to the popular tradition, was Meg's Original. There is, however, no reference to her in the Gutterbluid Minute Books, which in the most careful manner record every event of the slightest interest that took place in the Burgh. The omission is striking—unless, indeed, Marion died previous to 31st January 1823, when the Club was instituted. That might well be. It is strange to think that her name does not appear on the family tombstone in Peebles Churchyard. Miss Willie died on 9th July 1841 at the age of seventy-seven. In the Gutterbluid Book she is said to have been "long Inn-keeper at the Cross Keys," and *her* name is inscribed on the tomb-stone. In *Glimpses of Peebles*, the Rev. Dr. Alexander Williamson (a native) states that Miss Willie Ritchie resided in the High Street, and that Miss Ritchie (the elder) died in July 1841. This must be a mistake. The likelihood is that she died some time between 1820 and 1823. The Rev. James Campbell, who was minister of Traquair in the first-mentioned year, remembered her and used to relate some of her sayings. The Presbytery always dined at her house. " It would have broken her heart if they had coun-tenanced the ' hotle.' " One afternoon as the members were at

dinner, Marion Ritchie passed away. Almost her last words were, "Are the ministers a' right?" When they learned what had occurred, they immediately broke up the Club for the day. Marion's Bible, punch-bowl, etc., are still preserved in Peebles. The bowl is said to have been cracked by Scott, "who, rather than encounter Meg's wrath, stole unseen from the house with it in his handkerchief, and ordering his groom to follow him with the carriage, walked out on the road till the groom came up; then driving with all haste to Edinburgh, had it clasped, and returned to Peebles with it next morning, thinking his anxiety for the bowl would be some palliation of his offence. But he was met by Miss Ritchie with a perfect torrent of abuse for 'leaving her decent house in sic a clandesteen manner, at sic a late hour, and a' aboot a bit crockerie-ware that wasna worth fashin' ane's thoomb aboot.'"

Since this Note was written it has been found from a research in the General Register House that Marion Ritchie died 8th February 1822.

CHAPTER TWENTY

ST. RONAN'S WELL
"JOSIAH CARGILL"

" His preaching much, but more his practice wrought ;
A living sermon of the truths he taught."
DRYDEN.

THE REVEREND JOSIAH CARGILL, THE SAD,
shy, gifted, amiable, dreary recluse, is another of the
admirable Scottish figures who fill up the glowing canvas of *St. Ronan's Well*. Mr. Cargill was the son of a
small farmer in the South of Scotland. At much sacrifice he had been trained for the ministry. When a
private tutor, he fell in love with his clever and come
ly ward, the Honourable Miss Augusta Bidmore, but
dared not reveal himself. " To sigh and suffer in
secret ; to form resolutions of separating himself from
a situation so fraught with danger, and to postpone
from day to day the accomplishment of a resolution
so prudent, was all to which the tutor found himself
equal." But in Mr. Cargill's absence as travelling
tutor to her brother—the Honourable Augustus—Miss
Augusta changed her maidenly for that of a wifely condition, a contingency wholly unanticipated by the bashful wooer. Whereupon the distressed Josiah, broken
in body and in mind, beat a sorrowful retreat home-
ward. By the grace of my Lord Bidmore he was offered
the living of St. Ronan's, where he speedily buried
himself in his studies, straining forward in pursuit
of a nobler and coyer Mistress than the Honourable
Augusta—Knowledge herself. Immersed in his own
tastes and interests (but by no means neglectful of his
parochial work), he very soon became the prey of personal indifference; ludicrous habits clung to him ; and
to an over-fastidious world the state of both manse
325

and minister lent occasion for astonishment and ridicule : " He not only indulged in neglect of dress and appearance, and all those ungainly tricks which men are apt to acquire by living very much alone, but besides, and especially, he became probably the most abstracted and absent man of a profession peculiarly liable to cherish such habits. No man fell so regularly into the painful dilemma of mistaking, or, in Scottish phrase, ' miskenning,' the person he spoke to, or more frequently inquired of an old maid for her husband, of a childless wife about her young people, of the distressed widower for the spouse at whose funeral he himself had assisted but a fortnight before ; and none was ever more familiar with strangers whom he had never seen, or seemed more estranged from those who had a title to think themselves well known to him. The worthy man perpetually confounded sex, age, and calling ; and when a blind beggar extended his hand for charity, he has been known to return the civility by taking off his hat, making a low bow, and hoping his worship was well."

Touchwood scented an original in Meg Dods's account of her minister, and being weary of his own society, resolved to interview that same abstracted personage. Arrived at the manse, all was silent, damp, dilapidated. His knock unanswered, he strode in.

" Amid a heap of books and other literary lumber which had accumulated around him, sat, in his wellworn leathern elbow-chair, the learned minister of St. Ronan's—a thin, spare man, beyond the middle age, of a dark complexion, but with eyes which, though now obscured and vacant, had been once bright, soft and expressive, and whose features seemed interesting, the rather that, notwithstanding the carelessness of his dress, he was in the habit of performing his ablutions with Eastern precision; for he had forgot neatness, but not cleanliness. His hair might have appeared much more disorderly had it not been thinned by time, and disposed chiefly around the sides of his countenance and the back part of his head; black stockings, ungartered, marked his professional dress, and his feet were thrust into the old slipshod shoes which served him instead of slippers. The rest of his garments, as far as visible, consisted in a plaid nightgown wrapt in long folds round his stooping and emaciated length of body, and reaching down to the slippers aforesaid. He was so intently engaged in studying the book before him, a folio of no ordinary bulk, that he totally disregarded the noise which Mr. Touchwood made in entering the room, as well as the coughs and hems with which he thought it proper to announce his presence.

"No notice being taken of these inarticulate signals, Mr. Touchwood, however great an enemy he was to ceremony, saw the necessity of introducing his business as an apology for his intrusion.

"'Hem! sir—ha, hem! You see before you a person in some distress for want of society, who has taken the liberty to call on you as a good pastor, who may be, in Christian charity, willing to afford him a little of your company, since he is tired of his own.'

327

Of this speech Mr. Cargill only understood the words 'distress' and 'charity'—sounds with which he was well acquainted, and which never failed to produce some effect on him. He looked at his visitor with lack-lustre eye, and, without correcting the first opinion which he had formed, although the stranger's plump and sturdy frame, as well as his nicely-brushed coat, glancing cane, and, above all, his upright and self-satisfied manner, resembled in no respect the dress, form, or bearing of a mendicant, he quietly thrust a shilling into his hand, and relapsed into the studious contemplation which the entrance of Touchwood had interrupted.

" 'Upon my word, my good sir,' said his visitor, surprised at a degree of absence of mind which he could hardly have conceived possible, ' you have entirely mistaken my object.'

" 'I am sorry my mite is insufficient, my friend,' said the clergyman, without again raising his eyes, ' it is all I have at present to bestow.'

" 'If you will have the kindness to look up for a moment, my good sir,' said the traveller, ' you may possibly perceive that you labour under a considerable mistake.'

" Mr. Cargill raised his head, recalled his attention, and, seeing that he had a well-dressed, respectable-looking person before him, he exclaimed in much confusion, ' Ha !—yes—on my word, I was so immersed in my book—I believe—I think I have the pleasure to see my worthy friend, Mr. Lavender ? ' "

The upshot was that the "Nabob" prevailed on him to accept an invitation for dinner. Each found something to like in the other. Mr. Touchwood bubbled over with curious and inflated harangues of his adventures in the farthermost parts of the earth, and the minister's simplicity and forgetfulness aroused all his finer feelings. He repaired the tumble-down manse, effected a change in the garden, and civilised the tow-headed maid-of-all-work, for Touchwood was never so happy as when he was setting other people's affairs to rights !

According to Lockhart, the absent-minded divine of the Aultoon of St. Ronan's was drawn from Dr. Alexander Duncan, the minister of Scott's Smailholm boyhood. Professor Lawson of Selkirk has been spoken of as an Original, and there are points of resemblance between the scholarly Seceder and the erudite Josiah. Lawson, like Cargill, "was characterised by all who knew him as a mild, gentle, and studious lover of learning, who, in the quiet prosecution of his own sole object, the acquisition of knowledge, and especially of that connected with his profession, had the utmost indulgence for all whose pursuits were different from his own. His sole relaxations were those of a retiring, mild, and pensive temper, and were limited to a ramble, almost always solitary, among the woods and hills."

"'Pray, Mrs. Dods, what sort of a man is your minister ? [it is Touchwood who is speaking]. Is he a sensible man ?'

"'No muckle o' that, sir,' answered Dame Dods,
329

' for if he was drinking this very tea that ye gat down frae London wi' the mail, he would mistake it for common Bohea. I have gi'en the minister a dram from my ain best bottle of real cognac brandy, and may I never stir frae the bit if he didna commend my whisky when he set down the glass ! There is no ane o' them in the Presbytery but himsell—ay, or in the Synod either—but wad hae kenn'd whisky frae brandy.'

" ' But what *sort* of man is he ? Has he learning ? ' said Touchwood.

" ' Learning ? Eneugh o' that,' answered Meg ; ' just dung donnart wi' learning ; lets a' things a-boot the manse gang whilk gate they will, sae they dinna plague him upon the score. If I had the twa tawpies that sorn upon the honest man ae week under my drilling, I think I wad show them how to sort a lodging ! ' "

Mention may be made of Alexander Affleck, who was minister of Lyne and Megget from 1814 to 1845. Mr. Affleck, while occupying a very humble sphere, was one of the pundits of the Church of Scotland in his day. A bachelor to the end, he exhibited many of the peculiarities of the eccentric Cargill, and his name has been frequently associated with the character.

II

It is more than likely, however, that Scott had in view the good divine of his early happy days in Roxburghshire. When, " ordered South " for the sake of his somewhat fragile life, the little lamiter from the College Wynd came under the spell of the breezes and the ballads of Sandyknowe, the minister had been thirty years in his parish. He was destined to be its spiritual head long after Scott had attained to manhood. He served the cure for fifty-eight years in all. Still hale at sixty-five—his age on Scott's first acquaintanceship—we have in his portrait (reproduced for the first time) an excellent representation of a Scottish clergyman of the old school. The face furnishes an index to the character of the man, with no clue or suggestion of whimsicality. There is the scholar's look, the rapt eye of one who sees more than mere time-visions ; and about the natural sternness of the features there mingles the play of a deep, honest sympathy. In the Smailholm district traditions of absent-mindedness on the part of Dr. Duncan have long since vanished. He was a student and a recluse, and had gathered together a considerable library—a rare thing for a minister in those days. That there was some acidity in his manner Scott himself tells us. Spite of that, he was " a most excellent and benevolent man, a gentleman in every feeling, and altogether different from those of his order who cringed at the tables of the gentry and domineered and rioted at those of the yeomanry."

Two interesting occasions chronicled in the Ashestiel fragment, afford us a couple of graphic snap-shots. In the first—a winsome picture—the minister is visit-

ing old Robert Scott at Sandyknowe. The two men
are engaged in earnest conversation, when there is serious interruption. It is the boy Walter Scott spouting
"Hardyknute," a trial of patience to the worthy pastor.
" Methinks I now see his tall, thin, emaciated figure,
his legs in glazed gambadoes, and his face of a length
that would have rivalled the Knight of La Mancha's,
and hear him exclaiming, 'One might as well speak
in the mouth of a cannon as where that child is.' "
The second, twenty years after, is almost the closing
scene in the good man's ministry. Now it is Scott
—" that child "—who knocks at the door of the
manse of Smailholm. He was in the habit of paying a
yearly visit to his old friend. This is to be his last. "I
found him emaciated to the last degree, wrapt in a
tartan nightgown and employed with all the activity
of health and youth in correcting a *History of the
Revolution* which he intended should be given to the
public when he was no more. He read me several
passages with a voice naturally strong, and which
the feelings of an author then raised above the depression of age and declining health. I begged him
to spare this fatigue, which could not but injure his
health. ' I know,' he said, ' that I cannot survive
a fortnight, and what signifies an exertion which can
at worst only accelerate my death a few days ? ' I
marvelled at the composure of this reply, for his appearance sufficiently vouched the truth of his prophecy. I rode home musing what there could be in
the spirit of authorship that could inspire its votaries

with the courage of martyrs. He died within less than the period he assigned."

Haunting memories of these, and, doubtless, similar incidents, survive in the Introduction to the third Canto of *Marmion*. There Dr. Duncan is further immortalised. He is

> " that venerable Priest,
> Our frequent and familiar guest,
> Whose life and manners well could paint
> Alike the student and the saint.
> Alas ! whose speech too oft I broke
> With gambol rude and timeless joke."

III

Alexander Duncan, son of an Aberdeen weaver and burgess, was born in 1708. At seventeen, he entered Marischal College; was licensed by the Presbytery of Earlston, 7th January 1735 ; and ordained assistant and successor at Traquair, 2nd September 1738. Scott says he had been chaplain to the second Lord Marchmont, had seen Pope, and could talk familiarly of many characters who had survived the Augustan age of Queen Anne. In 1743 he was translated to Smailholm. Duncan did not turn author until thirty years afterwards, when he produced *A Preservative against the Principles of Infidelity* or The Nature and Design of the Christian Religion and the Evidences of its Truth and Divine Origin. Stated in a plain and familiar manner.

His other works are as follows : *The Devout Communicant's Assistant* (1777) ; *The Evidence of the Re-*

surrection of Jesus as recorded in the New Testament, preached before the Society in Scotland for Propagating Christian Knowledge (1783) ; *History of the Revolution of 1688 :* giving an Account of the Manner in which it was accomplished and its happy Effects, particularly to the Kingdom and Church of Scotland (1790) ; and the article on Smailholm in Sinclair's *Statistical Account of Scotland.*

Dr. Duncan (he was made D.D. in 1773) wrote a *Journal of the Rebellion of 1745*, which was not published. It seems certain that this is the work, the manuscript of which he was engaged in correcting at the time of Scott's last visit to him, and not his previously published *History of the Revolution*, as stated in Lockhart's *Life.**

Duncan died in 1795. His intimate friend, Professor George Stewart of the Edinburgh Chair of Humanity, composed a Latin epitaph which was intended to be inscribed on a Memorial Stone in the Church. For some reason that was not done. (The matter might be taken up even yet.) The epitaph, however, appeared in the *Scots Magazine* for June, 1796, without any memoir or notice of the Smailholm minister :

* The volume of *Miscellaneous Essays, Naval, Moral, Political, and Divine*, Edin. 1799, which is attributed to Dr. Duncan in the *Bibliotheca Britannica*, and elsewhere, was written by the Rev. Alex. Duncan, D.D., Vicar of Bolam (See British Museum Catalogue), and the " Sermon on the Design and Advantages of the Christian Dispensation" (from 2 Peter i. 18) published in *Sermons on Miscellaneous Subjects by Ministers of the General Association Synod* (vol. ii., 1860), which is put under his name in the British Museum Catalogue, was written by the Rev. Alex. Duncan, D.D., Secession Minister at Midcalder.

ST. RONAN'S WELL "JOSIAH CARGILL"

Dr. Duncan's wife was the fourth child of William Home of Greenlaw Castle, afterwards of Sharpitlaw, factor to Baillie of Mellerstain. Her mother was the daughter of Sir Alexander Purves of that Ilk. Her brother, Robert, was the father of Sir Everard Home, the surgeon, and his daughter Anne (authoress of the song " My Mother bids me bind my hair ") became the wife of John Hunter the anatomist. Another daughter, Mary, married Robert Mylne, architect of Blackfriars Bridge, London, and the Edinburgh North Bridge. Mrs. Duncan died young. Her husband, who had been devoted to and very much dependent on her, was disconsolate at his loss. He was a widower for nearly fifty years. Among his papers were found several versions of an effusive but heart-wrung eulogy :

335

THE SCOTT ORIGINALS

" Here rests in hope of the Resurrection of the Just,
Helen Home, Spouse to Mr. A. D., Minister of Smalholm ;
A Woman Exemplary in every office and Relation of Life,
A Daughter full of Duty and Affection,
A Sister disinterested, above rivalship,
A Wife blest with the Tenderest love and fidelity,
And a Mother who felt the wants of her Infant Children ere
they could express them.

Her heart was full of goodness and Generosity ;
Her uncommon Understanding, clear and extensive ;
Religion in her account was not words but actions ;
And thereby She was So much above the fashion (of) this
world
That she never was once charged with having fail'd in Duty or
Affection, to Friend or Relation.

She knew indeed the partialitys of friendship,
But thought ym the most forgivable failings of our Nature ;
Her Friends Prosperity She beheld without envy,
And was unwearied to Serve them, from ye alone Motive of See-
ing what she designed for them, by her Means, prove suc-
cessful.
While she had as much difficulty to prevail on her Self
To accept an obligation, as the most part have to prevail on one
to grant it.
She could truely have compassion on her Enimys,
Counscious they were never made Such by her conduct.
And never Saw a real object of Distress
Without divising to her Ability Some means of relief.
So Sensible and just was her heart, allways, that it was in power
of her
Friends to hurt her more than could her Enimys.

Her Husband, during the four (alas) short years She lived in ye
Relation,
And Double that time She had been his friend,
Never had discovered in her a failing ;
But upon every occasion felt, that if she could have devised
Any method to have made him happy, or more usefull in his
office,
The earnest ambition of her heart would have been eagerly to
promote it.

She was to him the Mother of four Children,
The Eldest of whom at her Death was not three years old.
And so helpless were those poor Orphans,
Deprived of her tender and watchfull care,
That in two months after, the Youngest George was laid in ye
grave by her Side.

The irrepairable loss of her, gave Such a shock to her Husband,
That he hath allmost ever Since been at the gates of Death.
So much goodness could not long be alleyed to clay.
Souls So Sensible Soon wear this frail tabernacle.
She therefore left this mortal estate to the unspeakable loss of
her family

And the undessembled Sorrow of all her Friends
To take possession of that glorious reward
Of all those who live agreeably to the hope of the Gospel.
And the frail Lodging of that worthy Soul
Was laid here 10th Janry 1748 and 37th Year of her Age.

SMALHOLM,* *9th May* 1750.

Of Dr. Duncan's family, Alexander became minister of Gordon. On 21st July, returning from Communion at Channelkirk, he was thrown from his horse, and was found dead on the road about six miles from his manse. William went into the service of the East India Company under Warren Hastings and Lord Cornwallis ; became Colonel ; returned to Scotland " with the highest character for military and civil merit " ; married his cousin Caroline Mylne ; and died at London in 1830. Agnes was the wife of Thomas Cleghorn, wine merchant in Edinburgh, afterwards Inspector-General of Imports and Exports, Dean of Guild, and a Magistrate of the City. He died in 1800. Their son Thomas succeeded his grandfather as minister of Smailholm. George, Dr. Dun-

* The old form of the name.

can's fourth child, was an infant when his mother was taken, and died two months after her.

In Dr. Duncan's library there was found a little Latin work *De Cadaveribus Damnatorum* (Concerning the Disposal of the dead bodies of Criminals). This was Scott's thesis on being called to the Bar.* It is now excessively rare, not more than about four copies having survived. The Dedication was given to his friend and neighbour in George Square—Macqueen of Braxfield, that terror of the law, the original Weir of Hermiston.

* Disputatio Juridica, ad Tit. xxiv. Lib. xlviii. Pand., de Cadaveribus Damnatorum, quam, etc., . . . Pro Advocati Munere consequendo, Publicæ Disquisitioni subjecit Gaulterus Scott, Auct. et Resp. Ad diem 10. Julii, hor. loc. sol. Edinburgi, apud Balfour et Smellie, Facultatis Juridicæ Typographos, 1792. 4to.

CHAPTER TWENTY-ONE

REDGAUNTLET

" Who will not mercie unto others show,
How can he mercie ever hope to have ? "

SPENSER.

CHAPTER TWENTY-ONE
REDGAUNTLET

NO SOONER WAS *ST. RONAN'S WELL* OFF
the anvil than Scott announced *Redgauntlet*. *Herries*
was its original title, and a considerable portion of the
novel was at press before Constable was able to persuade Scott to adopt the more euphonious and more
striking appellation. Published in June 1824, there was
no rapturous welcome for the new romance. It was
coldly received. A glance at contemporary annals reveals the disappointment which was felt in Scotland,
and the almost childish spirit manifested by critics
south of the Border, who, among other things, affected
to complain of having to review a novel by the Author
of *Waverley* about once a quarter. Scott cared little
for criticism, friendly or unfriendly. All the same,
Redgauntlet was the only novel of that year. But
what a novel! Out of its seemingly still-born condition the story awakened to life and vitality and
interest and affection, to take its place in the very
forefront of the Waverleys, and reaching—there are
those who think so—possibly the highest place.
Lockhart's forecast has been richly fulfilled. In the
variety and excellence of its characters, above all, in
its tender and winsome revelation of the author's
temperament and earlier life, *Redgauntlet* is specially
dear to all who value Scott either as man or writer.

Historically, the novel harks back to Jacobitism
and to " Chairlie." The same " Bonnie Prince " who
stole the Highland hearts—yet how different ! From
341

his flight at Loch-nan-uamh, through all the years he had been haunted by the memory of his misfortunes and shattered hopes. And, alas, those "sordid enjoyments," of which Scott speaks, had played havoc with his beauty and his gallantry! He was a broken and a prematurely-aged man—the transfiguration of *Waverley* clean vanished, the old fire burned to its ashes. Some there were who imagined that Jacobitism had still a chance. It was a vain hope. Charles was once capable of great enterprises—but not now. He was the wreck of his former self, and his liaison with Clementina Walkinshaw (whom he neither loved nor esteemed) was the last straw to break the devotion and sympathy of the few who were willing to follow. In *Redgauntlet*, Scott's pen writes almost the final page of the forlorn tale. Nor is there in the whole of Scott a scene more touching than that in which the last heir of the Stuarts—the most fascinating of a fatal line—walks towards the beach leaning on Redgauntlet's arm, "for the ground was rough, and he no longer possessed the elasticity of limb and of spirit which had, twenty years before, carried him over many a Highland hill as light as one of their native deer."

The novel is reminiscent of Scott's early years and experiences. It is this element of autobiography which is the distinguishing charm of the romance. The author's youth, his first and only love, that exquisite picture of his stiff, "pernickety" father in Saunders Fairford; of his bosom friend, Will Clerk, in Darsie

Latimer; and of himself, as Alan,—are possibly (of their kind) the tenderest and most heart-stirring word-paintings in the whole of the Waverleys.

So with the Geddeses, Joshua and Rachel, the Quakers of Mount Sharon (modelled from the Waldies of Hendersyde). Rachel Geddes is Ruskin's type of perfect womanhood,—as fair a rose as ever reddened to the sun in her delicious old-world garden by the Solway.* Of *dramatis personæ* less worthy but no less striking, Nanty Ewart (painted from Paul Jones perhaps), that wreck of a noble life, is a more convincing pirate than Cleveland. Cristal Nixon (sketched from Tom Purdie, curiously, but only as to externals) is a villain and traitor of the first water—his own victim's victim in the end. As for poor Peter Peebles, most persistent, most unfortunate of litigants, who but Scott or Dickens could have drawn him, making us pity him at first, despise him afterwards, and be interested in him all the time?

"Wandering Willie's Tale" † is, of course, the gem of *Redgauntlet*. This was admitted by even the most

* Ann Ormiston, daughter of Jonathan Ormiston of Newcastle, and wife of George Waldie of Hendersyde, was the real Rachel. She was of a well-known North of England family of Quakers. Scott, in his note to the novel, has confounded *young* Mrs. Waldie (the Quakeress) with her mother-in-law, *old* Mrs. Waldie, who lived with the couple in their Kelso house during Scott's halcyon days at Garden Cottage. The picture reproduced of Mrs. Ann Waldie shows her as she was in middle life.

† Train finds a prototype of "Wandering Willie" in a blind harper who, with his wife and family, perished from a landslide in a gravel-pit, near Twynholm Kirk, in 1816. The spot is still known as the Harper's Hole, and the graves of the unfortunate family are to be seen in the churchyard of the parish.

captious London critics. Indeed, it is possible to speak of it as the most perfect piece of prose from Scott's pen. Men like Sir Leslie Stephen, and John Ruskin, and Andrew Lang, and Professor Saintsbury, who can hardly be accused of being rapturists, have spoken of this little story, this *conté*, with the most singular appreciation.

" I think the reason that everybody likes to read Willie's tale," wrote Ruskin, " is principally that it is so short they have time to read it, and so exciting all through that they attend completely to it. The great works of Scott require far closer attention in their intricate design and beautifully quiet execution ; and nowadays nobody has leisure to understand anything—they like to have something to dream idly over—or rush through.

" In the second place, it is all of Scott's best. Few of the novels are without scenes either impossible to rational imagination, or a little padded and insipid. Sydney Smith thus condemns the whole of *The Pirate*, and I do not myself contend for the great leap out of the cave in *Old Mortality* ; the Bailie's battle, or suspension, in *Rob Roy* ; or the caricature of Margaret's father in *Nigel*. But every word of Willie's tale is as natural as the best of Burns, with a grandeur in its main scene equal to Dante, and the waking by the gravestones in the dew is as probable as it is sweet and skilful in composition." *

The proof-sheets are still extant and bear ample

* Letter to Lieut.-Col. Fergusson, 1885.

evidence in the large number of corrections and additions that Wandering Willie's Tale was elaborated and polished with an exactness and a precision utterly foreign to the rest of Scott's work. The like may be said of *The Highland Widow*, the next best of Sir Walter's short gems. It has been said that Scott is not a stylist, that he was a great story-teller but no artist. But what do people mean by artistry? If the term is to be restricted to decoration, to a display of fine phrases which are not capable of being improved upon, then Scott is not always artistic. He is often slovenly in style, involved, prolix, deadly dull, and, as is well known, the novels abound in errors and inconsistencies. Like Shakespeare, like Dryden, he rarely blotted or corrected his manuscript, he worked on a great scale; but, on the other hand, his style is nearly always reasonably good, and, when the occasion demands it, rises to splendid and noble heights. It is the tone and the spirit which make all the difference. Scott puts his entire self into his work and so identifies himself with his characters that, apart from the mere formal setting in which his language occurs, we feel we are following one who is a consummate master of the heart and the ways of men. The letters of Darsie, for example, are conceived in the spirit of Darsie, and the story of the blind fiddler is written as no man but Scott could have done it. The description of Steenie's interview with Redgauntlet in his "own place" has never been eclipsed.

345

II

The hero of the story to which Darsie Latimer listened spellbound as he and old Willie trudged along by the shore of the Solway, it is hardly necessary to say, was Sir Robert Grierson, Laird of Lag, persecutor of the Covenanters—a name held in the highest detestation all over Nithsdale, his own country. It is hardly possible to say anything good about Lag. And yet he was not all the hardened wretch which tradition has pictured him. There were gentler and more emotional traits about the man, especially in his later years. But in the heyday of his infamy none was so intolerant, so cruel, so heartless, so bloodthirsty as he. Lag's name was the synonym for all that was ignoble and inhuman. The barbarities he practised were of the most revolting type, and such was the impression produced upon the mind of the simple Lowland peasantry that it was the custom, less than one hundred years ago, to commemorate Lag's evil deeds by a rude theatrical performance in which he appeared in the guise of a hideous monster inserting its snout into every crevice, pretending to listen for any sound of Psalm-singing or devotional exercise which would betray the whereabouts of some zealous Covenanter lurking under the sideboard and other likely places. Generally an attempt would be made to seize some youthful member of the family, but as often as not, in the struggle that followed, the disguise would reveal itself amid the universal merriment.

346

REDGAUNTLET

Sir Robert Grierson came of old Dumfriesshire stock who claimed descent from Malcolm, son of the lame lord of MacGregor, Bruce's friend and ally. The lands of Lag (in Dunscore) are said to have been bestowed on Gilbert Grierson by Henry, Earl of Orkney, in 1408, and, in any case, the estate was in possession of the family before the close of that century. Sir Robert Grierson was the great-grandson of Sir William Grierson who was knighted by King James VI. in 1608, and appointed Keeper of the Rolls in 1623, and the son of William Grierson of Barquhar, by Margaret Douglas of Mouswald. The marriage contract is dated 1654. Grierson's birth may be placed in 1655. On 9th April 1669 he was served heir to his cousin, who died a minor. From the first, Lag supported the policy of the Government against the Covenanters. His initial act in open opposition to the Hillfolk was a bond which he required all his tenants to sign, obliging themselves with their wives and children and servants never to be present at conventicles, but "to walk orderlie and in obedience to the law under the paynes and penalties contained in the Actis of Parlat maide there against, and, further, that we shall not Resett, Supplie, commune with forfault persons, intercommuned ministers, vagrant preatchers." In the following year—the year of Sharp's murder—Claverhouse made his first appearance in Dumfriesshire, where Grierson blossomed into his most active agent. In a year or two he had charge of the Kirkcudbright Military Court, established for the administration of summary justice in Galloway. Under Claverhouse, who had succeeded Sir Andrew Agnew of Lochnaw (a non-Test man) as Sheriff of Wigtownshire, Lag found full scope for his persecuting energies. He held Courts of his own, enforced the obnoxious Test Act in every possible direction, and with all his well-known ferocity brought the terrible thumb-screws into operation. With the advent of 1685, the fires of persecution burned hotter and fiercer. In that year was passed an Act of the Privy Council punishing refusal to take the Abjuration Oath with instant death. Now it was that Lag and his compeers reached the acme of their infamy. Macaulay cites the proceedings of a single fortnight as illustrative of the crimes which goaded the peasantry of the western Border into madness. It is Lag's lurid figure around whom so many of the grim legends centre. In his house at Rockhall an iron hook is still shown on which he is said to have hanged his prisoners, and a hill is pointed out from which his victims were rolled down in barrels filled with knife-blades and iron spikes. He was the most callous, most cruel, most malignant of Charles's persecuting band. It is specially recorded of him that he invariably refused the request of his victims for a brief space for prayer before they were put to death. The case of the Lockenkeit martyrs is significant of "monstrous Lag's" barbarity, while his treatment of John Bell of Whiteside is one of the most deplorable things of its kind. Bell asked to be allowed a few moments for prayer. Lag answered, " What the devil have you been doing so many years on those hills—have you not prayed enough?" Bell's body was even refused burial. When Lord Kenmure remonstrated with Lag on the subject, Grierson swore, and said, "Take him if you will, and salt him in your beef barrel." Enraged, Kenmure drew his sword and would have run Lag through had not Claverhouse intervened. On the accession of James VII., Grierson was created a Baronet, and among other appointments which fell to him about the same time was the post of Lord-Justice of Wigtownshire. It was in this capacity that Lag presided at the trial of Margaret MacLachlan and Margaret Wilson, the Wigtown martyrs, who, having refused to take the oath of abjuration, were condemned to death by drowning, but afterwards reprieved. Reprieve notwithstanding, and even the promise of a full pardon, there seems to be no reasonable doubt that the dread sentence was carried out to the letter. Much argument has been used to bolster up both positions, but the evidence adduced by Dr. Archibald Stewart, minister of Glasserton, in his *History vindicated in the case of the Wigtown Martyrs* (1869), disposes once for all of any difficulty as to the fact of drowning. An old lady (Miss Susan Heron) who was alive in 1834, remembered her grandfather saying that "There were cluds o' folk on the sands that day in clusters here and there praying for the women as they were put down."

When at last the blow fell and Lag's royal master was forced to fly from his kingdom, Nemesis followed
349

hard on the heels of Grierson. Lord Kenmure seized him and carried him prisoner to the Tolbooth at Kirkcudbright. He lay for some time also in the Edinburgh Tolbooth, but ultimately obtained release on a large bail. On 8th July 1689, he was again apprehended on suspicion of being concerned with Claverhouse and others in a plot against the Convention Parliament. But about the end of August he was liberated on account of the state of his health, after giving bail to the amount of £1500. In 1692 and 1693 he was in ward in the Canongate Tolbooth, and for several years thereafter much of his time was passed in durance vile.

Lag took no personal share in the Fifteen attempt, but allowed two of his sons, William and Gilbert, to join Kenmure's unlucky expedition into England. At Preston both were taken prisoners. There is a tradition that William lay in the Tower of London for several weeks awaiting the headsman's axe, his coffin in a corner of his cell. A fine was ultimately imposed.

As for old Lag's exit from this life, the legends are thick as leaves in Vallombrosa. He died in the last hours of the year 1733—a night of portents! Before his end came, relays of men stood from the Nith to the Turnpike (Lag's Dumfries house) constantly passing up buckets of water to cool his burning gouty limbs, " and the instant his feet touched the water it fizzed and boiled." So corpulent was Lag that a breach required to be made in the wall ere his corpse could be taken out for burial (an ascertained fact). The Evil

One, fashioned as a " corbie," alighted on his coffin and accompanied the cortège to Dunscore. The horses sent to convey the hearse were unable to move it, but a team of beautiful Spanish chestnuts yoked to it and driven by Sir Thomas Kirkpatrick (Lag's nephew) dashed off at a gallop nor halted till the burial-place was reached, where they pulled up—and died! The accounts of the funeral expenses are extant, and indicate a considerable amount of hard drinking. Curiously, they confirm some mishap to the hearse, in the items: "Paid 5s. 6d. to Charles Herries, smith, for Iron work to the Hearse"; and " to the smith for Sir Thomas Kirkpatrick's horses, 2 sh." The smith may have attended in the capacity of farrier, or some slight accident may have occurred on rough roads in a winter's day.

"The evil that men do lives after them." In Lag's case it lives in that singularly pungent pasquin known as *Lag's Elegy*, one of the most popular chapbooks of the period and for at least fifty years after Lag's day, though few copies are to be met with now. The title-page affords the best explanation as to its nature :

AN
ELEGY
IN
MEMORY

Of that Valiant Champion
Sir Robert Grierson
Of Lag

or

The *Prince of Darkness*, his Lamentation for, and Commendation of, his trusty and well-beloved Friend, the *Laird of Lag*, who died Dec. 23d, 1733.*

Wherein the Prince of Darkness sets forth the Commendation of many of his best Friends, who were chief promoters of his interest and upholders of his Kingdom in the time of Persecution.

Very useful and necessary to be read by all who desire to be well informed concerning the chief Managers and management of the late Persecuting Period.

The Tenth Edition

Glasgow

Printed by John Bryce, and Sold at his Shop, Saltmarket. 1773

---

* The commonly accepted date, but the 31st has now been established as the actual date.

SIR ROBERT GRIERSON, FIFTH BART., OF LAG
"Hugh Redgauntlet"

MRS ANN WALDIE
"Rachel Geddes"

REDGAUNTLET

The authorship is claimed for William Irving, schoolmaster of Hoddam, who died in 1782, though Carlyle told his nephew, John Aitken Carlyle, that the
author was John Orr, the old schoolmaster so graphi-
cally sketched in the *Reminiscences* as a man "religious and enthusiastic, though in practice irregular
with drink." In its scope the *Elegy* embraces all the
principal and many of the subordinate actors in the
Persecution, Claverhouse leading the way, and receiving Satan's thanks for his services, but being somewhat cruelly reminded of his conduct at Drumclog.

The work interests us from the fact that Scott possessed a copy which almost certainly furnished him
with hints for "Wandering Willie's Tale." Possibly
that most distinctive touch in his description of Sir
Robert Redgauntlet was suggested by the line—

"He bore my image on his brow,"

although the horse-shoe frown is said to have been
borrowed from the sister of Weir the Warlock, that
Major Weir who gives name to the jackanapes in the
Tale. Not unlikely Scott had a vivid recollection of
the lampooner's picture of Lag sitting "in the great
chair" in hell where he represents the cavalier as pre-
eminent amongst the damned. "Bluidy Dalyell,"
"dissolute Rothes," Sir George Mackenzie, Sir James
Turner, Lauderdale, Westerhall, Sharp, Bonshaw,
Earlshall, and the rest has each his place grouped
round the infinitely darker figure of Lag—"none for-
warder among them all." It is thus that the Arch-
Fiend soliloquises:

353   z

THE SCOTT ORIGINALS

' What fatal news is this I hear !
On earth who shall my standard bear ?
For *Lag*, who was my champion brave,
Is dead, and now laid in his grave !
The want of him is a great grief ;
He was my manager in chief,
Who sought my kingdom to improve,
And to my laws he had great love.
Could such a furious fiend as I
Shed tears, my cheeks would never dry ;
But I would mourn both night and day,
'Cause *Lag* from earth is ta'en away.

It is no wonder I am sad,
A better friend I never had,
Thro' all the large tract of his time,
He never did my ways decline ;
He was my constant trusty liege,
Who at all times did me oblige ;
But now what shall I think or say ?
By death at last he's ta'en away.

He was no coward to relent,
No man dare say he did repent
Of the good service done to me ;
For as he lived so did he die.
He bore my image on his brow,
My service he did still avow ;
He had no other deitie
But this world, the flesh, and me ;
The thing that he delighted in,
Was what the pious folks call sin ;
——, ——, and such vice,
Such pleasures were his paradise.
T' excess he drunk beer and wine
Till he was drunken like a swine.
No Sabbath day regarded he,
But spent it in profanity.

But that which raised his fame so hie,
Was the good service done to me,
In bearing of a deadly fead
'Gainst people who did pray and read.

REDGAUNTLET

Any who reads the Scriptures thro'
I'm sure they'll find but very few
Of my best friends that's mention'd there
That can with *Grier* of *Lag* compare.

Although Cain was a bloody man,
He to *Lag's* latchets never came,
In shedding of the blood of those
Who did my laws and ways oppose.

. . . . . ◄

Doeg, the Edomite, did slay
Four score and five priests in one day ;
But if you'll take the will for deed,
Brave *Lag* did Doeg far exceed :
He of the royal blood was come,
Of Ahab he was a true son ;
For he did sell himself to me
To work sin and iniquitie.
Herod for me had a great zeal,
Tho' his main purpose far did fail
He many slew by a decree,
But did not toil so much for me
As *Lag*, who in his person went
To every place where he was sent
To persecute both man and wife,
Who he knew led a pious life."

. . . . .

The Mephistophelian speaker then passes into profane history—into the record of the Persecution, in which Grierson is ever his devoted champion. And at the end Lag's " place " is well defined in the significant remark :

"Now Lag lives hot and bien with me ! "

III

Of Hugh Redgauntlet (modelled from Scott's intimate, the fifth Sir Robert Grierson*), that fiery Laird

* The fifth Sir Robert of Lag died in 1839, at the age of 102. "Usually the kindest and best-hearted of men, as many of his race have been, it was a small matter that would bring out the horse-shoe upon his forehead ; and at such a moment he was a terror to his household."—*The Laird of Lag*.

355

of the Solway Loch who gives the novel its name, a word must be said. He is, as a matter of fact, the real hero—a remarkable figure throughout. Indeed, it may be doubted if Scott ever did a better piece of work. Nobody but Scott could have done justice to this so strongly-marked and romantic character, and at the same time have retained sympathy for the nominal heroes of the story. There was much that was noble about Hugh Redgauntlet. His pride, his fidelity to his principles, his determination to carry them into effect—if he could, even his turbulent passion, are (in his case) all commendable qualities. He could love and hate with all his heart, but his love depended on submission to his will. To Darsie all his soul went out—as the only son of his murdered brother, and the last hope of his race. And yet he spoke to him sincerely when he said: "If you yourself crossed my path in opposition, I swear by the mark that darkens my brow, that a new deed should be done —a new doom should be deserved!" At the end he was better than his words. His truer nature triumphed; and to Darsie, to whom he had looked for so much, and to Lilias, who would have been his comforter in exile, he gave his benediction as he left Scotland for ever. Amid a cloister's retirement he never spoke of his past, or of the part he had played (another Fergus Mac-Ivor) in seeking to inspire lukewarm partisans with his ardour. But he never forgot it, he never repented of it, and he died with the silver box about his neck inscribed with the motto, *Haud obliviscendum.*

CHAPTER TWENTY-TWO

CHRONICLES OF THE CANONGATE
"MRS. BETHUNE BALIOL"

" The endearing elegance of female friendship."

SAMUEL JOHNSON

SCOTT HAD MANY FRIENDSHIPS ON THE
spindle-side. He was a standing contradiction to the
notion held in his own day, but not in ours, that there
can be no real intellectual intercourse, no genuine and
simple friendship between men and women, " so un-
wholesomely is the imagination of man affected by
ideas of sex." History in every age has contradicted
this theory : Michael Angelo and Vittoria Colonna,
Leibnitz and the Princess Palatine, Swift and Stella,
Cowper and Mary Unwin, Burns and Clarinda, and
many another.   In the case of Sir Walter Scott the
theory absolutely falls to pieces. His friendships with
women and his relations to the women who rejoiced
in his friendship were of the highest, the knightliest
order.

In early life he had his sister Anne, alluded to so
tenderly in the Autobiography, an invalid, but with
much of his own imaginative and romantic temperament, without his power of controlling it. It was to
Aunt Jenny that he confided his intention of becoming a " virtuoso—one who must and will know everything." He had aunts on his mother's side (well-read
women) who were his very good friends and helpers in
the time of his intellectual growth. It was a woman
(as mentioned elsewhere) who announced his genius
to the world. Nor can we forget the kind Kelso
Quakeress. In his student days, Mary Anne Erskine
359

and Jane Anne Cranstoun were the sisters who kept house for their respective brothers, Scott's bosom cronies. Miss Erskine's letter to Scott on the eve of her marriage is the quintessence of single-mindedness and trust in the good sense and graciousness of her friend: "I can express but a very very little of what I feel, and ever shall feel, for your unremitting friendship and attention. I have ever considered you as a brother, and shall now think myself entitled to make still larger claims on your confidence. I cannot tell you my distress at leaving this house where I have enjoyed so much real happiness, and giving up the service of so gentle a master. I will therefore only commend him to your care, as the last bequest of Mary Anne Erskine, and conjure you to continue to each other throughout your pilgrimage as you have commenced it." Which they did. And Scott's heart almost broke when Will Erskine died, " slain by a silly piece of gossip." Scott's relations with Miss Cranstoun have already been dealt with. Her Letters, printed in the Life, are among the liveliest correspondence Lockhart has utilised. After Scott's marriage his friendships take on a different colour. He was hastening to the period of his literary successes, and we find him forming intimacies with the Swan of Lichfield and Joanna Baillie. Much of Anna Seward's verse Scott thought "execrable," but on her death he proceeded to edit it. When Joanna Baillie's *The Family Legend* was acted in Edinburgh Scott did all he could to make it popular. His correspondence with Maria Edgeworth is among the most delightful of those *Familiar Letters* which reveal Scott in his very best and noblest moods. Then there is that other most notable group of friends which comprised his lovely chieftainesses—the Duchess of Buccleuch; Frances, Lady Douglas *; and Lady Louisa Stuart, daughter of that unlucky statesman, John, Earl of Bute. In Scott's world of women Lady Louisa was almost the central figure. A Scots lady of the olden time, who discoursed in the Doric with admirable felicity and with that pride which ladies in her position could so well affect, she was at the same time the very best critic Scott ever had, and she never spared what she had to say. To her was due much of Scott's information regarding Jeanie Deans's Duke of Argyll, whose *Memoir* Lady Louisa compiled. And she set Scott right about poor Lady Suffolk.

Another of those old-time lady friends of Scott's, to whom he was indebted for many exquisite touches here and there throughout the novels, and for many of the facts on which the novels themselves were based, was Mrs. Anne Murray Keith, the Original of that fine portrait prefixed to the *Chronicles of the Canongate*—Mrs. Martha Bethune Baliol. When she died in 1818 Scott wrote of her: "Much tradition, and of the very best kind, has died with this excellent old lady: one of the few persons whose spirits and

* Lady Louisa Stuart thought that Scott had derived some of the traits of Jeanie Deans from Lady Frances.

cheerfulness, and freshness of mind and body, made old age lovely and desirable."

Anne Keith came of the stock of the Keiths of Craig, in Kincardineshire. The story goes that young Robert Keith of Craig " ran off " with Margaret Cunningham of Caprington. A happy husband she made him, but when her five children were all young the beautiful little mother " faded like a summer cloud away." Her eldest son became Ambassador Sir Robert Keith, following his father at the Court of Vienna. The second boy, Sir Basil, became Governor of Jamaica ; and of her three charming daughters, Anne, the youngest, is the best known, although Jannie (rendered a cripple by a burning accident) deserves to be remembered as one of the founders of the Longmore Hospital for Incurables.

Anne's long life (she survived the others) was spent chiefly in Edinburgh. For us it touches interest when, in 1794, she settled in a George Square flat with her " chum " (her own word), Anne, Countess of Balcarres (cousin also), and mother of the author of "Auld Robin Gray." There the two Annes lived for several years in close and joyous comradeship, entertaining their friends, enjoying their little whist-parties, nor ever neglectful of the higher things of mind and soul. By and by a little shrinking girl of eight years, orphaned through the sudden death of her parent, the Vienna plenipotentiary, came North—a legacy which the kind old aunt accepted with " tender gratitude." When the King (George III.) heard that the child was to be cared for by Mrs. Keith, he said: "It will be fortunate for the child. She is a sensible woman."

Anne Keith's personality has done duty for the pen of two novelists. Scott knew her well. With greedy interest he listened to her budget of tales, gave them a "cocked hat" on occasion, and when the mood suited, left them plain and unvarnished. All were like seed dropped into soil where fruitage was certain. The clear-headed old lady had never the smallest doubt as to the authorship of the novels: "D'ye think I dinna ken my ain groats among ither folks' kail?" she would say playfully when the talk turned on the subject. Long after the story-teller had departed, her sweet image looked out from the pages of the *Chronicles of the Canongate*. Mr. Chrystal Croftangry's account of the Baliol lodging is imaginary, but its characteristic treasures—the old-fashioned furniture, family portraits, cabinets of japan and *or molu*, books and china, the bronzes, and the "spontoon which her elder brother bore when he was leading on a company of the Black Watch at Fontenoy" —are all highly reminiscent of the home where Scott, in his own George Square days, had spent many an entertaining and profitable hour. Mrs. Bethune Baliol's "teas," the considerateness with which she brought her guests together, her punctiliousness, the old-world propriety with which she insisted on retaining Mrs. Alice Lambskin in her boudoir, when, at eighty, and after the fashion of the old Scottish school, she entertained her gentleman visitors, the avidity with which she met her impost charges, the unwonted hospitality which ordered a glass of wine for the astonished tax-collector—not least, her good Holyrood Scots, her legacy of the ring, are doubtless all drawn from life. Take, again, the portrait of this perfect little woman : She had " ordinary features, and an ordinary form. She said herself that she was never remarkable for personal charms ; a modest admission, which was readily confirmed by certain old ladies, her contemporaries, who, whatever might have been the youthful advantages which they more than hinted had been formerly their own share, were now in personal appearance, as well as in everything else, far inferior to my accomplished friend. Mrs. Martha's features had been of a kind which might be said to wear well : their irregularity was now of little consequence, animated as they were by the vivacity of her conversation ; her teeth were excellent, and her eyes, though inclining to grey, were lively, laughing, and undimmed by time. A slight shade of complexion, more brilliant than her years promised, subjected my friend amongst strangers to the suspicion of having stretched her foreign habits as far as the prudent touch of the rouge. But it was a calumny ; for, when telling or listening to an interesting or affecting story, I have seen her colour come and go as if it played on the cheek of eighteen. Her hair was now the most beautiful white that Time could bleach, and was disposed with some degree of pretension, though in the simplest manner possible, so as to appear neatly smoothed under a cap of Flanders lace, of an old-fashioned but of a very handsome form."

Mrs. Anne Murray Keith lives also as Mrs. Sydney Hume in the pages of that novel (now long forgotten) called *Probation*, the work of the little London ward grown into a woman.* Mrs. Hume's "snug little parlour" is a much humbler dwelling than the baronial mansion of the Canongate, but many of its interior characteristics are identical, and the pen-portrait of its mistress is much akin to Scott's—" her curls of ivory white, the lofty brow, the nose which must in youth have been somewhat strong for feminine beauty, the large blue eyes, and mouth around which smiles of good-humour and genuine enjoyment usually mantled, softened the manlier conformation of the other features; and joined to the pale, though not sickly hue of the once fair skin, gave altogether an aspect at once feminine and interesting."

Mrs. Keith's life drew to its close in quiet contentment and in a sort of stately dignity. When age crept on, the " chums " left Edinburgh for ever, and found their last resting-place (in a twofold sense) within the ancient Lindsay domicile at Balcarres, where first the one died, as has been mentioned, in 1818, the companion following two years afterwards.

"I have never known any one," wrote Scott to

---

* Mrs. A. Gillespie Smyth of Gibliston, author of *Selwyn, Tales of the Moors, Memoirs and Correspondence of Sir Robert Murray Keith*, etc.

Mrs. Lindsay of Balcarres, "whose sunset was so enviably serene. Such was the benevolence of her disposition, that one almost thought Time respected a being so amiable, and laid his hand upon her so gradually that she reached the extremity of age, and the bowl was broken at the cistern before she experienced either the decay of her organs or of her excellent intellect. Nothing could have been more acceptable to me than such a token of remembrance [the legacy of a ring], for I held very dear the place which she allowed me in her esteem, and it was not the less valuable to me that I owed it, as much at least to her kind partiality in favour of a friend, as to her judgment, which was too correct to have ranked me so highly as an author. We who have, so much longer than the ordinary period of human life could have warranted, enjoyed the society of this excellent woman, and who can never know any one who can be to us what she was, cannot but reflect upon her virtues, her talents, her exquisite elasticity, and at the same time her kindness of disposition. We must always hold everything sacred that is connected with her memory, as one who lived among us with all the recollections of a former generation, yet with all the warmth of heart and clearness of intellect which enabled her to enter into the events and interests of our own."

CHAPTER TWENTY-THREE

THE SURGEON'S DAUGHTER
"GIDEON GRAY"

" Luckless is he, whom hard fates urge on
To practise as a country surgeon."

QUIS (1817).

ANNE MURRAY KEITH
"Mrs Bethune Baliol"   [see page 359

DR EBENEZER CLARKSON
"Gideon Gray"

THE AVOWAL OF THE AUTHORSHIP OF
Waverley and its august company is one of the land-
marks not only of Sir Walter's life but of Literature itself. Scott chose neither the occasion nor the
moment of the great revelation. It fell out simply
and naturally and was void of all pre-arrangements.
The mask, " like Aunt Dinah's in *Tristram Shandy*,
was laid aside with a good grace " and in the most
honourable fashion, and attended by a demonstra-
tion of enthusiasm such as Edinburgh has seldom
witnessed. On the 23rd February 1827, at the Theatrical Fund Dinner, Scott declared that " he was the
author, the total and undivided author, that (with
the exception of quotations) there was not a single
word that was not derived from himself." November
of that same year saw the first series of the *Chronicles
of the Canongate*, containing *The Highland Widow*,
the tale of *The Two Drovers*, and *The Surgeon's
Daughter*. The last of these, the longer story, was
founded on a modicum of fact furnished by that indefatigable " jackal " Train (see Appendix to Introduction to the novel). At the commencement, the
locale is Scotland, but by and by the characters are
transferred to the pomp and glitter of an Indian
Court, where, however, Scott preserves them unchanged amid every turn of fortune and situation.
The Hindostan scenes are spirited—that is to say, for

one who had never been in India. Colonel Ferguson of Huntlyburn—the Mackerris of " Mr. Croftangry's Conclusion "—talked with Scott on matters connected with the East. The novel, especially towards its close, is crowded with improbabilities, and on the whole it is not particularly interesting. The dénouement is dramatic enough, but too glaring to be pleasing. One little incident—a tale within a tale—is worth pages of the story—where Sadhu Sing sits by the grave of his bride Mora to his own dying day.

As for the *dramatis personæ* from the old land, pretty Menie Gray, gentle and sweet, wins all hearts. Her lover (or once her lover), Richard Middlemas, is the most consummate, most unredeemable scoundrel in the Waverley series. Hartley, true-blue hero to the last, hardly gets his deserts.

With the surgeon himself, Gideon Gray—who has no connection with the Indian part of the tale—we are on ground in which Scott was at his best—the delineation of Lowland life and manners. The scenes in the street at Middlemas, which is held to be Selkirk, the race of the three Luckies, and the portrait of the country doctor, are wholly admirable. Scott's romances teem with representatives of law and divinity, but how seldom are the men of medicine admitted into the golden circle! Yet Scott had a supreme respect for the medical profession. Many of his forebears belonged to its honourable guild, and his own repeated illnesses brought him into close touch with some of the most noted practitioners of the day. It is Clarkson

of Selkirk, Scott's own Abbotsford doctor, who stands
before the world in the character of Gideon Gray,
" a man of such reputation that he had been often
advised to exchange the village and its meagre circle
of practice for Edinburgh. There is no creature in
Scotland that works harder and is more poorly re-
quited than the country doctor, unless, maybe, his
horse. Yet the horse is, and indeed must be, hardy,
active, and indefatigable, in spite of a rough coat and
indifferent condition ; and so you will often find in
his master, under a blunt exterior, professional skill
and enthusiasm, intelligence, humanity, courage,
and science."   Scott was unquestionably thinking of
Mungo Park (who is referred to in the passage quoted)
as well as of Ebenezer Clarkson, when he limned his
so sympathetic picture.* Scott and Park were on the
best of terms. In the Ashestiel years they met frequently. Once, on the top of Williamhope Ridge,
Park's horse stumbled and nearly fell, when Scott
and he were crossing the hill to Foulshiels : " I am
afraid, Mungo, that is a bad omen," said Scott. To
which Park made answer, smiling, " Freits follow
those who look to them." Returning from his first
African journey, Park settled as a surgeon in Peebles,
but the incessant and uncertain calls, and wandering
by night and day, which a rural doctor's life entailed,
forced him back to the Niger, whence he never re-

* Traits of Dr. Thomas Anderson of Selkirk no doubt appear
in the picture. See Dr. John Brown's " Our Gideon Grays " in
Horae Subsecivae.

turned. Dr. Clarkson, on the other hand, pursued his noble, self-sacrificing career for more than half a century. Few men were held in higher veneration all over the Border. Large-hearted and generous, he left no call for help unanswered, no case of need neglected. And, like all his brethren, much of his good and beneficent work was done with no hope of financial recompense. Clarkson was equally distinguished as a citizen. For many years he held the office of Chief Magistrate of Selkirk, and measures originated by him for the public weal are in operation still. After a life of surpassing usefulness, honouring to his profession, worthy of the kind and genial soul that he was, and the good Christian too, Dr. Clarkson died in the winter of 1847. He was born at Dalkeith in 1763, was married twice, and left two sons, one of whom was medical aide-de-camp to the King of Oude, the other, a physician in Melrose for over forty years—also Sir Walter's devoted friend, who performed the last sad offices to the dead hero slain in as noble a fight as any that history has recorded.*

* " I was present when Scott died. I shut his eyes, and opened his head for my father the next day—not that we had any doubt it was softening of the brain, but because the medical men at Edinburgh particularly wished it done. I was called away when watching by Sir Walter the day he died, and had to gallop up the hill towards Laidlaw's house to attend a patient, and, upon returning to send medicine, left my horse ready at the door to mount again immediately for Abbotsford. I then received a message from Lockhart saying, ' Do come for God's sake—I think Sir Walter is going.' When I got back he said, ' Doctor, you are barely in time,' but I had the melancholy satisfaction of closing his eyes while they all stood or knelt about the bed."—*From a conversation.*

CHAPTER TWENTY-FOUR

IS SCOTT SELF-REVEALED?

" Every author, in some degree, portrays himself in his works even be it against his will."

GOETHE.

THIS IS A QUITE PERTINENT QUESTION—
as pertinent as Professor Dowden's " Is Shakespeare
self-revealed ? " It can scarcely be doubted that in
the Waverleys we are constantly faced by a portraiture of the immortal author himself. More than any
other novelist, mayhap, it may be said that Sir Walter sat for his own picture in his own resplendent
studio. He makes himself not infrequently the hero
of the story, or one of its central figures at all events.
For those who are acquainted with Scott's history,
and who know their Lockhart, the difficulty in the
way of identification is trifling. Scott's character,
and sentiments, and foibles, shine with a conspicuous-
ness which is as remarkable as it is evident. Many
passages are autobiographic gems of the first water.
His early life at Smailholm, the years of delicate
health, his familiarity with the stories of Border romance and chivalry, and with the old-fashioned rural
life of Southern Scotland, all find an echo in the pages
both of the Poems and Novels. It was at Sandyknowe
that he became inspired with that sentiment of Jacobitism which produced the most touching passages in
Waverley and *Redgauntlet*. It is Scott's own boyhood
which is recalled in the account that Frank Osbaldistone gives of his nurse's tales of the Border. Old
Mabel Rickets is a Northumbrian, and tells her stories
from an English point of view, but the instances described are Scott's own, and it is his own youthful

mind which was fed upon the rhymes and ballads of the north country, and the legends of the Black Douglas and Wat the Devil. It is the quiet simple life of his native Lowlands which Scott has limned in *Guy Mannering* and the *Black Dwarf* and the *Monastery*. Innumerable passages might be quoted to show where and how his spoils had been gathered by the banks of the Tweed and the green braes of Sandyknowe and Brotherstone. Take his schooldays, again. Are they not recorded in the Letters of Alan Fairford and Darsie Latimer ? Scott was not a scholar in the exact sense, but he won praise for his appreciation of the classic authors, and his devotion to verse was keen and eager. From an early age he even tried his hand at it. The "bickers" or street fights which formed so common a feature in the school life of Edinburgh are recalled in *Redgauntlet* and in the Greenbreeks Episode of the General Introduction. Scott's College days, the time of his law apprenticeship, and his experience as an advocate have their undistorted reflection in the Waverley mirror. For Scott's early studies—the books which he read—one has to turn to the opening of *Waverley*—Shakespeare, Milton, Spenser, Drayton : the romantic literature of Italy, Froissart's *Chronicles* with their heart-stirring and eye-dazzling descriptions of war and of tournaments, English and Scottish and Spanish metrical romances, and all the lore of the Border. As with Edward Waverley, the education of Scott was of a somewhat desultory nature. Lockhart describes two notebooks, of date 1792, the year of Scott's calling to the Bar, which afford some idea of his private studies during that period. The whole gamut of European Literature seems to have engaged his attention, from the Norse Sagas and translations of Italian canzonets to Hall's Satires and *Albania*. Probably no other Scotsman of his years had a mind so stored with such a vast amount of curious and minute lore. Then the pursuits and the recreations of the young lawyer are constantly cropping up in the novels. His commissions to the Highlands and intercourse with such Highland gentlemen as Buchanan of Cambusmore and Ramsay of Ochtertyre, leave their indelible mark on the pages of romance. Nor can we overlook the social side of Scott's life, and its contribution to the triumph of his efforts in fiction. In depicting the "high jinks" of *Guy Mannering*, for instance, Scott was simply describing a feature of that wild conviviality which was fashionable among the Edinburgh youth of his time. He himself was dubbed "Colonel Grogg," always ready for any revel—to sail with the Clerks in their lugger, and lay the foundation of the sea knowledge displayed in *The Pirate*, to gain at Bayle's, Fortune's, and Walker's his intimate acquaintance with tavern life, to eat oysters in the Covenant Close, or drink delight of battle in street fight and playhouse riot.

It was about 1791 that Scott fell in love with pretty Williamina Belsches, and how he loved her is known to all who love Scott. The affair has been much discussed, but may be capable of a simple explanation.

Miss Williamina was a bit coquettish, Scott was a poor man, the parents did not favour the suit, and there was a wealthier Romeo. The great thing is that Scott's non-success did not damp his prospects, did not spoil him. It rather stimulated his literary leanings and activities. Whilst some other men no doubt would have become depressed, and fallen into careless habits, and lost interest in life, it was the reverse with Scott. He never ceased to remember his passion, and to carry to his latest day a haunting vision of the sweet face of his beloved, but that, in his case, rejection did not degenerate into dejection, is one of those happy concomitants for which the centuries must be everlastingly grateful. Scott's love affair was the immediate cause of his appearance in print : it inspired some of the finest passages in his longer poems and flung a tender melancholy round many scenes in the novels. His lost love lives in *Redgauntlet* as the Lady of the Green Mantle, and it is this experience that adds pathos to such characters as Jonathan Oldbuck and Josiah Cargill. There is a passage in *Kenilworth* which is almost certainly borrowed from personal experience, when Tressilian says, " Nothing is perhaps more dangerous to the future happiness of men of deep thought and retired habits than the entertaining an early, long and unfortunate attachment. It frequently sinks so deep into the mind that it becomes their dream by night and their vision by day—mixes itself with every source of interest and enjoyment, and when blighted and withered by final disappointment it seems as if the springs of the heart were dried up along with it."

The personal element in *Rob Roy* is especially striking. Frank Osbaldistone is Scott, through and through, more completely perhaps than any of his heroes. And the love episodes in that novel can, again, have only one basis—Scott's first and fondest attachment. The library scenes where Frank and Di read Ariosto together,—above all, that brief, tearful farewell spoken in the moonlight, are clearly autobiographic. It has been shown, too, that Frank's political creed is Scott's own: Jacobitism offends his judgment while appealing to his sentiment. He is no singer, but is said to have sung a song while drunk. The same incident happened to Scott. The Osbaldistones, like the Scotts, are a long-descended family of country gentlemen, and Frank's father, like Scott's, has been the first to engage in business. Frank, like Scott, hated the drudgery of a commercial life. It went against his grain, and so he escaped from its trammels. Even so Scott longed to be free from the weary round of purely mundane affairs and to occupy instead the coveted position of a landed proprietor.

The autobiographic element is further seen in the exquisite portraiture of Colonel Mannering, a man of the world, but a gentleman every inch of him. In those clever and ingenious letters to Richard Heber, by John Leicester Adolphus, particular mention is made of Mannering's high qualities as an argument that the author of *Guy Mannering* and of

Marmion are one and the same. " Colonel Mannering is one of the most striking representations I am
acquainted with of a gentleman in feelings and in
manners, in habits, taste, predilection . . . a gentleman even in prejudices, passions, and caprices. It
was no vulgar hand that drew the lineaments of
Colonel Mannering." Lockhart tells that when *Guy
Mannering* was published, Hogg said to Professor
Wilson : " I have done wi' doubts now. Colonel Mannering is just Walter Scott painted by himself."
When this was told to Scott he smiled in approbation
of the Shepherd's shrewdness, and often in speaking
to Ballantyne he referred to himself under the name
of Colonel Mannering. That the identification should
have been so possible and so just, was joyfully admitted by Scott. It was a tribute to the essentially
splendid character of the man, and coming as it
did from James Hogg, Scott was doubly gratified.
Mannering's characterisation corresponded closely to
those of his creator. He was a born gentleman. When
we first make his acquaintance he is a man who exhibits a deep and generous delight in nature. He has
a certain amount of family pride, and he was passionately in love. " Beneath his eye lay the modern
house—an awkward mansion indeed in point of archi-
tecture, but well situated and with a warm, pleasant exposure. 'How happily,' thought our hero,
' would life glide on in such a retirement ! On the
one hand, the striking remnants of ancient grandeur
with the secret consciousness of family pride which

they inspire : on the other, enough of modern elegance and comfort to satisfy every modern wish. Here then, and with thee, Sophia.' We shall not pursue a lover's day-dream any further. Mannering stood a moment with arms folded and then turned to the ruined castle." Years pass and he returned to Ellangowan : "His appearance, voice and manner produced an instantaneous effect in his favour. He was a handsome, tall, thin figure dressed in black, as appeared when he laid aside his riding coat : his age might have been between forty and fifty : his cast of features grave and interesting and his air somewhat military. Every point of his appearance and address bespoke the gentleman." He was then the famous Colonel Mannering from the West Indies, with all his blushing honours thick upon him—the relief of Cuddieburn, the defence of Chingalore, the defeat of the great Mahrattan chief Ram Jolli Bundleman. His servant says of him : " You never saw a plainer creature in your life than our old Colonel and yet he has a spice of the devil in him too." So had Scott. Again, Mannering's marriage was not altogether happy. " I told you," he writes to a friend, " I had that upon my mind which I should carry to my grave with me —a perpetual aloes in the draught of existence." His wife, a gay and thoughtless young thing, appeared to flirt with a young man, and her husband took fire. They came to an understanding, but the wife died shortly afterwards, leaving behind her the sprightly daughter who became Julia Mannering. " Julia is very like a certain friend of mine," said her father; "she has a quick and lively imagination and keen feelings which are apt to exaggerate both the good and evil they find in life. She is a charming girl, however, as generous and spirited as she is lovely. She was of middle size, or rather less, but formed with much elegance, piercing dark eyes and jet black hair of great length corresponded with the vivacity and intelligence of features in which were blended a little haughtiness and a little bashfulness, a great deal of shrewdness and some power of humorous sarcasm." This is clearly a picture of Charlotte Carpenter in the early married years of Scott's life. Elsewhere, Scott speaks of her as "a brunette as dark as a blackberry, but her person and face are very engaging." It was not entirely a love match. Lady Scott's temperament and tastes were very different from those of Scott. She had little interest in his studies, and it is said that she never read the Waverleys. She was "uppish," and made full use of her position as Lady of Abbotsford. Other hints have been handed down which do not need to be repeated here. On the whole, Charlotte Carpenter made Scott quite a good wife, and managed for him many things he could not have attempted himself. Scott's grief at her death, and his entries in the Journal, are among the most affecting things in the Biography.

To return to Mannering. Further points of resemblance between Scott and the Colonel are found in the latter's quick, though fairly well-controlled tem-

per, in his stoicism, and his interest in the occult
sciences. In his youth he studied with an old clergyman who was an astrologer and made himself pro-
ficient in the technical process of astrological research.
He is therefore able to read the horoscope of the
young heir of Ellangowan. Scott's fancy for occult
questions is one of the commanding things in his career. Lockhart touches on some aspects of this, but
the novels are our best sources of information. In how
many of these does Scott demonstrate the action of
mystical powers? They are seldom without a touch
of the supernatural. His presentation of the Unseen
is often a blemish in the Waverleys—the White Lady,
for example. Yet that was the way in which Scott
was built. He was capable of feeling supernatural fear
(as at Glamis Castle) and of imparting the feeling to
others. He was not altogether a believer, but the
subject had considerable attractions for him, as witness his *Letters on Demonology and Witchcraft*, a work
of Scott's declining age which, naturally, does not represent him at his best. The apparitions in the *Bride
of Lammermoor* (the vision of Blind Alice at the fountain—the best wraith in fiction) and in *The Betrothed*
are accounted for by the fact that the first of these
is part of the legend, and the second that it is but a
dream *et præterea nihil*. While Norna of the Fitful
Head seems in league with powers outside of life's ordinary realm, there is always a suspicion that the information which she gives, and in which she seldom makes
mistakes, may all be due to her paid agents, to her

weather wisdom, to her knowledge of the country and of human nature. The crowning triumph in Scott's treatment of the supernormal is Wandering Willie's Tale. "Perhaps he succeeded here because he wrote of the demon world in the manner of the great Scottish writers from Dunbar to Burns,—with bristling hair and leery eye, with fearful reverence, and comical attempt, with ludicrous horror, and familiar fear."

It is plain, then (not to further labour the point), that Scott affixed his own particular portrait in the Waverley Gallery. The merely physical man—his intellectual qualities, and tastes, and pursuits, his ambitions, his loves, and hopes, and fears, have been all strongly delineated. While he painted others, he did not pass himself over. While he judged others, he did not fail to sit in judgment on his own characteristics. He never praises himself unduly. On the contrary, he is often severely hard on himself, satirising, for instance, his own antiquarian foibles in Oldbuck, and unveiling the very secrets of his heart, and the haunting sorrows of his life, in the story of Chrystal Croftangry, that dweller in the Canongate whose autobiography is among the very best of Scott's work— haunted by heart-throbs which not even the dullest ear can miss.

CHAPTER TWENTY-FIVE

SCOTT'S CLERICAL CHARACTERS

"There goes the parson, oh illustrious spark!"

COWPER.

THAT SCOTT HAD IN HIM A VEIN OF GENU-
ine and reverent piety, admits of no dispute. He seldom talked on the subject of religion, as indeed he
seldom talked about any of the deeper feelings of the
heart. The Scots are a curiously silent folk where
such questions are concerned, and Sir Walter followed
the characteristics of the race. Essentially broad-
minded, Scott allied himself to no definite kind of orthodoxy. But that he had grasped something of the
innermost secret of the Christian faith is apparent all
through the Biography. Few men, Professor Saintsbury says, have ever so well observed the one half of
the apostle's doctrine as to pure religion : and if he did
not keep himself (in the matter of the secret partner-
ship and other things) altogether unspotted from the
world, the suffering of his last seven years may surely
be taken as a more than sufficient purification.

What was Scott's attitude to the organised Christian Church of his day ? He was a Presbyterian for a
considerable portion of his life and, as a matter of fact,
was elected an elder in the parish of Duddingston,
though he is never likely to have acted in that capacity. He was a member of the General Assembly for
1806 and 1807 and, at the same time, of the Edinburgh Presbytery. He had nothing but Presbyterian
blood in his veins. Brought up under parents whose
religion was strongly Calvinistic, he tells us how his
boyish nature rebelled against the discipline of the
387

Presbyterian Sabbath, and how it was that he turned to his beloved books to relieve the gloom of one dull sermon succeeding another and the tedium annexed to the duties of the day. " Eh sirs, mony a weary, weary sermon ha'e I heard beneath that steeple," was his remark when the spire of the Tron Kirk, where his father worshipped, perished in the great fire of 1824. A reconciliation to church-going seems to have come over him in early manhood. For it was in Greyfriars Churchyard on the dispersal of the congregation on a wet Sunday that he met the Lady of the Green Mantle, his first love, whom he was afterwards in the habit of escorting home.

Scott had strong leanings, however, towards the Episcopal Church of Scotland. Whilst resident in Edinburgh, he attended St. George's Chapel in York Place—the oldest existing Episcopal place of worship in the metropolis. He may have been attracted hither by the fact that the Rev. Alexander Cleeve, B.A., his tutor before he went to the High School, was incumbent. On the other hand, it should be mentioned that Scott's three elder children were baptized by the Rev. Daniel Sandford (afterwards Bishop) of Charlotte Chapel, at the west end of Rose Street (now a Baptist place of worship). It is probable that Scott and his wife sat under Sandford for some years after their marriage in 1797. There is no question that from 1810 to 1825, when Abbotsford was completed, St. George's was their church. An entry in the accounts records that the treasurer had " received from Mr. W.

Scott the sum of three guineas, being the rent of three sittings in Pew No. 81 for the year ending Whitsunday 1811." Scott's daughters, Sophia and Anne, were confirmed in St. George's, and on Saturday evening, 29th April 1820, Sophia was married to Lockhart by the Rev. Richard Quaile Shannon, the incumbent. In the Ashestiel years, and at Abbotsford, Scott was accustomed to read the Church of England Service on Sundays, adding sometimes a sermon from some divine whom he specially favoured, English or Scottish. He seldom went to church (*parcus et infrequens cultor deorum*), though he did make occasional worshipping visits to Yarrow, "the shrine of my ancesters"; and to Melrose, which was his own parish kirk. He attended Selkirk church in his capacity as Sheriff on official occasions. Not infrequently—more especially in later years —he turned to his task on Sundays as on week-days, a proceeding neither good for him nor his task: "The ladies went to church: I, God forgive me! finished the *Chronicles* [*of the Canongate*]."

All this notwithstanding, Scott's religion was honest and sincere, and his regard for the Church and the ministerial profession was borne out by his many clerical friendships on both sides of the Border. It is on record that he allowed his temper to get the better of him when informed that a Galashiels tradesman with whom he was in the habit of doing business at Abbotsford, was also a preacher.

The Waverleys abound with representatives of the cloth, and some of Scott's most pleasing characters are in the ranks of the clergy. It is a mistake to imagine that Scott banned the Reformation and the principles of Presbyterianism. He has not a word to say against either. In *The Monastery* and *The Abbot*, Scott recognised the preachers of the Reformed faith as exactly the sort of men "suited by Providence for the times." In Elias Henderson, for instance (who is thought to be John Knox on a small scale), he gives us a most admirable specimen of a Protestant chaplain— a man of solid accomplishments, of good natural parts, and, as is shown by his interview with Queen Mary at Loch Leven, courteous and courageous, civil-spoken, and possessed of fine delicacy of feeling. The Rev. Henry Warden is more pronounced in his views. The vehemence of his zeal made it necessary for him to fly from Edinburgh, and being sheltered by Julian Avenel there is a good deal of honest plain talk with that licentious and outlawed Baron (who, by the way, had his prototype in the laird of Black Ormiston). Warden insisted upon Avenel's marriage with the wronged Catherine :

"' Is she thy house-dame ? ' said the preacher . . . ' Is she, in brief, thy wife ? '

" Avenel answered that she was handfasted to him.

"' Handfasted ! ' repeated Warden.

"' Knowest thou not that rite, holy man ? ' said Avenel in the same tone of derision ; ' then I will tell thee. We Border men are more wary than your inland clowns of Fife and Lothian : no jump in the dark for us, no clenching the fetters around our wrists till we know how they will wear with us : we take our wives like our horses, upon trial. When we are handfasted, as we term it, we are man and wife for a year and a day : that space gone by, each may choose another mate, or at their pleasure may call the priest to marry them for life, and this we call handfasting.'

" 'Then,' said the preacher, ' I tell thee, noble Baron, in brotherly love to thy soul, it is a custom licentious, gross, and corrupted, and, if persisted in, dangerous, yea damnable. It binds thee to the frail being while she is still the object of desire: it relieves thee when she is most the object of pity: it gives all to brutal sense and nothing to generous and gentle affection. I say to thee that he who can meditate the breach of such an engagement, abandoning the deluded woman and the helpless offspring, is worse than the birds of prey : for of them the males remain with their mates until the nestlings can take wing. Above all I say is it contrary to the pure Christian doctrine, which assigns woman to man as the partner of his labour, the soother of his evil, his helpmeet in peril, his friend in affliction : not as the toy of his looser hours, or as a flower which once cropped he may throw aside at pleasure.' "

In *Guy Mannering* Scott has painted an excellent portrait of Dr. Erskine, the leader of the Evangelical Party in the Church of Scotland :

" The colleague of Dr. Robertson ascended the pulpit. His external appearance was not prepossessing. A remarkably fair complexion, strangely contrasted with a black wig without a grain of powder ; a narrow chest and a stooping posture ; hands which, placed like props on either side of the pulpit, seemed necessary rather to support the person than to assist the gesticulation of the preacher ; no gown, not even that of Geneva, a tumbled band and a gesture which seemed scarce voluntary, were the first circumstances which struck a stranger. ' The preacher seems a very ungainly person,' whispered Mannering to his new friend.

" ' Never fear, he's the son of an excellent Scottish lawyer ; he'll show blood, I'll warrant him.'

" The learned Counsellor predicted truly. A lecture was delivered, fraught with new, striking, and entertaining views of Scripture history, a sermon in which the Calvinism of the Kirk of Scotland was ably supported, yet made the basis of a sound system of practical morals, which should neither shelter the sinner under the cloak of speculative faith or of peculiarity of opinion, nor leave him loose to the waves of unbelief and schism. Something there was of an antiquated turn of argument and metaphor, but it only served to give zest and peculiarity to the style of elocution. The sermon was not read ; a scrap of paper containing the heads of the discourse was occasionally referred to, and the enunciation, which at first seemed imperfect and embarrassed, became, as the preacher warmed in his progress, animated and distinct ; and although the discourse could not be quoted as a correct specimen of pulpit eloquence, yet

Mannering had seldom heard so much learning, metaphysical acuteness, and energy of argument brought into the service of Christianity.

" ' Such,' he said, going out of the church, ' must have been the preachers to whose unfearing minds and acute, though sometimes rudely exercised, talents, we owe the Reformation.'

" ' And yet that reverend gentleman,' said Pleydell, ' whom I love for his father's sake and his own, has nothing of the sour or pharisaical pride which has been imputed to some of the early fathers of the Calvinistic Kirk of Scotland. His colleague and he differ, and head different parties in the kirk, about particular points of church discipline ; but without for a moment losing personal regard or respect for each other, or suffering malignity to interfere in an opposition steady, constant, and apparently conscientious on both sides.'

" ' And you, Mr. Pleydell, what do you think of their points of difference ? '

" ' Why, I hope, Colonel, a plain man may go to heaven without thinking about them at all ; besides, *inter nos*, I am a member of the suffering and Episcopal Church of Scotland—the shadow of a shade now, and fortunately so ; but I love to pray where my fathers prayed before me, without thinking worse of the Presbyterian forms because they do not affect me with the same associations.' "

Here he is fair to the character of Erskine ; and it may be said, generally speaking, he deals fairly with the clerical character throughout the series. None

393

of Scott's ministers are villains in disguise, or immoral men, or sneaking sycophants, or hypocrites, or anything approaching thereto. In the main they are all honourable men, no matter their weaknesses and failings. Scott followed Goldsmith and Fielding in depicting the average clergyman of his day. In the *Vicar of Wakefield*, Dr. Primrose is said to be rich in heavenly wisdom, but poor, indeed, in all worldly knowledge; amiable, charitable, devout—a pious, good man: and in Fielding's *Joseph Andrews*, Parson Adams is, according to Scott himself, one of the richest productions of the muse of fiction. It is divines of this school whom Scott introduces into his romances. He steers clear of a tendency common to Dickens and Thackeray to make the preachers of the gospel somewhat contemptible and unworthy creatures. Scott does not place his clerical characters upon a pinnacle height, making heroes of them and pushing them to the front in the evolution of his story. But they are mostly men of attractive personality, and with probably two exceptions there is nothing repellent about them. In *Waverley*, the parish minister of Cairnvreckan, Mr. Morton (Scott's ideal of a divine), preached and believed in practical religion. His creed may be summed up in his words to Waverley, "Evil to him that thinks otherwise, or who holds church government and ceremonies as the exclusive gauge of Christian faith or moral virtue."

In *Guy Mannering* the immortal Dominie is an incomparable figure. He never had a kirk of his own (as we have seen), but the singleness of his motives and the supreme candour of the man are exquisite. He was a dungeon of learning, too. The incident in which he goes off his road to argue with the Moffat schoolmaster as to a quantity in one of Horace's Odes, is one of Sir Walter's most illuminating asides. Sampson's account of what he had done as Lucy's tutor, and his pride in his pupil, are admirable: " By my poor aid you will find her perfect in the tongues of France and Italy and even of Spain—in reading and writing her vernacular tongue, and in arithmetic and book-keeping by double and single entry. I say nothing of her talents of shaping, and hemming, and governing a household, which, to give every one their due, she acquired, not from me, but from the housekeeper. Nor do I take merit for her performance upon stringed instruments."

Mr. Blattergowl in *The Antiquary*, who had been Moderator of Assembly, a portly gentleman equipped in a buzz-wig, upon the top of which was an equilateral cocked hat, was a good man, in the old Scottish Presbyterian phrase, Godward and manward. "No divine was more attentive in visiting the sick and afflicted, in catechising the youth, or instructing the ignorant, and in reproving the erring."

In *The Heart of Midlothian*, Reuben Butler passed through his college career with a considerable struggle. He had a weak constitution and was a little lame (was Scott thinking of himself?). He had to wait a long time for promotion, which only came through the

395

good offices of the Argyll family, after he had suffered many hardships and privations, including a brief but humiliating imprisonment, the result of his having been forced by the rioters to administer the last consolations to the doomed Porteous. Butler was a character in which worth and good sense and simplicity were the principal ingredients. When offered a living in England at twelve hundred a year, he makes this reply to Sir George Staunton : " I could not accept it. I have no mind to enter into a debate between the churches, but I was brought up in mine own, have received her ordination, am satisfied of the truth of her doctrines, and will die under the banner I have enlisted to." " What may be the value of your preferment," inquired Sir George, " unless I am asking an indiscreet question ? " " Probably a hundred a year, one year with another, besides my glebe and pasture land." " And you scruple to exchange that for twelve hundred a year without alleging any damning difference of doctrine betwixt the two churches of England and Scotland." " On that, sir, I have reserved my judgment. There may be much good and certainly saving means in both, but every man must act according to his lights. I hope I have done, and am in the course of doing, my Master's work in this Highland parish : and it would ill become me for the sake of lucre to leave my sheep in the wilderness." Excellently spoken, and typical of the man who seems to carry the fortunes of the story in his hand !

In *The Bride of Lammermoor*, the Reverend Peter

Bide-the-Bent, the minister whose aid Lady Ashton invoked to assist her in dissolving the engagement between Ravenswood and Lucy, is of the strictest order and the most rigid orthodoxy; but with all the more severe prejudice and principles of his sect he possessed a sound judgment and had learned sympathy even in that very school of persecution where the heart is so frequently hardened.

The Rev. Josiah Cargill in *St. Ronan's Well* is one of the most beautiful of Scott's portraits, " a man of singularly sweet disposition, with bright, soft, expressive eyes." His love-story accounts to a great extent for his hermit life and his utter absent-mindedness. In him Scott has painted the best type of the Scottish rural pastor of the olden time. He is a man of taste and refinement, scrupulous as to his person, though careless as to his dress, and absolutely conscientious in the discharge of his public duties. He is not afraid to speak boldly on occasion and to reprove irreverence, as witness his interviews with Touchwood and the gossipy Lady Penelope Penfeather (whom he mistakes for Clara Mowbray) and the false Earl of Etherington, Lady Binks's acknowledged gallant. Cargill cut a good figure in the pulpit, and he had long won the love of his little flock. He might at times preach over the heads of his people ; " but what of that, as I am aye telling them," said the indomitable Meg Dods, " them that pays stipend get aye the mair for their siller ! "

In *The Highland Widow*, the Rev. Michael Tyrie is a pleasing specimen of the parish clergyman—a kind and faithful friend to Elspat MacTavish and her son.

The Rev. Nehemiah Solsgrace, in *Peveril of the Peak*, an ejected Presbyterian divine, who appears only a few times, is characterised as a good but illiberal man, and the Rev. Nehemiah Holdenough, of *Woodstock*, combined with his kind-heartedness and courage a temperament somewhat irascible and disputatious.

To return to the clerical characters in *Old Mortality*. They are four in number—Gabriel Kettledrummle, Peter Poundtext, Ephraim Macbriar, and Habakkuk Mucklewrath. Ugly names, and admittedly suggestive of an attempt to besmirch the memory of men who (spite of all their faults) were singularly in earnest, and magnificently heroic. Scott had no such intention. It is inconceivable that this big-hearted, high-minded, always generous Scotsman could have employed his pen with so ignoble an object. Dr. M'Crie believed that he did, and fell virulently foul of the picture given in *Old Mortality*. He will listen to no word in defence of his great contemporary. Knox's biographer, it must be allowed, is quite as fanatical in his own way, as he maintains Scott to be in his. Scott built up his story, he says, on prejudice, on a determined aversion to the Hill-men, on a narrow distorted view of their whole circumstances. He wrote from the standpoint of a convinced prelatic. He could see no good in the " beastly Covenanters," hence his tirade. But what are the facts? No one nowadays will deny that the Covenanters (good men though they were) in many respects were misguided men and themselves guilty of gross exaggerations. They magnified many times the differences which separated them from their opponents. They clung to the notion that there was only one true Cause, and they held that all who were outside that Cause were traitors and on their way to perdition. That they were bigoted, selfish, fanatical, revengeful, seems to be the reading of history. And it was this one-sided and rancorous element which Scott put in the pillory. He caricatured Covenanting manners, but not the men themselves. Scott would be the first to admit that in most of the Christian virtues, prayerfulness, diligent study of the Scriptures, self-control, the men of the Covenant were a long way ahead of their antagonists. Even Kettledrummle, that contumacious thunderer, and the wild and maniacal Mucklewrath are characteristically better men than the profligate Sergeant Bothwell or the scapegrace Tam Halliday, both of whom fought on the side of Charles. The period was such as to produce enthusiasts. The situation was desperate, and both parties went to extremes. It was in the very nature of the Covenanters to behave as they did, faced by wrongs and oppressions which they believed were remedial, but persistence in which burned into their breasts, rousing within them the bitterest resentment, and obsessing them with the idea that, like the Children of Israel, they were under a divine mandate to extirpate, root and branch, from the land whatsoever, according to their fancy, savoured of anti-Christ, what-soever was derogatory to that true-blue faith for which they had sworn to shed their last drop of blood. It must be confessed that Scott did paint a rather lurid picture in the fiendish Mucklewrath. But such a being as Habakkuk Mucklewrath never existed, or if he did, his mental balance had become unhinged under the terrible strain. Kettledrummle is a clumsy caricature of the more rigid divine. About Poundtext there was much of the man of the world. " Warfare had little charm for him in comparison with a theological treatise or pipe and a jug of ale which he called his studies." Macbriar is far the most natural of the group and was probably modelled (as said elsewhere) from Hugh M'Kail, whom he closely resembles in his youth, his eloquence, his ardour, his renunciation of the Stuarts, his claim to the right of defensive arms, and, finally, in his exultant death. In actual men of the Covenant, heroes and martyrs such as Alexander Peden, Richard Cameron, Donald Cargill, James Renwick, and others, Scott had historical data of the best sort lying to his hand which he might have devoted to the noblest ends. He did, however, make some atonement for what have been called the " excrescences " of *Old Mortality* when he wrote *The Heart of Midlothian*. There the all-pervading character is that most winsome of the daughters of the Covenant, true-hearted Jeanie Deans. And, later, in the *Tales of a Grandfather*, Scott is conspicuously fair in his treatment of the Covenanters—

those men of the moss-hags and the rough corries of the south country, of whom, despite all cavilling and criticism, it must unhesitatingly be said that they sealed Freedom's Sacred Cause.

To sum up : there is very little in Scott's work to throw discredit on Presbyterianism or ministers of that persuasion. Scott, as we have seen, favoured the Episcopal mode of worship. " He took up early in life," says Lockhart, " a repugnance to the method in which public worship is conducted in the Scottish Establishment and adhered to the sister church, whose system of government and discipline he believed to be the fairest copy of the primitive quality, and whose litanies and collects he reverenced as having been transmitted to us from the age immediately succeeding that of the apostles." Snatches of the *Te Deum* and the *Dies Iræ* were repeated amid the delirium of the death-bed, and on his funeral day ministers of the Church of Scotland conducted a service at Abbotsford, while the beautiful burial service of the Church of England was said at the grave by one of his oldest friends. Religion comforted Sir Walter at the last. For him there was only " one Book," out of which Lockhart read the message of the eternal hope. There is not one of his own books which does not bear in some aspect of it genuine testimony to the moral and religious convictions of its author. The passage has often been quoted in which it is said that he never wrote a line that could have embittered the bed of death. " His works teach the practical lessons of

THE SCOTT ORIGINALS

morality and Christianity in the most captivating form—unobtrusively and unaffectedly." "The few passages in his Diaries in which he alludes to his own religious feelings and practices, show clearly the sober, serene, and devoted frame of mind in which he habitually contemplated man's relations with his Maker: the modesty with which he shrank from indulging either the presumption of reason or the extravagance of imagination in the province of Faith: his humble reliance on the wisdom and mercy of God: and his firm belief that we are placed in this state of existence, not to speculate about another, but to prepare ourselves for it by actual exertion of our intellectual faculties and the constant cultivation of kindness and benevolence towards our fellow-men."

APPENDIX

APPENDIX

Trial of Isobel Walker, the Original of " Effie Deans " (*now first published*).

CURIA ITINERIS JUSTICIARII S.D.N.

Regis tenta in Praetorio Burgi de Dumfreis Secundo die Mensis Maii anno domini 1737 Per Honorabilem Virum Alexandrum Fraser de Strichen Armigerum Unum dominorum Commissionariorum Justiciarii Dict S.D.N. Regis.

Curia Legitime Affirmata.

Present—The Sheriff Depute of Dumfreis The Stewart Depute of Annandale The Stewart Depute of Kirkudbright.

Intran Isobel Walker, daughter to the deceast William Walker in Clouden now Prisoner in the tolbooth of Dumfreis Indicted and accused at the instance of Duncan Forbes of Culloden Esqr. his Majesties Advocate for his Highness Interest as guilty actor art and part of the unnaturall and detestable crime of Murder and paricide upon the body of her own child in manner mentioned in her indictment in the porteous roll for the Shire of Dumfreis, *Pannell.*

Mr. Hugh Forbes, *Advocate Depute for the interest of the Crown.*	*Prors. in Defence*—Mr. James Fergusson, Younger of Craigdarroch, *Advocate.*

Fergusson objected agt any procedure in this tryall in regard that by the 82d Act parl: 11th of James the 6th Intitled of the forme how Justiceairs shall be holden twice every year in the months of Aprile and October it appears that two Lords of Session Advocats or other proper persons appointed under the Great Seall were to go to each Division or District And therefrom it would appear that two of them were a necessary quorum And more particularly

405

from the Act 1672 concerning the Regulation of the Judicatories in the fifth clause concerning the Justice Court it is expressly Ordained that once a year in the months of Aprile or May two of the number of the Judges are appointed to keep Circuit Courts att Dumfreis and Jedburgh two at Stirling Glasgow and Air and other two at the Towns of Perth Aberdeen and Inverness and therefore that as His Lordship is here a single Judge he with great deference apprehends he cannot competently proceed in this tryall.

ADVOCATUS Answered that the objectiom made to the competency of the Court in regard that his Lordship is only a single Judge appears very naturally to arise from the express words of the Acts mentioned by the Objector particularly from the Statute 1672 But that it is notour from many instances where single Judges have tryed at their Circuit Courts crimes of all sorts even capitall crimes and that this practice was sufficient to authorise His Lordship to proceed in this tryall but nevertheless in case any scruple remained if his Lordship thought it proper to remitt the tryall of these crimes to the Justiciary Court att Edinburgh he would not oppose it.

THE LORD STRICHEN Before answer to the above Debate Remitts the Indictment agt the said Isobel Walker Pannell to be tryed before the Lords of Justiciary at Edinburgh the twenty first day of June next and for that effect Grants Warrand to and Ordains the Sherriff Depute of Dumfreis to transport the said Isobel Walker from the tolbooth of Dumfreis upon the twenty fifth day of May current under a sure guard to the Stewarty of Annandale and deliver her to the Stewart Depute thereof who is hereby required and ordained to transport her under a sure guard to the Shire of Peebles and deliver her to the Sherriff Depute yrof Who is hereby required and Or-

APPENDIX

dained to transport her under a sure guard to the Shire of
Midlothian and deliver her to the Sherriffe Depute yrof
who is hereby required and ordained to imprison her within the tolbooth of Edinr The Magistrates whereof and
keepers of their tolbooth are hereby required and ordained to keep and detain her prisoner therein untill she be
thence liberate in due course of law.

" ALEXR. FRASER."

Note.—The High Court Record contains no entry of
date 21 June 1737.

Among the papers in the case is a petition of date 13th
June 1737 by Isobel Walker designed prisoner in the Tolbooth of Edinburgh praying for banishment—with deliverance of same date by the Lord Justice Clerk, *I.P.D.*,
ordaining same to be seen and answered by His Majesty's
Advocat or his Deputs betwixt and Wednesday next. Answers were lodged containing a short abstract of the
Crown precognition " submitting to the Court whether the
" desire of the Petition ought to be granted or not." No
farther Deliverance.—Isobel Walker's Petition is signed
by two Notaries, she not being able to write. There is a-
mong the papers in the case another Petition, dated 1 May
1738 by Isobel Walker praying to be transported beyond
seas never to return (signed by Notaries) but there is no
consent by A.D. or deliverance or any marking thereon.

CURIA ITINERIS JUSTICIARII S.D.N.
REGIS TENTA IN PRAETORIO BURGI DE DUM-
FREIS PRIMO DIE MAI ANNO DOMINI MIL-
LESIMO SEPTINGENTESIMO TRIGESIMO OCTA-
VO PER HONORABILES VIROS DOMINUM
JACOBUM MCKENZIE DE ROYSTON ET MA-
GISTRUM PATRICIUM GRANT DE ELCHIES
DOMINOS COMMISSIONARIOS JUSTICIARII
DICT S.D.N. REGIS.

THE SCOTT ORIGINALS

Curia Legitime Affirmata.

Present—THE SHERRIFF DEPUTE OF DUMFREIS THE STEWART DEPUTE OF ANNANDALE THE STEWART DEPUTE OF KIRKUDBRIGHT.

INTRAN Isobel Walker daughter of the deceast William Walker in Cluden within the Paroch of Irongray and Stewarty of Kirkudbright now prisoner within the Tolbooth of Dumfreis Indicted and accused at the instance of His Majesties Advocate for the crime of murder and Paricide in manner mentioned in the Porteous Roll for the Shire of Dumfreis.

Pursuer—	*Advocats in defence*—
SIR JAMES ELPHINSTONE,	MR. JAMES FERGUSSON.
Advocate-Depute	MR. JAMES GEDDES.

GEDDES for the Pannell objected That as to the Lybell so far as it relates to the actual murder He had nothing to object against the relevancy for surely if the Pannell is guilty of that horride crime of murdering her own child she well deserves the highest punishment to be inflicted upon her But if the relevancy is also to be founded on the presumptive murder he humbly conceives that the Statute upon which that presumption is founded should have been libelled particularly And besides the facts lybelled against the Pannell are not so specially lybelled as to make her fall within the presumption of the Act of Parliament The Act says that concealing being with child during the whole space presumes murder Now it is neither said that the child found was a child come to the full time nor that when the Pannell was inspected were there the signs such as women have who bring forth children to the full time.

SIR JAMES ELPHINSTON for the Crown answered that there is no occasion for lybelling the Statute for if the facts charged against the Pannell are sufficient to infer the conclusion of the Lybell the law or Statute upon which that conclusion is founded is left to the Judge who is presumed to know the law And as to the other point pled for the pannell he humbly submitts if it is not sufficient in generall to lybell that the pannell concealed her being with child during the whole space.

The Lords Commissioners of Justiciary having considered the Indictment raised at the instance of Charles Ereskine of Tinwald Esqr. His Majesties Advocat against Isobel Walker Pannell with the above debate thereupon Find that the pannell having time and place lybelled brought furth a child and murdered the same relevent to infer the pain of death and confiscation of moveables, and find it Separatim relevent to infer the like pains that the pannell time and place foresaid did bring forth a child which was thereafter found dead or amissing and not found and that the pannell during the whole time of her pregnancy did conceal her being with child and did not call for help and assistance in the time of the birth But sustain it relevent to eleide the branch of the Lybell last above mentioned that the pannell revealed her being with child or called for help the time of the birth and Allow also the pannell to prove that the child was born before the usuall time and repell the haill other defences proponed for the pannell And remit her and the Indictment as found relevent and her said defences hereby admitted to proof to the knowledge of an Assize.

" JA. MACKENZIE."

" P. GRANT."

Then the Lords proceeded to make choice of the following persons to pass upon the pannells assize :—

Adam Johnston of Craigielands
Robert Henderson late Bailie in Lochmaben

THE SCOTT ORIGINALS

John Carruthers of Denbigh
Willm Carruthers of Braes
John Irving of Whitehill
William Johnstone yr of Lockerbie
Andrew Johnstone of Damm
Samuel Johnston of Broadmeadows
John Johnston of Banks
Francis Carruthers of Whitecroft
William Carruthers of Hardriggs
Robert Herris Merchant in Dumfreis
Archd. Malcolm Writer in Dumfreis
James Maxwell of Elchieshiells
John Rae Merchant in Dumfreis

The assize being lawfully sworn and no objections in the contrary the following witnesses were adduced for the Pursuer Compeared Elspeth Ferguson relict of William Welsh in Wigston aged sixty or yrby who being solemnly sworn, purged of malice Examined and Interrogate DEPONES that she was desired by one of the Elders to go and visit the pannell as a person who was suspected to have born a child That accordingly she went and after proper inspection and examination found her in such a condition as a woman lately brought to bed should be By various simptoms she judged that she had born a child to the full time That this was about Hallowmass was a year Depones that at that same time she saw a dead child lying upon the pannells knee which had been brought from Holywood That the said child appeared to be a ripe child and come to the full time both by its size colour and that it had nails by which it appeared to be so But she heard the pannell say that the child was none of hers That she had thrown the child which she had born into the Water of Cluden and that it was not a ripe child Depones that when she saw the child it had a napkine tyed strait about its neck with several knots upon it and the child was naked

APPENDIX

And this is truth as she shall answer to God And depones she cannot write. *Causa scientia* the Deponent is a midwife and saw what she depones.

" JA. MACKENZIE."

Compeared Jean Johnsone relict of James Walker in Cluden aged sixty six or thereby sworn and interrogate as above DEPONES That sometime before Martinmas was a year the pannell having been suspected to have born a child she the deponent went to visit her and that it appeared to her she was latly brought to bed but whether the child was come to the full time she does not know there was such confusion in the room That she then saw a dead child lying on the pannells knee that it was almost naked and had a cloath tyed about its neck which child seemed to be comed to the full time and that the pannell denyed it was hers and said that the child that she had born was not bigger than her two fists and that she had thrown it into the Water of Cluden and that Elspeth Ferguson the preceding witness was present at the same time *Causa scientia* tho she's not a midwife by trade yet she sometimes assists in bringing women to bed and saw as she depones And this is truth as she shall answer to God and depones she cannot write.

" JA. MACKENZIE."

Compeared Jean Alexander daughter to James Alexander in Cluden aged twenty two years or yrby unmarried, who being solemnly sworn purged of malice examined and interrogate DEPONES That upon a Sabath day about eight days before Hallowmass in the year imvii thirty six the deponent went to the pannells mothers house in the town of Cluden where the deponent found the pannel and her mother That soon after the deponents coming into the house the pannel retired to the other end of the house which was separated from the place where her mother and the deponent was by a thin wattle wall That

411

the deponent stayed thereafter in the house for the space of an hour dureing which time the pannel did not again return and then it being near sun setting the deponent went away That dureing the deponents stay in the house and likewise in her goeing out of the house she heard a person moaning in the other end of the house which she knew to be the pannel not only by the voice but likewise because she knew there was no other person in the house That the deponent had then no suspicion of the pannels being with child or of her being about to be delivered otherwise she would have called for assistance But a very few days thereafter some other people in the same town suspected the pannel's having brought forth a child and therefore upon the Thursday of the same week the two preceeding witnesses and some others went to inspect the pannel and the deponent went at the same time and upon the inspection the deponent as well as the other women present were of opinion that the pannel had lately brought forth a child That about the same time that the pannel was inspected as above a dead child was found in the Water of Cluden at a very little distance below the town That the deponent was not present when the child was found but saw it in about ane hour and a half thereafter at which time the child was naked but had a rag of a napkin striped blew and white tyed very strait about its neck with three severall knots That the deponent thought she knew the napkine and could go far to be positive that about a month before she had seen the very same napkine about the pannels neck and she knew the napkine the better not only for the colour but likewise because a rag had been tore off from it That the child so found had all the usual simptoms of a ripe child that had been born at the full time Depones that the said child was brought to the pannels mothers house and shown to the pannel and that the Deponent heard the pannel own her having brought forth a child but said that that was not her child because her child was a female and not the bigness of her two fists whereas the child found was a male and fully ripe and Depones that the pannel own'd that she had told nobody of her being with child *Causa scientia* the deponent lived at the time foresaid in the same town with the pannel vizt. the town of Cluden and saw and heard as she depones And this is the truth as she shall answer to God and depones she cannot write.

" P. Grant."

Compeared Emelia Walker spouse to Samuel Walker in Cluden aged fourty three years or thereby solemnly sworn purged and interrogate as above Depones that a considerable time before Hallowmass in the year imvii and thirty six the deponent and others in the town of Cluden suspected the pannel's being with child but the pannel still denyed it However the suspicion still continuing the deponent in conversation with one of her neighbours said that if they allowed her to go on she would beguile them all and deny her ever being with child and therefore desired her said neighbour to send for the deponent the first time the pannel should come to her house That accordingly upon the Thursday before Hallowmass the deponent was sent for and at that time she again remonstrated to the pannel the suspicion she lay under That about the same time a dead child had been found in the Water of Cluden and laid in Church That the deponent went and fetched the child from the Church and brought it where the pannel then was in her mothers house That the said child when the deponent saw it was naked but had a rag of a blew and white striped napkin tyed about its neck but which as the deponent was informed had been loosed by the people who had found it before That the deponent remembers she has seen napkins of the same collour about the pannels neck before but cannot say that they were the same That the child found in the water

413

was a ripe child but when it was shown to the pannel she denyed that it was her child But at last the pannel acknowledged that she had brought forth a child but said she knew that was not her child because hers was a female whereas that was a male child That the pannel said that she had thrown it into the Water of Cluden and that it was only of the bigness of her two fists *Causa scientia* the deponent lived in the same town with the pannel and saw and heard as she has deponed and depones she cannot write And this is truth as she shall answer to God.

" P. GRANT."

Compeared John Stott in Cluden aged sixty five years or thereby married solemnly sworn purged and interrogate as above DEPONES that about a quarter of a year before the pannel was discovered to have born a child which was some days before Hallowmass imvii thirty six the deponent suspected that the pannel was with child he said to several of his neighbours that he would wager a guinea of gold she was with child but the pannel threatening to call him before the Session for scandal denying she was with child whereupon there was no more talk of it neither by the deponent nor others for some time That two or three days before the pannel was discovered to have born a child the deponent upon seeing her look pale and sickly and small and lank in the body did then suspect she had bore a child and having come to Dumfreis upon his return he found she had been apprehended and being viewed by midwives and other women was found to be a woman who was lately brought to bed And dureing this time a child was found in the water of Cluden dead a little below the town and brought into the house where the pannel lived dureing the time the deponent was there and being then challenged if that was her child she said that she had born a child but that was not her's the child born by her being no bigger than her two fists That the child found seemed to be a ripe child and was naked all except a rag about the neck which was then loosed but that the child's neck was blae and seemed to be twisted by tying something hard about it *Causa scientia* he lives in Cluden where the pannel dwells and heard and saw what he depones And this is truth as he shall answer to God.

" JOHN STOTT."

" JA. MACKENZIE."

Compeared William Johnston in nether Cluden aged forty two years or thereby married who being solemnly sworn purged and interrogate as above DEPONES that in the end of October imvii and thirty six years as the deponent was walking from his walkmiln down the water of Cluden a little below the town he discovered a dead child on the side of the water but did not touch it till he called some of his neighbours and then they took up the child which was a male and seemed to be a ripe child That there was a piece of an old blew and white napkin tyed about the child's neck with severall knots so tight as possibly could be done That there was a piece of a clout tyed over the child's mouth and nose and one of its hands tyed up to the side of its head and this cloath was so strait tyed that the child's nose was turned aside That this was the same day upon which the pannel was found by women to have bore a child but the deponent did not see her that day *Causa scientia* the deponent lives in the neighbourhood with the pannel and this is truth as he shall answer to God.

" WILLIAM JOHNSTON."

" JA. MACKENZIE."

Compeared William Crokat in Nether Cluden aged seventy years or thereby married sollemnly sworn purged and interrogate DEPONES that upon a Thursday being two or three days before Hallowmass imvii and thirty six William Johnston the preceeding witness called the deponent to come and see a dead child that he had found in the water of Cluden and the deponent haveing called some other neighbours they went together and found a male child lyeing dead on a sand bank at the side of the water and which seemed to have been thrown out there by the water while it was great That the child was quite naked except some lining cloath tyed about the face and a napkin or rag tyed about the neck and which the women in company did take off That the deponent thinks the woman who loosed it was Mary Haining *Causa scientia patet* and this is truth as he shall answer to God.

"WILLIAM CROKAT."
"P. GRANT.

Compeared Mary Haining spouse to John Crockat in Nether Cluden aged forty years or thereby solemnly sworn purged and interrogate DEPONES that two or three days before Hallowmass imvii and thirty six years William Johnston a preceeding witness called the deponent and others to go to see a dead child which he had found by the water of Cluden Accordingly the deponent went and found a male child dead upon the sand bank close by the water which the deponent thought had been thrown out by the water while it was in flood the day before That the child was quite naked except a bit of harden rag tyed about its face and a napkin stripped blew and white tyed about its neck with three or four knots which had been tyed so ticht that the childs neck was drawn in to the ordinary bigness of a childs arm of six years old That the deponent untied these knots but wraped the napkin loose about the childs neck and in that manner it was carried away to the Church *Causa scientia patet* and this is truth as she shall answer to God.

"MARY HAINING."
"P. GRANT."

APPENDIX

The Lords Commissioners of Justiciary Ordain this Assize to enclose in this place instantly and to return their verdict by their conveniency and the whole fifteen to be present under the pains of Law And Ordain the Pannel to be carried back to prison.

Post meridiem Lo. ELCHIES, *pres.*

CURIA ITINERIS JUSTICIARIAE S.D.N REGIS TENTA IN PRAETORIO BURGI DE DUM-FREIS PRIMO DIE MAI ANNO DOMINI MIL-LESIMO SEPTINGENTESIMO TRIGESIMO OC-TAVO PER HONORABILES VIROS DOMINUM JACOBUM MACKENZIE DE ROYSTON ET MAGISTRUM PATRICIUM GRANT DE ELCHIES DOMINOS COMMISSIONARIOS JUSTICIARII DICT S.D.N. REGIS.

Curia Legitime Affirmata.

INTRAN Isobel Walker indicted and accused as in the former Sederunt The above assize being called and they answering to their names their Chancelour gave in the following verdict :

At Dumfreis the first day of May imvii and thirty eight years The above assize haveing enclosed did choose John Carruthers of Denbigh to be their Chancelour and John Irving of Whitehill to be their Clerk and haveing considered the Indictment raised at the instance of Charles Areskine of Tinwald Esqr. his Majesties Advocate for his Highness interest against Isobel Walker pannell and the Lords Commissioners of Justiciary their Interloqr yron with the deposi-tions of the witnesses adduced for proveing yrof They all in one voice find it proven that the pannel Isobel Walker time and place lybelled did bring forth a child which was thereafter found dead or amissing and not found And that the said pannel dureing the whole time of her pregnancy did conceal her being with child and did not call for help and assistance in the time of the birth In Witness Whereof our said Chancelour and Clerk have subscribed these presents for us and in our names place and date forsaid. (Signed) JOHN CARRUTHERS, *Chancelour*. JOHN IRVING, *Clerk*.

The Lords Commissioners of Justiciary haveing considered the above verdict of Assize returned against Isobel Walker pannel They in respect thereof DECERN and ADJUDGE by the mouth of David Bane Dempster of Court the said Isobel Walker to be taken upon Wednesday the fourteenth day of June next to come from the prison of Dumfreis to the ordinary place of execution and there betwixt the hours of three and four o'clock in the afternoon to be hanged by the neck upon a gibbet untill she be dead And Ordain her whole moveable goods and gear to be escheat to his Majestie which is pronounced for DOME And Ordain the Magistrates of Dumfreis to see the sentence put in execution And in the meantime Ordain her to be detained in sure prison.

" P. GRANT."
" JA. MACKENZIE."

NOTES.

1. Books of Adjournal of 12 June 1738 contain Respite for two months, viz. :—until 15th August, as follows :—

   CURIA JUSTICIARIAE S.D.N. REGIS TENTA IN PRAETORIO BURGI DE EDINBURGO, DUO DECIMO DIE MENSIS JUNII 1738 PER HONORABILES VIROS ANDREAM FLETCHER DE MILTOUN JUSTITIARIUM CLERICUM, DOMINUM JACOBUM MACKENZIE DE ROY-

APPENDIX

Curia Legitime Affirmata.

This day the Lord Justice Clerk delivered a letter directed to his Lordship from his Grace the Duke of Newcastle, one of His Majesty's Principal Secretaries of State, whereof the tenour follows :—

Whitehall, 6th June 1738.—My Lord, Application having been made to His Majesty, in behalf of Isobel Walker lately condemned at Dumfreis for the murder of her bastard child ; I am conmanded to signifie to your Lordship his Majesty's pleasure That the execution of the sentence pronounced against the said Isobel Walker be Respited for two months from the time appointed for her execution ; and that a state of her case be laid before his Majesty, whereupon his Majesty will declare his further pleasure. I am, My Lord, Your Lordship's most obedient humble servant, (Sic subscribitur) Holles Newcastle (Directed thus) To the Right Honourable the Lord Justice Clerk at Edinburgh. Holles Newcastle.— Thereafter the said Lords gave their Warrant to the Magistrates of Dumfreis for stopping the said execution, whereof the tenour follows :—By the Right Honourable the Lord Justice Clerk and Lords Commissioners of Justiciary, Whereas his Majesty has been graciously pleased, by a letter signed by his Grace the Duke of Newcastle one of his Majesties principall Secretaries of State, to signifie his pleasure to their Lordships that the sentence of death pronounced against Isobel Walker, Prisoner in the tolbooth of Dumfreis which was to have been execute upon her upon the fourteenth of June current, be Respited for two months from the time appointed for her execution ; These, therefore, in obedience to his Majesty's commands, DISCHARGED and PROHIBITED the Magistrates of Dumfreis, and all other officers of the law from putting the foresaid sentence of death in execution upon the said Isobel Walker till the fifteenth day of August next to come ; on which day the said Magistrates of Dumfreis were hereby required and ordained to put the former sentence of death in execution upon the said Isobel Walker, in all points as they would be answerable. Given att Edinburgh the Twelfth day of June 1738 years. (Signed) ANDR. FLETCHER. JA. MACKENZIE. GILB. ELLIOT. P. GRANT.

2. Remission to Isobel Walker is dated 12 July 1738 and is granted on condition that she, within the space of forty days after she is liberated in virtue of the remission, shall transport herself from the dominions of Great Britain and Ireland, never to return without licence from the Sovereign under his sign manual and Privy or Great Seal previously obtained.—If she be found within the Kingdom after that time the remission is declared to be void.

3. On the margin of the original Minute Book of Record, opposite the entry of the two months respite, there is written the following, viz. :—" Isobel Wal-" ker remitted and the Remission is dated the " Twelfth day of July 1738, pass the Great Seall " the seventh day of August the said year with this " express condition that she depart the Kingdoms " of Great Britain and Ireland within fourty days " after she is liberate in virtue of the said Remis-" sion never to be seen therein unless she obtain a " licence from his Majestie or his Royal successors " for that effect. If she be seen within his Majes-" ties dominions foresaid the foresaid remission to " be void and the sentence to be put in execution " against her." This entry, which is in the same

APPENDIX

handwriting as that of the entry of Respite is not authenticated by any one and has not been transferred to the Books of Adjournal. The Books of Adjournal may have been written up prior to the writing of this marginal entry.

4. From the tradition which makes Isobel marry and settle in Whitehaven, we must conclude that liberty to return had been granted, unless, indeed, an absolute pardon had been bestowed upon her. Careful research in Whitehaven has failed to elicit any information respecting Effie Deans's prototype.

INDEX

INDEX

425

INDEX

INDEX

INDEX

INDEX

429

INDEX

430

INDEX

INDEX